THROW
YOURSELF AWAY

THINKING LITERATURE
A series edited by Nan Z. Da and Anahid Nersessian

Throw Yourself Away

WRITING AND MASOCHISM

Julia Jarcho

The University of Chicago Press
Chicago and London

The University of Chicago Press, Chicago 60637
The University of Chicago Press, Ltd., London
© 2024 by The University of Chicago
Published 2024
Printed in the United States of America

33 32 31 30 29 28 27 26 25 24   1 2 3 4 5

ISBN-13: 978-0-226-83502-0 (cloth)
ISBN-13: 978-0-226-83503-7 (paper)
ISBN-13: 978-0-226-83504-4 (e-book)
DOI: https://doi.org/10.7208/chicago/9780226835044.001.0001

The University of Chicago Press gratefully acknowledges the
generous support of the Brown University Humanities Research
Fund, in the Office of the Vice President for Research, toward the
publication of this book.

Library of Congress Cataloging-in-Publication Data

Names: Jarcho, Julia, author.
Title: Throw yourself away : writing and masochism / Julia Jarcho.
Other titles: Thinking literature.
Description: Chicago : The University of Chicago Press, 2024. |
   Series: Thinking literature | Includes bibliographical references
   and index.
Identifiers: LCCN 2024002361 | ISBN 9780226835020 (cloth) |
   ISBN 9780226835037 (paperback) | ISBN 9780226835044
   (ebook)
Subjects: LCSH: Sadomasochism in literature. | Masochism
   in literature. | American literature—History and criticism. |
   American literature—Themes, motives. | European literature—
   History and criticism. | European literature—Themes, motives. |
   Authorship—Psychological aspects.
Classification: LCC PS169.S25 J37 2024 | DDC 810.9/3538—dc23/
   eng/20240229
LC record available at https://lccn.loc.gov/2024002361

Contents

Another Book about Masochism

Everyone already knows all about masochism. As Freud put it a hundred years ago, "the material is very uniform and is accessible to any observer, even to non-analysts."[1] By now it seems indisputable: there are too many books and essays on masochism already. Nobody needs another one—especially at the well-trodden intersection of late-twentieth-century literary criticism, "French theory," queer theory, and psychoanalysis, where much of this book, the one you're reading now, takes place.

It gets worse: masochism is *basic*. To the extent that it still makes sense to refer to something like a mainstream of popular culture—and even if it doesn't, I grew up in the nineties, so I probably can't stop—there's no denying that masochism has been bobbing brightly and placidly in its midst for quite some time. The most obvious instance and, no doubt, a major contributing cause of this banality has been the *Fifty Shades of Grey* franchise, whose movies had grossed over a billion box-office dollars by 2018, five years after *The Guardian* reported that E. L. James had become the world's highest-earning author, the fastest-earning in history.[2] But *Fifty Shades* hasn't exactly cornered the market; today you find frank references to masochism in the most ubiquitous pop songs, from teen crooner Billie Eilish's "Bad Guy" to rap star Cardi B's "WAP" (short for "Wet Ass Pussy," as you know), and all over TV, as in the Hulu series based on Sally Rooney's bestselling 2018 novel *Normal People*. Ten years before I wrote this sentence, a writer for the Modern Love column of the *New York Times* observed that "it has become fashionable in certain millennial circles to announce an interest in bondage or other forms of sadomasochism."[3] I could keep listing examples, but you see what I mean.

Freud notwithstanding, the utter banalization of masochistic desire would seem to be a relatively recent—a millennial—phenomenon, as the *Times* writer suggests. The controversial status of sadomasochism for

1970s and 1980s feminism is well known; in rereading work like Gayle Rubin's momentous 1984 essay "Thinking Sex," you can't help but notice the confidence with which Rubin includes sadomasochists among "the most despised sexual castes," not just for antiporn feminists but in "modern Western societies" writ large; sadomasochistic practices, Rubin observes with some irony, are typically "viewed as unmodulated horrors incapable of involving affection, love, free choice, kindness, or transcendence."[4] In today's post–*Fifty Shades* world, who could imagine S&M proclivities as a barrier to any of these delights? The strand of second-wave feminism that condemned sadomasochism along with (and as the heart of) pornography—and that sex-positive thinkers like Rubin fought to challenge—seems to have lost that battle so hard that affirming masochistic sex as a subversive cultural force would now seem almost as bizarre as excoriating it.[5]

And yet some of us do seem to feel an unaccountable urge to go on writing about masochism, even if we have to fabricate a motive for doing so. For instance, in the brief introduction to their 2021 anthology *Kink*—whose front matter features effusive praise from *Time*, *Kirkus Reviews*, Oprah's *O Magazine*, and *Cosmopolitan*, among others—the editors R. O. Kwon and Garth Greenwell maintain that "kink is often pathologized in popular culture, the attendant desires flattened, simplified, and turned into a joke, a cause for only shame."[6] Reading this, I'm reminded of a moment in Gilles Deleuze's 1967 essay "Coldness and Cruelty" when the author fumes about a "popular joke"—concerning a sadist and a masochist—that "foolishly claims competence to pass judgment on the world of perversions."[7] One wonders: Is a judgmental world really the problem, or is it just that any "popular" rendition of a complex phenomenon is likely to flatten, simplify, and/or poke fun? And does masochism really need to be rescued from this kind of rough treatment? After the *New York Times* published a review of *Kink* that quoted the editors' introduction, the venerable film critic Molly Haskell wrote a letter mocking their language as "the stuff of high parody": "How 'transgressive' is B.D.S.M. (an abbreviation which apparently needs no introduction to *Times* readers) when it comes from a major publisher, and presents itself in the anodyne jargon of academe?" Haskell demanded. "In other words, how pervy is kink anyway?"[8] Her exasperation marks what some of us rightly fear: that masochism is by now at once too familiar *and* too academic to be at all interesting (let alone subversive), on paper or, for that matter, in bed.

It may be that the most relevant problem facing enthusiasts of sadism and masochism today, then, is not pathologization but something more like thematic exhaustion, with its attendant threat of aesthetic failure. For example, in "Safeword," Kwon's own contribution to the *Kink* anthology, a man is bemused when his wife wants him to start hurting her during sex. "They tried reading *Fifty Shades of Grey*, but soon dropped it," Kwon's narrator informs us; "it was so badly written that it made her laugh."[9] In another contribution, "Impact Play" by Peter Mountford, the protagonist is a successful Seattle curator who's terrified of being ostracized for his secret BDSM lifestyle but finds himself even more overwhelmed by the uncoolness of a local fetish convention.[10] While racism, transphobia, misogyny, and poverty all operate as oppressive forces in these stories, the kind of normative kink-shaming the editors refer to in the introduction looks, in fact, pretty thin on the ground. What the stories seem intent on redressing is less the social marginalization of sadists, masochists, and other sexual deviants than the aesthetic quality of their everyday representation—as if what sexual perversion needs today is less a social defense than a literary redemption.

But isn't this position itself somewhat perverse? In other words, if the world is finally OK with our *having* sadomasochistic sex, why insist on continuing to (of all things) *write* about it? In a certain way, this question is the real motivation for this book. Struck by the fact of how much I have wanted to write it, despite every evidence of its gratuitousness, I have thus wanted to understand that perverse wanting. In the following pages, then, I have tried to figure out how masochism can operate as a sexual disposition inextricable from a desire to write, a desire for writing. And because that desire is also, in me and I know not only in me, bound up with a desire to keep reading, I have pursued the question mainly by digging into a handful of late nineteenth- to early twenty-first-century texts.

The chapters of this book are thus all readings of works that in different ways invest desire in getting hurt and identify this investment with writing. Masochism, or the concerted intertwinement of sexual desire and suffering, appears in all these writers' imagination as a relation that plays out not only between lovers but also between an individual and a field of literary endeavor. These texts bear out Amber Jamilla Musser's argument—grounded in the history of sexology—that masochism was always "fundamentally a literary disease," a phenomenon whose meaningfulness only became possible through its "intimate connection with literature and its attendant practices of reading and writing."[11] More pointedly, they show that masochism produces writing *as the best kind of sex*, because writing offers the subject a way to approach, over and over, what's unbearably bad—what's really painful—and to elaborate that pain into something she can almost handle. In masochistic writing, that is, the unbearable becomes something to which the subject can give form, and something from which, accordingly, she can remove or distance herself, in order thereby to survive. But this is only half the story: as we'll see, the remove writing offers is never just a site of safety; again and again, the formalizing "escape" it offers loops back into new devastations. Writing doesn't only keep the subject from destruction but also conducts her toward it: it is a treacherous machine for wresting pleasure from the real dangers that threaten to consume her, and it's *because* writing is treacherous that it proves irresistible. This is the main point of the readings that follow: by demonstrating how literary practice operates as sexual practice in particular writers' imaginations, they offer masochism as a way to understand the force literature can wield in our lives.

Wait, "our lives"? Whose exactly? Or as David Marriott puts it, reading Jacques Lacan: "Who is this we? And why does it feel so symptomatic?"[12] Any project indebted to psychoanalytic thought, as this book is, will be haunted by the specter of white universalism. I'll have more to say about this problem below, but lest you think I'm after a grand theory of sexuality (or even of masochism) "as such"—eliding the historical specificities and the social categories that have always determined the sexual—let me be clear about my intentions. The claims about sex that come up in this book are the claims that I understand these particular texts to be making; they are *fantasies* about what sex is, just as they are more and less explicitly fantasies about writing, gender, theater, and race. The work of articulating how these fantasies take form in the texts I read requires me to formulate propositions on the texts' behalf, in free indirect discourse, as it were. But these are not claims about what sex and writing really are; they are claims about what these texts have imagined them to be. Sometimes—as in Freud, for instance—the texts themselves obviously universalize; to my mind, the fact that their implications (e.g., "writing is masochistic sex") may turn out to be false for most people, and indeed that the works that make these claims often *do not care*, doesn't mean that the only valid approach to such works is one of correction or redress. The latter aim might focus on explicit sociocultural or historical delimitation, which would emphasize the empirical boundaries of the populations (cultural, social, or literary-historical) for whom a given text can in fact be seen to speak. I don't consider such historicizing work unimportant or uninteresting, but I do find myself more insistently interested in elaborating on these texts than in situating them. I am ultimately less curious about how and why they came to be the way they are than I am about how they are, which of course means something like: how they do what they do to me.

This mode of reading aims to discover patterns of desire that certain cultural objects manifest and cultivate, because doing so illuminates those objects' power: their ability to draw subjects into aesthetic and erotic relations with them. By attending to texts' complexity this way, what I seek is not to confirm that they could only have issued from the culturally, histor- ically, geographically, socially, and economically specific experiences of those who have produced them, a fact that is never in doubt. Rather, the hope is to understand the texts' powers of seduction, which may operate largely within homogenous sociocultural fields but may also exceed them. Even if we were to grant that a subject must identify with a text in order to enjoy it, we know that the paths of identification are often socially coun- terintuitive and even painful.[13] The works I read here register that kind of pain to different degrees, and sometimes manage to relish it.

It also seems important to acknowledge, however, that *my* charged identification with many of the texts I engage—texts that have been show- ing me for decades how to think with masochism—is an identification lu- bricated by my own whiteness, particularly where these texts proceed as if untroubled by the structures of white supremacy. Those very structures have decisively shaped masochism itself, as becomes blindingly obvious when, for example, Freud notes that *Uncle Tom's Cabin* is invariably one of the books that has stimulated beating fantasies in his patients.[14] And yet the implications of this history are nowhere to be found in many of the texts and the authors I read, and read with, several of which are stal- warts of what is now widely held to be an outdated, oppressively and un- selfconsciously white "queer theory" canon. For instance, Leo Bersani and, in chapter 2, Lee Edelman are among my most important theoretical interlocutors; both have been widely criticized for their limitations and exclusions, including by Musser, who incorporates both in a genealogy of masochism theory from Krafft-Ebing to Foucault that "has disavowed difference in its quest to decenter the subject" and accordingly "produces the idea of a universal subject, a subject who is most easily legible in these accounts as a gay white male."[15] Another white queer theorist, Eve Ko- sofsky Sedgwick—who in fact writes explicitly about identifying as a gay white male in her literary and erotic life but whose analyses almost always privilege sex and gender over race—is the main focus of chapter 4. Kaja Silverman, yet another white critic whose work on masochism from the 1980s belongs to the same disciplinary nexus, has also profoundly influ- enced my thinking here; and throughout the book, I engage repeatedly and centrally with both Deleuze and Freud, just as the aforementioned critics do.[16] I can't deny that this rather endogamously nested critical ap- paratus scaffolds my reading: these are the authors who taught me how to read for masochism, and I have not yet learned to find them dispens- able, even as I also seek to excavate the fantasies that drive *their* work. This kind of insistent iteration extends to some of my "primary" texts as well: chapter 1 focuses on a story by Mary Gaitskill, whose work has already been subject to readings by the Sedgwick-adjacent theorists Lauren Berlant and Maggie Nelson; and chapter 2 turns—it will surprise no one—to Henry James.

In a book about the writing of masochism and the masochism of writing, it would be inappropriate to disavow the book's own drivelike eros of textual production as repetition of, or return to, what one really ought to have moved beyond: in this case, a discourse whose characteristic avoidances have by now marked it out more properly for critique than for reelaboration. As we'll see, however, there seems to be something in masochism itself that makes this very distinction unstable. Analyses of masochism often end up reinstantiating the masochistic fantasy they purport to scrutinize. And this understanding of masochism as an erotics of textual reiteration helps explain how something like a "masochism canon" is produced in the first place, through a series of returns to erotically charged source texts—for instance, Freud's article "A Child Is Being Beaten," the darling of so much subsequent theory; or the sexological case studies to which Freud's own work refers. The erotic dimension of these returns in the works of theory that make them is a fundamental component of what my book seeks to describe, in full awareness that describing them also implicates my own analysis in this erotic series. In fact, part of the fantasy my book is articulating is often the fantasy of a textual object to which one can always return in one's own writing: this amounts to offering a theory of how or why canons acquire the enduring power they have over some readers, which is to say, a partial theory of how there can be canons at all.[17]

The white writers in the genealogy I've named above don't all have the same canonical status; nor, for that matter, do they inhabit the same version of whiteness. But in different ways and proportions, they all inevitably leverage their whiteness to access a spuriously universal subject position from which to speak. They—or, to return to Marriott, "we"—symptomatically both rely on that access and repress that reliance. Because I don't want to repeat this repression, I'll use a substantial part of this introduction to review some different ways masochism, as a modern sexological concept, takes shape around the violence of white supremacy, following work on the subject by Musser and other scholars. I hope this discussion will help situate all of the texts I read in relation to the conditions that have made their masochism possible, while also laying some useful groundwork for readings of two Black American authors who bring white supremacist violence into upsettingly intimate perspectives: Adrienne Kennedy, whose plays are the subject of chapter 3, and Gary Fisher, whose story "Red Cream Soda" I'll examine briefly in chapter 4.

Before moving into that discussion, however, it seems useful to preview some other things *Throw Yourself Away* will suggest about masochism, to give a sense of what I think is to be gained from returning to this historically troubled conceptual field. The first is a new way of thinking about both sex and literature in relation to dramatic theater. It strikes me that drama—especially realist drama—has received very little attention from the queer-theory literary-critical nexus referred to above. This is no doubt partly because of a tendency, in that milieu, to privilege literary instances of antinarrativity, indeterminacy, stylistic flourish, and formal excess, all of which realist drama has seemed precisely designed to exclude; I suppose it takes both a filthy imagination and a high tolerance for stodginess to find Ibsen profoundly perverse, the way I do in chapter 2.[18] Throughout this book, however, dramatic theater will turn out to be an indispensable referent and tool of the masochistic literary imagination, both inside and outside of actual plays.

What difference does this attention to drama make? While figurative references to theater are de rigueur in masochism theory, Lynda Hart has pointed out that most often "the way in which 'theater' is used as an implied synonym for 'fantasy' ignores the complexities of both. What *kind of theater* we are talking about is scarcely ever mentioned."[19] The sustained interest with which this book interrogates masochistic writing's relationship to theater, by examining literary works that are for and about the stage, is, I believe, unusual, and this focus reveals a distinctive account of how writing can function erotically. In particular, theater turns out to furnish a specific fantasy of writing modeled, as it were, on playwriting: writing as a practice of writing toward *something else*, something like enactment, which will be unpredictably dangerous to the writing's and the writer's integrity, and is nevertheless (and therefore) writing's insistent aim. This account of masochism's theatricality becomes key, moreover, for thinking about desire that emerges in proximity to actual harm and oppression, and as an anticipatory strategy of response to psychically untenable situations. Throughout its readings, *Throw Yourself Away* will thus repeatedly discover an erotics of pain that cannot be reconciled with the premises of autonomy, safety, and existential or aesthetic stability that often seem to attend masochism in Freud and in many of his readers. Instead, the literary masochism we encounter can function as a mechanism of ambivalent survival, a means of negotiating and navigating injurious realities, rather than an indulgence best pursued from a position of unassailed security.[20]

Less surprising, no doubt, is the fact that throughout these readings, writing shows up again and again as a sexual practice in itself: a system of erotic gratification, however precarious or untenable the desires and pleasures thus set in motion. I don't believe this possibility will require much introduction, let alone a defense; see, for instance, Roland Barthes's entire body of work, or Michel Foucault's famous argument that in modern Europe "sex became something to say," an account in which sexual and discursive practices emerge as coconstitutive.[21] It takes Foucault's *History of Sexuality* fewer than forty pages to discredit the "often-stated theme, that sex is outside of discourse"; surely by now there is no need to argue that writing can be a way of having sex.[22] Indeed, the safety of this assumption is one reason why it has seemed to me (and to many other authors before me) reasonable to write a book about masochism without, say, visiting dungeons or interviewing practitioners.[23] Nor do representations of what might be called "actual BDSM sex" take place in most of the texts I read. But this raises a definitional question: how do I know masochism when I read it?

Perhaps the defining feature of what I've come to understand as literary masochism is that in these texts, writing is not only the expression or representation of desire attached to pain but is also imagined as what makes their conjuncture possible: as sustaining a coincidence between the two that would otherwise be unattainable. This admittedly somewhat instrumentalizing perspective on writing marks a difference between my readings and more concertedly formalist approaches to masochism's textual force. Thus for the Victorianist scholar Clair Jarvis—who, like Musser, emphasizes that "from its earliest uses by sexologists, the concept of masochism has been connected to literary analysis"—masochism is most interesting as a "primarily formal, not psychological" term.[24] In her 2016 monograph *Exquisite Masochism*, Jarvis calls attention to a tendency in Victorian novels whereby the unfolding of a marriage plot is suspended or interrupted by erotically charged but narratively static *scenes* of negotiation, arousal, and refusal between dominant women and the men who are not going to end up marrying them. The compositional importance of such scenes, Jarvis argues, complicates and often undermines the apparent values, and imaginaries, seemingly promoted by the novels' plots. These masochistic passages even offer to reshape what reading itself can feel like, since "by virtue of their static presentation, they force greater readerly attention to their constitutive elements—that is, to form."[25] My "masochism," like Jarvis's, becomes available with or as a sexualization of literary form. And yet even as I think some of my readings will resonate with Jarvis's account, for me, masochism *is* irreducibly psychological and indeed experiential; it always implies someone's desire to be hurt, dispensed with, or destroyed. In these texts, such desire avails itself of—and develops through—an erotic engagement and production of form, which is something subjects imagine and experience: form, as the possibility of a depersonalizing literary achievement, manifests *within* masochistic fantasy, rather than being merely the result or the sign or the shape of that fantasy.[26] In other words, it's not just that the masochistic imagination privileges specific formal attributes; it's also, more crudely, that masochists fantasize about literary form.

Indeed, it's precisely because of the ways Freud's theories of masochism point toward literature's importance for sex (and, of course, vice-versa) that I have found the psychoanalytic discourse on masochism indispensable for these readings—and have in fact been drawn to privilege Freud's accounts over the Deleuzean model Jarvis adapts.[27] It's true that Deleuze, unlike Freud, explicitly insists on the validity of a "literary approach" to the study of masochism; but Deleuze's argument that "the clinical specificities of sadism and masochism are not separable from the literary values peculiar to Sade and Masoch," and his subsequent elucidation of a theory of masochism produced entirely through a reading that contrasts the latter author with the former, ultimately confines masochism to a singular literary aesthetic.[28] While echoes and anticipations of this aesthetic can of course be found in the works of other authors, which can then be claimed as masochistic on that basis, I have never felt moved to grant Masoch's texts this degree of definitional authority over masochism—not because I think masochism is a "real" phenomenon that exists prior to its specific literary history, but because it seems to me that the other texts that constitute this history, including Deleuze's own, are always also revising and redefining masochism, nomenclature notwithstanding. In this respect, Freud's more sporadic but insistent references to a more generalized sphere of literary experience, while sometimes irritating in themselves, have often seemed to me more flexible and hence more suggestive for thinking about what is afoot in the texts I examine. Freud's accounts are also often more helpful in encounters with scenes in which what is erotic is not (or not only) a specific literary sensibility—say, the decadence of indulgently detailed description—but a fantasy of experiencing something like *the* literary itself.

The more we read Freud on masochism, however, the harder it becomes to decide whether masochism is a particular kind of sexuality or a feature of all sexuality—and thus whether or not it is even meaningful to speak of "a masochist."[29] This is not exactly surprising, since Freud's work characteristically relocates deviance to the heart of the normal, but it does produce a certain conceptual tension. As masochism becomes increasingly central to Freud's account of subjectivity, that is, masochists still also appear in his work as distinctive characters whose conscious fantasies—let alone their "real-life performances" (*Veranstaltungen*)—are by no means assumed to be typical of the population at large.[30] And yet in his 1924 article "The Economic Problem of Masochism," for example, the pervert serves less as an object of clinical concern than as a kind of illustration, acting out the "masochistic trend in the instinctual life of human beings"—of human beings in general—that seems to be the real topic of interest.[31] As Musser notes, masochism here "is at once a marginal perversion and a necessary universality."[32] Men who like to be "gagged, bound, painfully beaten, whipped, in some way maltreated, forced into unconditional obedience, dirtied and debased" are ultimately adduced in an attempt to show us all something about ourselves.[33]

Sounding this dimension of Freudian masochism, Leo Bersani's 1986 book *The Freudian Body* famously discerned that "sexuality—at least in the mode in which it is constituted—could be thought of as a tautology for masochism."[34] For Bersani, that is, all sexuality is masochistic, grounded in an experience of self-shattering, and art itself is fundamentally a "replicative elaboration of masochistic sexual tensions": the encounter with artistic form offers a site—or more precisely, an endless series of sites—where the ego can experience shattering, i.e., pleasure, with a body to which it remains unattached and that it thus does not actually need to destroy.[35] We might expect that Bersani's account of art as masochistic would privilege representations of violence, but instead he asks us to see masochistic sexuality at work in texts and images that diffract, displace, and proliferate violence by, so to speak, fucking with our perception at the formal level. This means that for Bersani, something like "literary masochism" would operate without any necessary reference to masochistic characters or even painfully sexy scenes: masochism would simply always be at work in the formal disruptions that constitute literary language.

On this point my account parts ways with Bersani's, since I am interested in the way investment in the literary collects around people—characters and implied authorial subjects—whose erotic lives also exhibit a marked or remarkable attachment to suffering. I am interested, that is, in a masochistic sexuality that is distinctive enough not to be "a tautology," at least in the sense Bersani means here. I'd be willing to entertain the notion, asserted both by Bersani and by Freud, that perverse masochism—the particular enjoyment of violent sex or violence as sex, real or imagined—fundamentally just *shows* us something about normative sexuality: "a kind of melodramatic version," as Bersani puts it, of the way sexuality would unobtrusively be working anyway.[36] But if that's so, then what interests me is the logic of those melodramatics: why and how it is that masochism seems to press desire toward emphatic expression, as it does in the works I look at here.

Of course, these terms—"melodrama," "showing," "emphatic expression"—bring us back to theater. The masochist's overweening drive to express her otherwise unremarkable desire might well seem continuous with the familiar characterization of masochism as a rather embarrassingly *stagey* perversion. "To the masochist," as Timothy Murray puts it, "an external audience is a structural necessity since the body is centrally on display."[37] This trope shows up widely across masochism theory from Freud's "Economic Problem" essay onward, especially in accounts of masochistic men. The dramaturgies we'll encounter, however, take the stage as a more complicated erotic opportunity: again and again in these texts, masochism invests in a notion of theatricality that subordinates self-display to self-displacement and self-erasure. Here theater isn't only a place for viewing and being viewed; it's also, even more centrally, a place for disappearing into darkness, and for delegating pleasure to others.

In this sense, masochism eroticizes a rather trickier "theatricality" of writing, closer to the kind found in poststructuralist accounts of textuality like Jacques Derrida's or Paul de Man's, or indeed throughout the essays in Murray's 1997 anthology *Mimesis, Masochism, and Mime: The Politics of Theatricality in Contemporary French Thought*—a discourse whose influence I bet you've discerned in some of my formulations above. In these accounts, theatricality appears as the attrition of self that takes place each time I duplicate or "stage" my self by writing it down, dislocating my being by consigning its truth to the alterity and contingency of the inscription.[38] The piece of writing whose point, like an actor's, is to be there *for* me—as in Derrida's "dangerous supplement"—becomes sexualized in masochistic desire as a technology for making myself disappear.[39] Or to return to Foucault, it's as if these masochistic texts were intent on wresting the maximum erotic charge from his observation that the written work "now possesses the right to kill, to be its author's murderer" as "the writing subject cancels out the signs of his particular individuality."[40]

Does all this mean that—at least in these theoretical systems—masochism would be "a tautology for" writing as well as for sexuality, threatening to lose its descriptive specificity in that direction too? If, as Bersani suggests, masochistic sex is merely a kind of *exaggerated rendering* of the drive to get yourself shattered that may be the most basic feature of sexuality as such, then this heightening or sensationalizing function of masochism would seem to manifest also in relation to the ordinary logic of textuality, which would, if you agree with Foucault, Derrida, and de Man, always be making us disappear anyway. But this is where, again, I'd want to insist on the specificity of the masochist's unseemly insistence: it's as if the masochistic writer is essentially someone who can't just enjoy the self-subverting structures of sex and text but has to keep making a scene about them. By chewing the scenery, as it were, of both sex and writing, the masochistic subject's confessional performances help illuminate the logic of both structures, as Jean-Jacques Rousseau does for Derrida in *Of Grammatology*, or as Freud's masochistic patient does for Jean Laplanche and

J.-B. Pontalis, who derive from the fantasy of "A Child Is Being Beaten" a theory of fantasy as such.[41] What the readings in this book will argue, however, is that the masochist's insistence on *making structure explicit*—which one might almost gloss as: her insistence on being emphatically basic—is not merely a heuristic convenience for those who would use it (her) to theorize basic structures; it (she) also *produces* theories, which is to say, in these texts, masochism is what writes. The masochist is one who has to make a thing of it, who insists on falling roughly out of sync with reality, with the body, even with her own discourse, encountering the facets of her life as if they weren't hers, and demonstrating her displacement from pleasure by documenting it, inscribing it. Where others might *have* sex and *do* writing, the masochist will tend to *elaborate on* both of these.

The term "elaboration," which also comes from Bersani—art, recall, is the "replicative elaboration of masochistic sexual tensions"—has seemed to me richly suggestive for specifying the masochistic attachment to writing. For Bersani, "elaboration" helps to name the ground where sexual desire and literature converge: "There is no scene of desire which is not an *elaboration*, a kind of visual interpretation, of other scenes," he writes in *A Future for Astyanax*. "Like literature, desire is inseparable from repetition, but they are both modes of repetition which produce difference."[42] Psychoanalytic theory at least since Freud's *Beyond the Pleasure Principle* has posited repetition as fundamental to sexuality, so fundamental that Berlant, for instance, defines "pleasure" as "a reiteration that makes a form, not necessarily something that feels good."[43] In the texts this book will consider, this kind of restive reiteration or recitation typically occurs as a desirous return to the act of writing. In this respect, my account takes its cue even more directly from "elaboration" as presented by Darieck Scott, whose reading of Samuel Delany renders writing, in Delany's erotic work, as a kind of perpetual motion machine: "one responds to the desire experienced by writing about it, in part to satisfy the desire by, in a sense, controlling it as one does in fantasy, but since the conventions of language always write us as we manipulate them, such control fails, so that the desire becomes *ever more elaborated*, it proliferates."[44] This vision of the scene of writing, as a practice that courts both compositional "control" and the latter's failure, will reappear throughout the readings in this book.

Published in 2010, Scott's *Extravagant Abjection: Blackness, Power, and Sexuality in the African American Literary Imagination* shows how another series of authors has seized on the literary as a privileged site for moving through the conjuncture of violation and pleasure; Scott's readings thus demonstrate both the complexity and the necessity of thinking this conjuncture in relation to race. *Extravagant Abjection* theorizes a counterintuitive form of Black power in scenes of masculine sexual abjection; to do so, it draws on Bersani and Edelman as well as Hortense Spillers and Frantz Fanon. Like other readers, Scott criticizes the "defining whiteness in Bersani's conception of gayness," and he is careful to maintain Bersani's Freudian account of masochism as "a useful analogy" for his own description of Black abjection, "rather than [as] definitive" for the latter.[45] Nevertheless, he nimbly incorporates psychoanalytic and white queer discourse on masochism into his own account of desire in Black texts, in readings that explicitly trace that desire's emergence in and as a relation to the history of white supremacist domination. In this work, Scott goes a long way toward showing how a critical project centered on masochism can productively bring these different interpretive registers into dialogue.

Perhaps not all the way, however: registering Scott's "anxiety about using [the term] *masochism*" itself—as opposed to sexualized "abjection"—Musser suggests that this ambivalence may be inevitable given the history of masochism's vexed relation to race, which she explores in her own book, *Sensational Flesh: Race, Power, and Masochism* (2014).[46] Musser observes that the term "masochism" carries considerable "baggage … when applied to black bodies," noting that "the problem is compounded when one is speaking of black women."[47] Musser elucidates this "baggage" throughout the book, tracing the intellectual history of masochism's racial implications. To begin with, there is the fact that Fanon's account of masochism—probably the most influential theoretical account of masochism in relation to race—posits masochism as a structure of white fantasy about "the Negro's aggression," a fantasy that directly serves the interest of white supremacy insofar as it has "made whites feel both justified in their racism and punished for it"; in this account, "white practices of domination are laced with the guilty pleasures of masochism."[48] Here masochism is a defensive (and illusory) structure that functions primarily to protect the continued enactment of domination; constitutive for white subjectivity, it would seem to have no place in the subjectivity of the dominated. Fanon, indeed like Freud and Deleuze, conceives masochism as an inherently "performative" representation of suffering, a conception that renders the concept inapplicable to the psychic lives of those who are actually, systematically oppressed; if Black male masochism is even remotely thinkable in Fanon, Musser writes, it is rendered "unrecognizable because … it becomes folded into [the Black man's] subjectivity and naturalized": actual domination has stripped him of the agency required for performing a masochistic position.[49]

Here masochism's whiteness is twofold: masochism is a perk of white privilege—only the powerful can play at powerlessness—but it is also a psychic support for the system that creates that privilege, because it helps white people manage their guilt through exclusively fantasmatic expiation.

Indeed, the pleasure this expiation provides would tend to redouble white subjects' attachment to the same oppressive structures that render whites (punishably, hence pleasurably) guilty, an erotic fixation that supplements the material incentive to domination. The masochist who keeps doing ill in order to be punished for it appears in Freud's famous conceptualization of "moral masochism," which we'll consider in chapter 1. And while Freud doesn't seem to be thinking about either race or structural oppression here, his rather startling parenthetical note that moral masochism is "exemplified in … many Russian character-types" does associate the concept with a society whose historical dependence on unfree labor was notorious.[50] Less oblique, though equally glancing, is Freud's aforementioned reference to *Uncle Tom's Cabin* as one of the books that had stimulated masochistic fantasies in his patients: "In my patients' *milieu* it was almost always the same books," he notes in "A Child Is Being Beaten."[51] Citing an earlier case study by Richard von Krafft-Ebing, in which a masochistic patient would excite himself by reading that novel's whipping scenes, David Savran has argued that this kind of eroticized identification with figures of Black suffering "allow[ed] the white male subject to take up the position of victim" in a manner that would become constitutive of white masculinity during the twentieth century, across the political spectrum.[52]

The point is not only that masochism feeds on and feeds into white supremacy but also that its very coherence as a concept emerged from patterns in white people's ways of abiding in their own perpetuation of colonialism and slavery. Indeed, Aliyyah Abdur-Rahman has argued that Black authors of mid-nineteenth-century abolitionist autobiography—in particular, Frederick Douglass and Harriet Jacobs—produced "representations of sexual perversity under conditions of enslavement" that would become fundamental for subsequent "theories of sexual perversion"; as theorized by these authors, "racial slavery provided the background—and the testing ground—for the emergence and articulation of [medical] theories" of sadomasochism.[53] Their discourse anticipates sexological theory not only by articulating white masters' and mistresses' cruelty as sexually sadistic but also by instituting a masochistic circuit in the "implicitly nineteenth-century white female" reader: their narrative text "provokes fantasies of sexual assault and thereby prompts an alliance with antislavery politics as a way to disassociate from the sexual perversions that precipitate and permeate enslavement—and that to some extent are the reader's own."[54] Abdur-Rahman suggests that the white women who read these narratives experienced an intolerable enjoyment; in this schema, their impulse to "disassociate from" their own sexual fantasy of being harmed—a dissociative impulse that will remain crucial in Freud's account of female masochistic patients, and that will be central to my own understanding of masochism throughout this book—establishes, in this case, the gendered and raced position of the white ally.[55]

Abdur-Rahman also cautiously discerns a second masochism at work here, which she calls a "literary masochism … in the text of the black author."[56] In this formulation, however, the "literary" seems to replace, not stimulate, the sexual: "the slave's masochistic relation to his master inheres in textual representation; the masochistic payoff, *belonging to the narrator*, is neither her pleasure nor [the enslaved character's] but exposure of the master's shameful sadism."[57] In a certain way, this treatment of masochism is a kind of perfect obverse of Scott's: Scott—as noted—hesitates to describe Black writers' investments in racialized abjection as masochistic, but he argues strongly for the function of pleasure in their literary renderings of sexual violation; Abdur-Rahman retains the term "masochism" for her authors but transposes its meaning: now it refers, not to pleasurable suffering but to a relish for enacting "exposure" (exposure of the captors, not of the narrators themselves). With this counterintuitive formulation, Abdur-Rahman implies that the term "literary masochism" might find its proper meaning *in* a self-contradictory enactment, discerning a mode of authorial desire that both absents itself and thereby constitutes itself at—or as—the site of the literary. This mode of authorial desire is, of course, historically specific, and specifically Black. And yet it seems to me that echoes of this dialectical structure recur in the self-displacing dramaturgies we'll encounter throughout *Throw Yourself Away*, in late nineteenth- and twentieth-century work by white as well as Black authors. If this is right, then what the similarity shows is not that the structure transcends historical specificity but, on the contrary, that this is yet another way in which fantasies that have typically passed as racially unmarked owe their erotic logic to the modern history of race—and here, to Black literary achievement in particular.

I'm aware that this hypothesis betrays a certain drive, in my own writing, to discern structures of fantasmatic experience that might be available to people of different racial identities, even though the structures themselves have been historically determined by those differences' violent production. Perhaps this is a symptom of obtuse liberal humanism on my part. But if masochism emerged as an erotic periphenomenon of white supremacist domination, and sometimes continues to operate as such, it has also circulated between subjects across a range of intersectional positions: its social dimensions and potential alignments cannot be exhaustively defined by its origins, any more than its literary possibilities are all contained in Sacher-Masoch's novels.

Thus Musser, while she explores the historical, conceptual, and political deterrents to theorizing Black women's masochism, also warns that refusing to theorize it can repeat the violence that has historically denied Black women any claim on pleasure or desire.[58] Her argument echoes Scott's caution against the "risk ... that in being scrupulous about the *difference* the practices and conditions of slavery make for putative universalities such as pleasure and desire, we begin to conclude that what is different about this pleasure, desire, and so on is that it is virtually nonexistent."[59] Denying the possibility of pleasure and desire under conditions of domination would, Scott argues, mean refusing to recognize a particular kind of power that may emerge under such conditions: "the *taking* of pleasure out of the maw of humiliation and pain, and the utilization of that pain that windows into pleasure and back again for an experience of self that, though abject, is politically salient, potentially politically effective or powerful."[60] Ariane Cruz develops a related argument in *The Color of Kink: Black Women, BDSM, and Pornography*, a study that analyzes artistic and pornographic work alongside interviews with Black BDSM practitioners. Challenging the "long-standing imagining of BDSM as a kind of Anglo phenomenon," Cruz contends both that Black women's participation in sadomasochistic sexual practice, including "race play" that explicitly sexualizes white supremacist domination, ought to be centered in critical accounts of BDSM, and also that race play "delineates the [everyday] performance of racialized sexuality more generally."[61] Most recently, Takeo Rivera has theorized Asian American identity as a masochistic formation, tracing its constitution through the fantasmatic repercussions of the Vincent Chin murder, the "model minority" myth, and what Rivera argues is a masochistic fantasy of Blackness "as a racial superego for the Asian American political imagination."[62]

To the question we began with—"why another book about masochism?"—these projects suggest in reply that in some contexts, the concept of masochism can help illuminate certain fundamental structures of BIPOC experience, an aim whose validity no one could contest. Correspondingly, Fanon, Saidiya Hartman, and Savran have all demonstrated the political stakes of theorizing a specifically white masochism, an endeavor to which most of the readings in this book—its readings of masochistic work by white authors—might earnestly try to contribute. If I have hesitated to announce these readings throughout as the engagements with whiteness that they obviously also are, this is partly because the operation of whiteness in these texts has often seemed to me too clear to warrant much explication. But it's also because I don't want to delimit in advance the social field of the erotic structures I discover, which are first of all textual structures and therefore prone to circulate, compelling identification and disidentification in unpredictable ways—as shown, for example, by Rivera's uptake of Deleuze to describe Asian American subjectivation, or Scott's careful use of Bersani in theorizing Black masculine abjection. Again, the point is not that these erotic configurations exist prior to, or somehow "above" or "beneath," the racialization that structures modernity but that they can and do echo each other, with varying degrees of distortion, across modernity's constitutive divides—and indeed, that the distortion itself may sometimes feed back into fantasy, complicating and compounding desire.

I'd offer this sonic feedback as another figure for the "universal sound of psychoanalysis" to which Spillers wryly refers in her essay "'All the Things You Could Be by Now, If Sigmund Freud's Wife Was Your Mother': Psychoanalysis and Race." The essay extends and reshapes the Fanonian project of staging a transformative intimacy between psychoanalysis and critical race theory, asking: "how might psychoanalytic theories speak about 'race' as a self-consciously assertive reflexivity, and how might 'race' expose the gaps that psychoanalytic theories awaken?"[63] Elaborating on some of these "gaps," Spillers writes:

> It seems that Freud wrote as if his man/woman were Everybody's, were constitutive of the social order, and that coeval particularities carried little or no weight. The universal sound of psychoanalysis, in giving short shrift to cultural uniqueness (which it had to circumvent, we suppose, in order to win the day for itself and, furthermore, in order to undermine, to throw off the track, the anti-Semitic impulses of Freud's era), must be invigilated as its limit: in other words, precisely because its theories seduce us to want to concede, to "give in" to its seeming naturalness, to its apparent rightness to the way we live, we must be on guard all the more against assimilating other cultural regimes to its modes of analyses too quickly and without question, if at all.
>
> But for all that, I have no evidence that what are for me, at least, the major topics of its field are not in fact stringently operative in African-American community.[64]

Pointing out psychoanalysis's own subjection to the history of white supremacy ("the anti-Semitic impulses of Freud's era"), Spillers goes on to argue that while Freud and Lacan have systematically misrecognized the particularity of their own cultural perspectives, psychoanalytic theory—and in particular, its ways of attending to desire's contradictions and incoherencies—can nevertheless be productive for articulating the conditions of Black life. Indeed, her entire body of work, and the manifold projects that draw from it, bear out this conviction.

Spillers's call for vigilant suspicion of psychoanalysis's "universal sound" harks back again to Fanon, who produces a paradigmatic critique of Freudian universalization in *Black Skin, White Masks.* In the book's fourth chapter, Fanon skewers the white psychoanalytic theorist Octave Mannoni's ascription of a "dependency complex" to colonized people in Madagascar, a complex which, according to Mannoni, supposedly preceded colonization. In seeking an ahistorical psychic source for subjects' behavior under colonial oppression, Mannoni—as Fanon ironically puts it—discovers "that the white man acts in obedience to an authority complex, a leadership complex, while the Malagasy obeys a dependency complex. Everyone is satisfied."[65] Fanon argues that this dehistoricizing mode of interpretation is absurd: colonized subjects' feelings of inferiority are rooted not in innate psychological "complexes," but in the real violent domination that conditions their lives. Challenging Mannoni's Oedipal interpretation of a series of dreams among his Malagasy analysands, Fanon writes: "the discoveries of Freud are of no use to us here. What must be done is to restore this dream *to its proper time*, and this time is the period during which eighty thousand natives were killed—that is to say, one of every fifty persons in the population; and *to its proper place.*"[66] In Fanon's hands, Mannoni's deployment of psychoanalysis to naturalize colonial subjects' suffering, and thereby to neutralize political action against that suffering's real, historical causes, demonstrates the damage (not to mention the absurdity) that can be wrought when a universalizing white discourse on desire is brought to bear on a real scene of racial violence and domination.

As the chapter on Mannoni, along with Fanon's other work, makes explicit, and as readers invested in psychoanalysis never tire of pointing out, Fanon himself is a psychoanalyst and psychoanalytic thinker, determined not to jettison but to retheorize such terms as "complex" and "masochism" so that they can be used to understand, treat, and empower the oppressed subjects produced through global white domination.[67] Nevertheless, the critique of universalism—which echoes in Spillers's reminder to be watchful—has perhaps been better heeded in recent decades than the argument for engaging psychoanalysis in the first place, especially when it comes to cultural studies of sexuality. In particular, as we've noted, the critique of universalism has been leveled against the constellation of late-twentieth-century white American queer theorists who mark masochism's critical heyday, and upon whose work the book you're reading frequently elaborates.[68] Accused of seeking to "distanc[e] queerness from ... the contamination of race, gender, or other particularities that taint the purity of sexuality as a singular trope of difference" (José Esteban Muñoz), this work fell foul of a widespread frustration with universalizing accounts of (queer) sex, and the appeal of masochism as a critical model sagged therewith.[69]

At the same time, however, another critical trajectory unfurling from Spillers's invitation to pursue "an apposite psychoanalytic protocol for the subjects of 'race'" has pressed Freudian and post-Freudian discourse on desire to become something that can meaningfully address this historical axis of difference and domination.[70] Scott's *Extravagant Abjection* has been decisive in shaping this trajectory, as has Christina Sharpe's *Monstrous Intimacies: Making Post-Slavery Subjects*, also published in 2010, which will be a key text for my readings in chapter 3. Both books boldly excavate traces of "pleasure" at the site of racialized "humiliation and pain" (Scott); but what's perhaps even more surprising, given the preponderance of the antiuniversalist critique, is the fact that both also argue for something like a renewed universalism. That is, while Sharpe and Scott both locate their analyses along sharp lines of racial difference and particular histories of racial enslavement and domination—and while both their analyses are acutely alive to the differences made by and to gender[71]—they both also insist upon a category of subjectivity (and desire) that extends across these determinations.

Scott begins *Extravagant Abjection* by referring to a first-person plural, an "Us," which he defines as "all who are connected by dint of ancestry or culture to the practices of chattel slavery in the Americas, all who bear any relation at all to the concept of blackness"—that is to say, presumably, everyone, though this collectivity is obviously internally differentiated, as Scott's analysis always reflects.[72] Somewhat more programmatically, Sharpe in *Monstrous Intimacies* theorizes "the ongoing processes of subjectification during slavery and into post-slavery to which all modern subjects are made subject," even as "post-slavery subjectivity is largely borne by and readable on the (New World) *black* subject."[73] At various points in her readings of works by writers and artists of the Black diaspora, Sharpe is careful to insist that the "monstrous" structure of pleasure on which this subjectivity depends—the practice of fantasmatically "entering into black bodies for enjoyment"—occurs in "those who already inhabit the black body as well as those whose inhabiting of it is fleeting"; conversely, she criticizes white readers "who white themselves out of the scenes" they confront, such that "race, like slavery, is read as entirely about black people."[74] Perhaps most surprisingly of all, Sharpe ends *Monstrous Intimacies* with a sentence that aligns her own critical project with precisely the universalizing dimension of Freud's: "And just as Freud insisted on the universality of psychoanalysis (it was not, he maintained, a Jewish science), so do I read [the artist Kara] Walker's positioning of her big black mammy ... as the mother, the 'mythic source' of *all* U.S./American post-slavery subjects."[75] Sharpe, that is, decides to leave her readers with a claim that the subject formation she has been describing—here specifically in Kara Walker's work, but by implication, throughout all the works Sharpe reads—*is* universal; she leaves us with what Spillers calls the "universal sound" of psychoanalysis ringing in our ears.

If, for these writers, desire and pleasure still offer themselves as conceptual objects through which it becomes possible to approach something like the universal, their work also encourages us to ask how desire and pleasure might slip out of their passive position *as objects* of this inquiry, to show up again in the theorizing impulse itself. It is, Spillers writes, "precisely because its theories *seduce us to want to concede, to 'give in'* to its seeming naturalness, to its apparent rightness to the way we live" that vigilance against uncritical extensions of psychoanalysis is necessary; she thus acknowledges that desire inhabits her own critical practice, and more specifically, frames universalism as a *seduction* that operates there. Universalism's tantalizing promise of "rightness," moreover, addresses the intellectual subject—who in Spillers's case is a Black American woman in the late twentieth century—precisely in her embodied, socially specific particularity: "the way we live." Of course, Spillers is saying that this promise of rightness is treacherous, that the lure is one to which her particular "we" must not succumb. But in framing as a scene of seduction the actual incommensurability that obtains between a universalizing system and a particular subject for whom it promises, falsely, to speak, Spillers raises the question of how desire might operate through the very negativity—the sonic distortion—of this nonrightness. The connection Spillers draws between the falseness of the Eurocentric universal's promise to be "right" and the dangerous desire that promise may evoke suggests, I think, a question of how the universalizing edge of any theory—including theory implicit in works of literature—might wield some of its appeal precisely *by* its falseness: its way of cutting *against* the particular experience of the real subjects whom it also claims to address. It seems to me, therefore, that an analytic of masochism, even as it may necessarily partake of universalism, can also help us understand the seductive power of universalism itself. *Throw Yourself Away* tries to contribute to this effort of understanding.

The images of masochistic elaboration, or literary form making, that will emerge in this book demonstrate a recursive insistence on (melo)dramatizing the familiar psychoanalytic story wherein desire's repetitions keep bringing us back to what hurts—both in order to control it, and in order not to. In returning repeatedly to the site where our capacity for enjoyment wavers, masochistic writing lays claim to unpleasure exactly where unpleasure would unmake the subject and shatter her claim; it does this by being at once a conduit to suffering and a means of separation from it, what Freud will call, somewhat enigmatically, an "escape." Through the mediation of writing, the masochist attempts to make eluding destruction a way of submitting to it, and vice-versa. Masochistic writing is writing that can't stop insisting on its own textual condition, because that condition is what makes the coincidence of utter brokenness and coherence possible; it is the reason there can be a subject of masochistic desire at all. But this is also why the masochistic text must keep circling back to reiterate and "proliferate" (Scott) its attachment to scenes of destruction, since if it didn't do so it would, as a text *on* getting destroyed, simply have mastered (or at least survived) the latter. Accordingly, the masochistic text will keep taking itself as an object, not only in order to neutralize the danger of its desire but also in order to reactivate that danger outside the frame that defines its ostensible content. This is to say that masochistic literary elaboration will tend to involve some version of what the narratologist Gérard Genette calls "metalepsis," literally "taking hold of (telling) by changing level."[76] For us, this means that the masochistic writing subject will tend to use writing to vault outside sexual experience, a shift that is achieved not only in the move from undergoing experience to writing about it but again (and again) within writing, each time the writing imagination finds a new way to reflect on its own procedure. Each time this happens, the writing subject relocates herself to a new remove from the violent experience being desirously described; this remove, however, offers both a respite from suffering and a different venue for its return.

In chapter 2, I'll describe this self-removal as a "dramaturgical" operation, grounding it in the Freudian patient's refusal to take up a place in her own fantasy, and see how this sexual logic of self-displacement unfolds as a fantasy of theatrical authorship (and gender) in *Hedda Gabler* and in James's "Nona Vincent." In chapter 3, reading three plays by Kennedy, we'll see how authorship—a notion of writing once again modeled, I'll argue, on theater—itself functions both as a necessary means of desirous self-assertion and as a painful, purposeful repetition of the self's violent systemic erasure. The move of removing the self from the scene can also manifest as an erotics of abstraction, as we'll find in reading Deleuze and Freud by the lights of Gaitskill in chapter 1, and again in the readings of autotheoretical texts by Paul Preciado and Sedgwick that, along with a short swerve into the writing of Sedgwick's friend Gary Fisher, comprise chapter 4. Endlessly elaborating their own desire, the masochist may sometimes show up—in literature, in theory, in sexual common sense, and on the stage—as a creature incredibly self-involved; but in the texts we'll read, their self-elaborations always also insist on unleashing, and perversely dramatizing, textual mechanisms of self-erasure or what de Man calls "de-facement."[77] Determined not only to succumb to this negative movement but also to reiterate or stage it, these writers imagine writing's negativity as both theatrical adventure and erotic force. That's why I couldn't resist using a phrase addressed to modern drama's most awesomely perverse and irreducibly theatrical heroine—"Hedda, how could you throw yourself away!"—as the book's title.[78]

And speaking of heroines, it's time to say something about the masochist's pronouns, which I render most frequently as she/her, but sometimes as they/them, and occasionally as he/him, depending on which text we're discussing. I have hesitated to impose a consistent pronoun for the composite figure I am calling, across these texts, "the masochist," even the usually preferable they-series, because gender—and in particular, binary gender—often seems erotically crucial to the particular fantasies each text constructs. This has been true throughout masochism's conceptual history: it's a familiar observation that nineteenth-century sexology, and sometimes psychoanalysis, conceived masochism as perverse *because* feminizing, a logic that implies a properly masculine subject. Deleuze, who in some ways challenges this tradition, still (as Silverman puts it in her own classic book on male masochism) "elaborates a theoretical model of masochism in which the suffering position is almost necessarily male."[79] In the first chapters below, we'll see women as well as men fantasizing femininity; in chapter 4, we'll see Preciado and Sedgwick both making gender a central point of erotic as well as theoretical concern. All these texts insist, in different ways, upon the abstract negativity of binary gender, demonstrating its powerful erotic affordances as a feature of masochistic elaboration. Masochism would thus be both an especially lively field of what Robyn Wiegman calls "the desire for gender," and a site that demonstrates with concerted force the erotics of gender as theorized by Andrea Long Chu, for whom gender is always "the self's gentle suicide in the name of someone *else*'s desires."[80]

Gentle—or not. For most of the protagonists who show up in these chapters, femininity is rough stuff, and it's precisely this roughness that opens an erotic investment in gender. Throughout the twentieth century, authors critical of masochism in women—from Simone de Beauvoir in *The Second Sex* to the writers of the 1982 anthology *Against Sadomasochism*—typically emphasized the continuity (and causal link) between women's fantasies of being hurt and dominated by men and the underlying reality of a society structured by patriarchal violence.[81] Pro-S&M authors have, in turn, variously emphasized the productive critical distance between sadomasochistic pleasure and social structures of domination, as when Cruz argues that "violence for black female performers in BDSM becomes not just a vehicle of intense pleasure but also a mode of accessing and critiquing power."[82] Analyses like Cruz's, however, also suggest that this mode of enjoyment depends upon feeling—indeed, may be a way to survive feeling—the prox-imity of actual historical (and ongoing) structural harm.[83] As Musser puts it, masochism is never separable from "the question of what it feels like to be enmeshed in various regimes of power."[84] Against the assumption that masochism is necessarily the province of subjects who are structurally re-moved from endangerment and are thus free to fantasize about it, these accounts suggest a model of desire as a means of navigating an unthink-able intimacy with something that already hurts, something that should be, and will be, impossible to want.

In the texts I examine, writing often appears as the means of this pur-posely impossible engagement. And this means that repeatedly, begin-ning with Gaitskill, Freud, and Deleuze in chapter 1, we'll encounter a structure wherein masochistic fantasy sets itself up to fail. This is not simply because of the masochist's naïveté or romantic idealism but more profoundly because this version of the masochistic imagination depends upon the proximity of a threat that neither that imagination's aesthetic achievements nor its erotic tolerances will be able to comprehend. Writ-ing appears as an erotic technology for approaching this threat, which is imagined—and felt—as something unimaginable, something writing will invoke and provoke but not finally manage or contain.

This notion of masochistic writing as writing toward a threatening something else suggests why writing for the stage would be one of mas-ochism's privileged genres, as I said earlier, and as the readings in chap-ters 2 and 3 will show. It may also hint at why the genre of autotheory—a mode of writing that offers to expose the writer's self to multiple forms of negation launched from points outside that self—would offer powerful masochistic affordances, as we'll see in chapter 4. And it points to some resonances between masochism and motherhood, which chapter 5, itself succumbing to the pervy lure of the autotheoretical, will try to sound. But more generally, this way of thinking about masochism and writing can help us reckon with some of the most puzzling content of stories about mas-ochistic sex. In particular, it might get us out of having to decide whether masochism is fundamentally "relational"—as Jarvis, for instance, asserts, and as work oriented by BDSM practice tends to reiterate—or "nonrela-tional," as Deleuze's insistence on aesthetic autonomy seems to imply, and as Bersani's account of masochism as tautological ego-shattering fa-mously asserts.[85] The fact is, stories about masochism very often seem to center around what might be called failures of relation: not just relations that turn out to fail but relations that turn out not to *be* relations. And yet this incommensurability is exactly what masochistic desire seems deter-mined to produce for itself.

We'll see this play out starkly in Gaitskill's "A Romantic Weekend," but any number of kinky texts exhibit this dynamic. For instance, Garth Greenwell's "Gospodar"—included in the 2021 *Kink* anthology Greenwell coedited with Kwon—details a sadomasochistic sexual encounter in which the narrator, a racially unmarked native English-speaker living in Sofia, goes to meet a dominant he doesn't know in the latter's "Soviet-style" apartment, hoping that the rough sex will help him get over a former lover.[86] "I had told him I wasn't Bulgarian in one of our online chats, warning him that when we met there might be things I wouldn't understand," the narrator relates. "We'll understand each other, he had said, don't worry, and maybe it was just to ensure this understanding that he had taken me in hand, firmly but not painfully guiding me to my knees."[87] Indeed, the dominant's violent treatment initially engenders not only a great deal of pleasure in the narrator but also moments of something like intimacy: "And you like me too, he said, feeling how hard I was; he gripped me tightly before letting me go. Very much, I said, I like you very much, and it was true ... I had never been with anyone so skilled or so patient."[88] At a certain point, however, the sex turns nonconsensual, and when the narrator resists, the other man becomes woundingly violent; ultimately, the narrator barely escapes after the dominant attacks him a final time in the staircase, injuring his foot and wrist; he cries uncontrollably as he races home, awash in "pain and relief and shame and panic."[89] But while the narrator excoriates himself for risking his life ("I had brought it all upon myself"), he also realizes he'll want to take such risks again: "I would come back ... maybe not to this man but to others like him; I would desire it, though I didn't desire it now."[90] The terrifying revelation that the sadistic partner isn't just playing a mutually agreed-upon role but truly has no sense of the narrator as anything but an object to brutalize—and that the narrator himself cannot consent to the pain and humiliation that result, much less enjoy them—doesn't finally chasten masochistic desire but renews it. This passionately nonrelational relation, an attachment to what will flout relation and shatter fantasy, structures masochism in many of these works; and my readings will often attend to variations on its logic.

In "Gospodar," too, gender is indispensable for making this difference: for producing the radical incommensurability between desire and event that makes this paradoxical mode of enjoyment possible. Greenwell's story could be glossed as the tale of a man who finds himself endangered by his own sexuality *precisely to the extent that it subjects him to feminization.* From the outset of the encounter, it is femininity that signals the unbearable turn things will take: "No, he said, fold your clothes nicely before you come in, be a good girl. At this last, something rose up in me, as at a step too far in humiliation. Most men would feel this, I think, especially men like me, who are taught that it's the worst thing, to seem like a woman.... Something rose up in me at what he said, this man who barred my way, and then it lay back down."[91] Later, when the narrator begins to resist the top's violence, the stakes of this submission to feminization become clear, and the masculinity that "lay back down" turns out to have been "personhood" itself "laid aside," now unrecoverable: "Open, he said, but I didn't open, my whole body clenched in refusal.... I was used to being the stronger one in such encounters, being so tall and so large, I was used to feeling the safety of strength, of knowing I could gather back up that personhood I had laid aside for an evening or an hour. But he was stronger than I was, and I was frightened as he held me down and pressed against me, shoving or thrusting himself."[92] Enraged, the sadist beats the narrator viciously with a leather strap: "The pain of it made me cry out, a womanish cry,... stop, I said in English, I'm sorry, stop."[93] Running home at the end, the narrator tells us, "I was still ashamed of my tears."[94]

How close are we, here, to Bersani's famous vision of the gay male bottom succumbing, through sex, to the "suicidal ecstasy of being a woman"?[95] Whereas Bersani is offering an account of everyday gay male sexuality, and ultimately of sexuality tout court, Greenwell's harrowing story goes out of its way to insist on the exceptional nature of its encounter—exceptional, that is, for a big strong white man. (What must it be like, some of us will wonder, to be "used to feeling the safety of strength" in sexual situations?) For Greenwell as for Bersani, the subject's masochistic identification as a "girl" is what guarantees his susceptibility to sex as destruction—which is what he wants, what he needs, even as it's what he can't bear. In this sense, both Bersani and Greenwell help us understand masochism's classic profile as a male pathology. It's not just that—as is often observed—a desire for pain and submission has traditionally been naturalized in women, so that it can't appear as a perversion in them. It's also that by maintaining an imaginative *distance* from femininity, masochistic men like Greenwell's narrator access femininity *as the form* of what would otherwise be a life-threatening formlessness, guaranteeing that there *is* a discrete position alien to their masculine "safety," a position that can serve as the referent and enabling limit-case of their erotic lives. The difference, of course, is that while Bersani suggests this need for unbearable femininity is just the logic of sex as such, Greenwell casts the need as a life-threatening dependence on the prospect of actual harm. His story suggests that wanting to be a "girl" isn't just a threat to normative models of sovereignty, it's also really dangerous—as many women's lived experiences would also testify.[96]

How can desire survive this kind of danger? "Gospodar" suggests it's by running away in the nick of time, knowing one will come running back again. But for those who can't find such clear paths of retreat from what threatens to destroy them, other erotic strategies emerge. The following chapters will suggest that the most reliably unreliable of these strategies are literary ones. As you might suspect, this book is just one more of them.

"You're Not a Masochist" [CHAPTER 1]

Sadism, Realism, and Fantasy in Gaitskill, Deleuze, and Freud

*I may ... want only the discomposure I can imagine, plus a
little of the right kind extra, and how can I bear the risk of
experiencing the* anything *that might be beyond? How can I
bear not seeking it?*

—LAUREN BERLANT, *Cruel Optimism*

Anything

When Gilles Deleuze argued in 1963 that sexual perversions must be understood through "the literary values" of their canonical authors, he based
his own analysis of masochism on the nineteenth-century stories of Leopold von Sacher-Masoch, after whom that perversion had been named.[1]
Perverse readers today, however, know a literature of masochism that extends far beyond the works of its namesake. This literature includes the
fifty-odd years of bestselling BDSM erotica running from the midcentury
sensation of *The Story of O* to the millennial success of *Fifty Shades*; and
alongside these works of ebullient fantasy, in a kind of adjacent but apparently distinct canon, a succession of more sober stories about masochism,
whose attitude toward this mode of desire often seems painfully unerotic.
Among the latter group we might place, for example, Elfriede Jelinek's
1983 novel *The Piano Teacher*, about an obsessive spinster whose fantasies
are shattered when her strapping male student viciously enacts them; or
the works of Mary Gaitskill, including the 1991 novel *Two Girls, Fat and
Thin* and the stories in her 1988 collection, *Bad Behavior*.[2]

At first glance it would seem fairly easy to distinguish between these two
groups of texts. Where Susan Sontag argued in 1967 that pornographic writings could be divided into "trash" and "authentic literature," today we might
be more inclined to categorize masochism texts not only in terms of their
cultural (and, often inversely, financial) capital but also in terms of the genre
of reading experience each seems to offer us.[3] Frankly erotic texts like *O* or
Fifty Shades, that is, just *are* masochistic fantasies for readers to get off on;
whereas texts that situate their characters' fantasies within a "real" world
hostile to fantasy, as Jelinek and Gaitskill do, invite us to the more sardonic
pleasures of recognizing the ways masochistic desire may be doomed.

As you'll have guessed, my aim in pointing out this intuitive distinction is to observe that the works themselves actually undermine it: that a surprising kind of continuity obtains between these two groups of texts. This continuity, moreover, is due less to any definitional stability of masochism than to what we might call its profoundly destabilizing tendency—its tendency to destabilize not only the masochistic subject herself but also the classifying distinction between what (or who) belongs *in* masochistic fantasy and what belongs outside of it. To see this, we can begin by focusing on a trope that recurs throughout all this literature, wherein I, a character, declare that there are no limits to what I will do or suffer for your enjoyment. In this gesture—or "figure," to adopt Roland Barthes's use of that term in *A Lover's Discourse*—rather than tell you all or indeed any of the particular things I want us to do, I renounce the particularity of fantasy altogether, ceding it to you.[4] "I will do whatever you command," says the hero Severin in Sacher-Masoch's *Venus in Furs*, "I am ready to endure anything."[5] "I'll do whatever you like," says O in *The Story of O*; and we read later that "no pleasure, no joy, no figment of her imagination could compete with the happiness she felt ... at the notion that he could do anything with her, that there was no limit, no restriction in the manner with which, on her body, he might search for pleasure."[6] And in Gaitskill's story "A Romantic Weekend," Beth—who longs to be "crush[ed] like an insect"— tells her lover: "Anything you do will be all right"; "I would do anything with you."[7]

Anything: in other words, all I want is whatever you want, and to get to feel you wanting it, "on [my] body," as O's narrator says. For all its earnest passion, this "anything" has the tactical advantage of obscuring my own particular fantasies, which might disgust or (worse) amuse you: there is something cowardly in the way this figure cajoles you into presenting your fantasy so I won't have to. But "anything" is more than just a demurral; if it weren't, then stories of masochistic desire would just become showplaces for the specific, surprising desires of tops—which they rarely do. While "anything" is manifestly my invitation to you to disclose and enact your desire, and simultaneously a refusal to specify mine, it is also always a kind of self-fashioning and self-display. I will be the one who was able to want the most repugnant, cruel things you could do to me; the more unbearable they are, the better they will prove my powers of wanting. Because in fact, saying I will do or suffer "anything" is above all an attempt to circumscribe every possible event within the radius of my permission, to make traumatic infraction impossible by enclosing you inside the fiery circle of my proleptic consent.

As a moment of elated bluster, "Do anything to me!" bears out Deleuze's claim that "in masochism the ego triumphs."[8] But there is also something slightly embarrassing about this boast, in a way that's a bit like participatory theater: while pretending to unleash your activity, all it does is delimit it. Somehow, the term through which I shirk the particularity of my own desire has the effect of neutralizing yours. "Anything" you do to me will be because I want you to; whatever it is you do will pale against the backdrop of my own impressive capacity for having wanted it. Thus masochistic erotica tends to operate as a frenzied elaboration not of your desire but of mine. This focus becomes hyperbolically dogged in *Fifty Shades of Grey*: although the tender sadist Edward Grey inducts the narrator Ana into a landscape of sexual ritual he has already created, the narrative itself consists of a relentless blow-by-blow account of every twinge Ana feels in the course of her relations with this handsome but troubled billionaire; it is difficult to imagine a narrative more intent on making sure we are tracking the protagonist's desire.[9] In the climactic scene of the first novel, Ana— initially reluctant to indulge her new boyfriend's violent proclivities— suddenly asks him to hurt her. "I can soothe him," she reflects. "Join him briefly in the darkness and bring him into the light.... 'Show me,' I whisper. 'Show you?' 'Show me how much it can hurt.'"[10] Through rhetoric that presents her own desire as an empty mirror of the other's, the masochist in fact turns the other's behavior into a reflection of her own erotic courage.

But as anyone familiar with this literature knows, things can never be so simple. The arrival of actual jouissance exceeds the fantasy and shatters the desire that had propelled us toward it; this account of sex is not specific to masochism, but masochism renders it in stark burlesque, yielding stories of subjects who get what they want only to find it unbearable—even within the tales that seem designed to get us (and them) off. "You take my fantasies too seriously," Severin whines in *Venus in Furs*; Ana storms out of the *Fifty Shades* playroom in tears.[11] Even O begs not to be whipped again: "Even if I agree to it now," she says wisely, "I couldn't bear it."[12] The desire for Anything that had comprised the masochist's heroic identity runs aground on the particular Something that her partner uses this license to do. In the event, all the masochist wants is for the biting or burning or flogging to stop; actual suffering makes her desire to suffer suddenly inaccessible, and with it, the vision of self that desire was supposed to sustain. In sex, that is, she finds she cannot *be* a masochist.

An awareness of this problem is built into all of the examples of masochistic literature I've mentioned, and even drives their narratives. We might be tempted to regard its presence in these texts as a sign of intellectual or even ethical integrity, a commitment to telling at least a little bit of the truth about desire, which would distinguish this literature from the unchecked fantasy machine of pure porn (porn being the genre in which you can love everything someone does to you). But the fact that the failure of masochistic desire is so ubiquitous and central in these texts suggests something else: that the failure of desire is not a check on masochistic fantasy that comes from without but a key feature *of* the fantasy itself. Paradoxically, the masochist desires a shattering even of her own desire. What's more, she cathects this paradoxical structure itself: her fantasy features an awareness of masochism as an *untenable position* and attaches her desire to its impossibility. The emptiness of the Anything figure testifies to this negativity: since "anything" is exactly not a particular scene or object, the word furtively articulates the masochist's commitment to the unimaginable. "What do you want to do?" the unnamed lover asks the protagonist Beth in Gaitskill's "A Romantic Weekend." "I can't just come out and tell you," Beth says. "It would ruin it."[13] Manifestly, this just means: I need the desire to be yours, not mine. But Beth's phrase is telling: "*it* would ruin *it*," a repetition suggesting that her desire will always nullify *itself*, failing to provide the stabilizing force that fantasy is supposed to offer the subject. "You're not a masochist," says her lover, after she screams at him for burning her with a cigarette lighter.[14] As a statement, this utterance is both true and false; as an erotic act, however, its very duplicity will turn out to make it perversely felicitous.

In tone as well as in content, the stories in *Bad Behavior* seem very far indeed from the sexy reveries of *Venus in Furs*, let alone *The Story of O* or *Fifty Shades of Grey*. In Gaitskill's 1980s American landscape, pleasure is erratic, precarious and lonely; hostility and alienation abound, along with other bad affects; relationships not only don't end well but feel awful from the start. According to the book's epigraph, from a poem by W. H. Auden, we are "Lost in a haunted wood, / Children afraid of the night / Who have never been happy or good."[15] Where masochism shows up in the stories, it's tempting to see it as just one of many manifestations of this lostness, alongside drug use, sex work, other shitty jobs, and various kinds of cruelty and betrayal. At the same time, Gaitskill's prose manifests a wry but intensely patient, curious attention to nuance, both sensory and psychological. Her descriptions as well as her plots work to produce the sense of an encounter with unresolved complexity, expressing and encouraging in readers the kind of negative capability that tolerates a wealth of detail—including details of characters' psychic lives—alongside a refusal of intellectual explanation or moral resolution. This production of complexity corresponds, as Gaitskill herself has observed, to a certain contemporary norm of American realist writing.[16] But Gaitskill's provision of a phenomenal richness that refuses to make good sense—that is, refuses to organize content into clear moral or explanatory value—also comports with realism as formulated by Barthes, apropos of nineteenth-century French texts like Gustave Flaubert's, in his famous essay on the "reality effect."[17] While Flaubert is in various ways an evident ancestor of Gaitskill's work, I'm most interested here in pinpointing the way a certain version of the realism Barthes locates in Flaubert's text is made to operate masochistically in Gaitskill's—since this is precisely the aspect of Gaitskill that might make us initially, and I think wrongly, assume we can distinguish her writing from erotic literature.

For Barthes, the reality effect occurs when a text provides descriptive details that seem not to mean anything. By appearing to resist interpretive comprehension, however, they do mean something: access to an unmediated—that is, unmeaning—"real." This structure's relevance to masochism hinges on the determining role negativity plays in it. In Barthes, it is in rupturing the expectation of meaningfulness that the Flaubertian barometer—"an object neither incongruous nor significant, and therefore not participating, at first glance, in the order of the *notable*"— manages to locate the entire narrative in an apparent proximity to realness: if the barometer has *no reason* for being mentioned in the sentence, it must be a manifestation of the text's absolute fidelity to how things really are.[18] In other words, a detail lends the feel of the real through its loud refusal to contribute to a sense of coherent meaning; it's in negating the value of what Barthes calls "the notable"—apparently refusing to participate in a literary project of making sense of being—that the detail produces resistance to the value of meaningfulness, a resistance that itself designates the opposing literary value of realism. To be sure, the literary regime against which Barthes sees realism thus defining itself is not the specific genre of erotica but the entire "ancient mode of verisimilitude" that had located truth value in an "opinable," rather than a referential, mode of discourse.[19] But in realism's rejection of this verisimilitude, Barthes discerns realism's attempt to distance itself from the domain of erotic fantasy: "by positing the referential as real, by pretending to follow it in a submissive fashion, realistic description avoids being reduced to fantasmatic activity"—unlike the earlier order, which "in a sense institutionalized the fantasmatic" and openly attempted to "impar[t] to representation all the luster of desire."[20] That realism behaves "in a submissive fashion" even as it disavows its own desire suggests, of course, that this apparent rejection of desire in fact obeys a perversely prurient motive.

When "A Romantic Weekend" begins, its protagonist Beth finds herself in what we might describe as a hellscape of Barthesian barometers. As she waits for her lover to meet her so they can go away for the weekend, Beth is racked by "a sense that the world was disorderly and unbeautiful. She became acutely aware of the garbage on the street. The wind stirred it; a candy wrapper waved forlornly from its trapped position in the mesh of a jammed public wastebasket. This was all wrong, all horrible. Her meeting with him should be perfect and scrap-free."[21] This landscape of scraps— "neither incongruous nor significant," as Barthes puts it—suggests a kind of hyperrealist world that is dominated by reality effects, except that Beth is working overtime to endow all this meaningless stuff with a totalizing aesthetic and moral meaning: "all wrong, all horrible." The evident impossibility, for Beth, of letting a candy wrapper just be a candy wrapper introduces her as someone who cannot tolerate unmeaning materiality; more specifically, as someone whose fantasy life ("Her meeting with him should be perfect") operates by attempting to negate the contingent material detail, the "scrap" that both violates her fantasy and spurs it on. Gaitskill is establishing a scene that is emphatically "real" ("the mesh of a jammed public wastebasket") and—in the tradition of *Madame Bovary*— placing her character's sexual subjectivity directly at odds with that very realness. As in Barthes's Flaubert, this would seem to be an instance of the literary value of realism constituting itself *against* an abstractive, fantasmatic totality—for Barthes, "the order of the notable" in its interdependence with "the fantasmatic"; for Gaitskill, the desperate perfectionism of Beth's fantasy life. But just as Barthes ultimately shows how the apparently rebarbative barometer actually restores totalizing signification by signifying the "realness" of the entire scene, Gaitskill presents a heroine bent on discovering in the world's messy incoherence a fantasmatic, albeit distressing, consistency.

The very features that seem most clearly to mark "A Romantic Weekend" as *not* a piece of erotica, then, will actually turn out to be its means of proving the strange capaciousness of masochistic erotics, which are always striving to comprehend whatever would appear to be beyond their pale. This "beyond" extends not only to the burgeoning horrors of the urban landscape but more centrally to scenes of bad sex—bad sex being perhaps the most effective "reality effect" an author can use to insist that what we are reading is *not fantasy.*

> Queasily, he stripped off her clothes and put their bodies in a viable position. He fastened his teeth on her breast and bit her. She made a surprised noise and her body stiffened. He bit her again, harder. She screamed. He wanted to draw blood. Her screams were short and stifled. He could tell that she was trying to like being bitten, but that she did not. He gnawed her breast. She screamed sharply. They screwed. They broke apart and regarded each other warily.[22]
>
> … In the morning they agreed that they would return to Manhattan immediately. Despite their mutual ill humor, they fornicated again, mostly because they could more easily ignore each other while doing so.[23]

I wouldn't describe these scenes as sexy, and I don't think you would either. Yet this relentless representation of sexual disappointment shares with masochistic erotica its investment in what I referred to above as the attachment to impossibility: the more painfully Beth's fantasy has to collide with reality's sharp edges, the more robustly her fantasy rallies. When the story ends, as we'll see, both characters seem determined to continue their liaison. Masochism thus sexualizes the very mechanism that is supposed to secure literary realism's *difference* from fantasmatic idealization. And through this perversely sexualized realism, Gaitskill offers a theory of how narrative fiction can support masochism's paradoxical dependence on "anything," and thereby sustain the masochistic subject.

"Not a Masochist"

The premise of "A Romantic Weekend" could be summarized as follows: two white people who hardly know each other go on a trip together. The man, unnamed, has to fly to Washington, DC, to pick up his grandmother's car and drive it back home. Beth will come with him so they can have violent sex, which they've done once before; in the wake of that previous encounter, Beth has "abruptly fallen in love" with him, an intensity of feeling that seems neither justified nor mutual.[24] As Beth waits for her beloved inside a flower store by the appointed street corner, she has "a paroxysm of fantasy. He held her, helpless and swooning, in his arms. They were supported by a soft ball of puffy blue stuff. Thornless roses surrounded their heads. His gaze penetrated her so thoroughly, it was as though he had thrust his hand into her chest and begun feeling her ribs one by one. This was all right with her.... None of this felt stupid or corny, but she knew that it was. Miserably, she tried to gain a sense of proportion."[25] But what would a well-proportioned desire even be? The stories in *Bad Behavior* are all about the ways desire can turn out to have been disproportionate, both to the realities of the given situation and to the wherewithal of the subject herself, whose longing will always leave her "unraveling in every direction."[26] In "A Romantic Weekend," this erotic inaptitude quickly comes to center around the dark comedy of an insistent mismatch between Beth's masochism and her lover's sadism. "We just had the wrong idea about each other," Beth says to him near the end of the story. "It's nobody's fault that we're incompatible."[27]

To manifest this wrongness throughout the story, Gaitskill uses the technique of variable focalization, alternating between Beth's perspective and her lover's to confirm continually that neither character is getting through to the other.[28] These shifts in perspective are usually unobtrusive, with passages of direct dialogue serving as neutral bridges between the two characters' points of view. Sometimes, however, Gaitskill chooses to emphasize the narrative's double penetration, presenting a staccato alternation of thoughts.

> "I'm not in a bad mood," she said wearily. "I just feel blank."
> Not blank enough, he thought.
> He pulled into a Roy Rogers fast food cafeteria. She thought: He is not even going to take me to a nice place. She was insulted.[29]

The narrative certainly seems to be conducting a cynical exposure of sexual nonrelation. Thus Maggie Nelson writes: "language here bores through the self-esteem and dignity of the characters, along with any possibility of compassionate communication between them…. The characters are fully exposed to the cruelty of the elements (which here means to each other and, more crucially, to Gaitskill's merciless authorial voice)."[30] On this reading, the story seems to echo Deleuze's famous argument that sadism and masochism are not complementary: "The sadist and the masochist might well be enacting separate dramas, each complete in itself, with different sets of characters and no possibility of communication between them, either from inside or outside," Deleuze writes. "Only the normal 'communicate'—more or less."[31] It's hard to imagine two characters less able to communicate than Beth and her lover, who can barely make sense of each other's words, much less each other's desires, throughout the two-day affair.

But the same device that cements the failure of Beth and her lover to communicate also emphasizes another function of narrative writing here: holding both characters in a kind of structural alignment. On the last page of the story, for example, when the narrative moves from his perspective to hers and then back to his, this shifting establishes a striking parallelism of content. "He was beginning to see her as a locked garden that he could sneak into and sit in for days, tearing the heads off the flowers," we read; and a couple of sentences later: "she was scrutinizing him carefully from behind an opaque façade as he entered her pasteboard scene of flora and fauna. Could he function as a character in this landscape?"[32] Beth's private vision of floral scenery mirrors her lover's daydream of the garden; while she wonders whether he can "function" in her interior "landscape," the narrative shows us that he is already inside.

The twist here is that masochistic Beth and her sadistic lover are not exactly incompatible after all. The story's last line reads: "He thought: This could work out fine."[33] And though everything we have read up to this point lets us know that things will *not* be fine in any conventional sense—especially for Beth—it would be a simplification to say that these last words are purely ironic. Similarly, the story's title, "A Romantic Weekend," is obviously laden with irony, but if we take it as *only* a skewering of its own literal meaning, the title comes off as sophomorically arch. In fact, romance is not exactly the opposite of what is going on here; as Lauren Berlant observes, in Gaitskill's work, "romance narrative and violent sex are twins."[34] Beth is a romantic, someone who invests disproportionately in fantasy; and this romantic bent serves her masochism, because the vulnerability it confers offers her a prime way of getting hurt. This produces a version of "romance" that is simultaneously threatened and sustained by reality's harsh intervention. As such, it establishes a kind of attachment to the other that cathects, precisely, their capacity to break our desire.[35]

As a phenomenon of everyday life, this kind of attachment is probably something most of us have observed, if not experienced. I'm suggesting that it also has a specifically literary function: it drives resolution to the level of discursive construction, demanding a compositional coherence that brings the characters into alignment in order to hold us in the paradox of their conjoined incommensurability. The incoherence in the "material" of this story—what demands that coherence be found at the level of form—is not just the erotic mess that erupts between the characters, but the disaster of desire itself as it manifests in each character separately. This is why we meet them separately: Beth while she is still waiting for her lover, and then her lover as he watches her from across the street. What is wrong in the world of "A Romantic Weekend" is not that the characters can't make each other feel good, but more fundamentally, that they can't do it for themselves: this is not a story of failed relation, but rather, we might say, of failed nonrelation, where the character's separate fantasy lives are both in crisis.

As we saw, the story begins with fantasy's breakdown: Beth's vision of the gaze that would penetrate her ribcage in order to "feel her ribs one by one," as if taking inventory, *fails* to constrain and contain the radical chaos of her lust, leaving her "miserabl[e]." Her lover is initially more successful in producing fantasies that lend coherence to his experience, as when he watches Beth from across the street, musing that "it might be entertaining to see how long she waited."[36] His interest in her, we learn, springs mainly from her resemblance to a previous lover, "whom he had tormented on and off for two years.... On meeting Beth, he was astonished at how much she looked, talked, and moved like his former victim."[37] This history promises to equip him with a kind of narrative template for his current desire. Soon, however, it starts contributing to an unmanageable multiplicity: "These images lay on top of one another, forming a hideously confusing grid. How was he going to sort them out?"[38] And later: "He lay wound in a blanket, blinking in the dark, as a dislocated, manic and unpleasing revue of his sexual experiences stumbled through his memory in a queasy scramble."[39] Throughout the story, desire, solitary to begin with, keeps falling apart of its own accord. Relation merely fails to correct *this* failure.

And yet something does correct it. The "happy ending" of "A Romantic Weekend" comes about not through any overcoming of communicative obstacles, but through a sudden surge in fantasy's ability to organize itself:

> He saw her apartment and then his. He saw them existing a nice distance apart, each of them blocked off by cleanly cut boundaries. Her apartment bloomed with scenes that spiraled toward him in colorful circular motions and then froze suddenly and clearly in place. She was crawling blindfolded across the floor. She was bound and naked in an S&M bar. She was sitting next to him in a taxi, her skirt pulled up, his fingers in her vagina.
>
> ... And then they would go back to her apartment. He would beat her and fuck her mouth.
>
> Then he would go home to his wife, and she would make dinner for him. It was so well balanced, the mere contemplation of it gave him pleasure.
>
> The next day he would send her flowers.[40]

This latter sentence gets a line to itself: after all, it is a kind of punch line, since the story begins with Beth's own flower-shop vision: "She stared at the flowers. They were an agony of bright, organized beauty. She couldn't help it. She wanted to give him flowers."[41] Her lover's fantasy culminates in unwittingly returning this gesture, and mirrors the "bright, organized beauty" that Beth had seen in the florist's earlier. Whether or not Beth would relish the specific images he sees, one senses that she would appreciate the coherence they impart to her body almost as much as he does. Gaitskill is of course ironizing the "pleasure" Beth's lover takes in the "well balanced" composition his fantasy finally attains; but the narrative also exhibits a version of that self-possession on its own account, deftly bringing together beginning and end, and layering its own gesture of formal closure neatly on top of the character's, as if narrator and character were somewhat smugly turning the page together.

If the lover's fantasies manage to respond to Beth's without there being, as Nelson puts it, "compassionate communication between them," that may be because the story's logic of desire aligns the possibility of experiencing pleasure with something other than dialogue—something precisely other, in terms of narratological categories. It's when fantasy approaches the condition of diegesis or *narrative*, rendering interior life independently of characters' embodied self-expression, that self-destroying desire can stabilize into a sustainable form. The trajectory of Beth's lover's fantasy entails a shift from a register of embodied self-display—the "manic and unpleasing revue"—to one of narrative progression: "*Then* they would go back to her apartment.... *Then* he would go home to his wife." Narrative itself offers the perspective in which fantasy can become bearable; fantasy is bearable when it colludes, not with speech or behavior (as in mimetic expression) but with a kind of discursive emplotment—the kind of writing that the story itself is. The relevant kind of communication here is not the compassionate but the compositional, achieved through a process of sorting and surveying, where relation is not interaction but structural rhyme.

In the last pages of the story, we thus find the pair of lovers driving happily back to New York, Beth's earlier sense that her lover is a "hostile moron" now eclipsed by the pleasure she takes in "the sound of his voice, the position of his body, and his sudden receptivity"—a receptivity occasioned, in turn, by Beth's revelation that when she took LSD in college, she "had often lost her sense of identity ... completely"—a remark that "br[ings] back her attractiveness in a terrific rush."[42] The image of Beth as someone who can disappear, I think we can infer, excites him by implying that he could be the agent of her future disappearance: if her "sense of identity" is detachable, then he can take it away from her. This could be the ground of a profound sexual compatibility—and from his perspective, it is—except that for Beth, the revelation seems incidental, not intended as a sexual invitation, and there is no sense that she understands why this particular anecdote has reignited her lover's interest, even if she notices "the quick dark gleam in his eyes."[43] This same asymmetry orders the characters' placement in relation to the narrative: even if the story establishes Beth as the privileged site of readerly identification, it ultimately brings her lover's perspective closer to the story's own.

In particular ways, then, the unnamed male sadist of "A Romantic Weekend" operates as a kind of surrogate for both author and reader. This is all the more remarkable given that he is a relentlessly unsympathetic figure. Gaitskill secures our alienation from him not only through his cruelty but more powerfully, I think, through his numbingly stupid thrall to gender norms. I imagine that for many readers, Beth's lover is at his most off-putting in passages like this: "They got undressed. He contemptuously took in the mascular, energetic look of her body. She looked more like a boy than a girl, in spite of her pronounced hips and round breasts. Her short, spiky red hair was more than enough to render her masculine. Even the dark bruise he had inflicted on her breast and the slight burn from his lighter failed to lend her a more feminine quality."[44]

The bite and burn themselves are less obnoxious than the fanatic allegiance to binary sexual difference that seems to guide his sexual behavior, making him seem not only cruel but pathologically unimaginative.

What's more, his fixation on feminine propriety feeds on a repellant orientalism: "He was married," we read in the third sentence, "to a Korean woman whom he described as the embodiment of all that was feminine and elegant"; he fantasizes repeatedly about his wife preparing meals for him, or "painstakingly applying kohl under her huge eyes" (he is presumably white, with "a pale, narrow face and blond hair that wisped across one brow").[45] Beth's fantasy life is tinged with its own version of orientalism—her bedroom wall is decorated with "pictures of huge-eyed Japanese cartoon characters," and at the end (as we'll see) she happily imagines "sitting across from him in a Japanese restaurant"—but her basic white-girl taste for exoticized commodities seems to pale (as it were) in comparison to his compulsive objectification of actual people.[46] His moral and imaginative failings make hers look comparatively mild over the course of the story, and the revelation of his puerility is markedly the most painful part of their adventure for Beth: "How, she thought miserably, could she have mistaken this hostile moron for the dark, brooding hero who would crush her like an insect and then talk about life and art?"[47] Beth's own fantasies may be, as she suspects, "stupid or corny," but most of them have a hyperbolic, impossible quality that compels sympathy much more readily than does her lover's devotion to the most generic misogynistic imaginary: "He longed for a dim-eyed little slut with a big, bright mouth and black vinyl underwear."[48]

And yet his eye for Beth's failings means that he does, almost in spite of himself, grasp something fundamental about her. "She had said that she wanted to be hurt," we read, "but he suspected that she didn't understand what that meant."[49] As we've already seen, Beth's lover is right to suspect this incoherence: in masochistic desire, the subject that wants and the subject that gets hurt will never coincide. Over the course of the story, each thing her lover actually does or even proposes is unbearable to Beth, a fact he uses to taunt her: "You're not a masochist." Whether or not he knows it, the lover's "You're not a masochist" has a specifically sadistic function. By exploding her self-image *as* a masochist he adds insult to injury, which brings him more pleasure.

> She spoke dreamily. "I would do anything with you."
> "You would not. You would be disgusted."
> "Disgusted by what?" ...
> "Have you ever been pissed on?"
> He gloated as he felt her body tighten.[50]

What the sadist has to enjoy is precisely the failure of the masochist's desire—he enjoys her nonenjoyment, which is to say that he enjoys the violence *for* her, a kind of erotic outsourcing which is necessarily a zero-sum game. We might assume that this process would need to occur behind the masochist's back, as it were; but in fact, it is precisely what she calls for with her Anything, which announces the irrelevance of particular sexual experiences in the face of this totalizing math. "Anything you do will be all right" really means, not "I'll love whatever you do to me," but "I love that you'll love that I'll hate whatever you do to me." This third-order formula can indeed comprehend, because it is entirely independent of, any particular act of violence. In this sense, the Anything is not a relinquishment of fantasy but a specific instance of it; and sadism itself is the content of that fantasy.

Enjoying the masochist's disappointment and his own power to inflict it, the sadist in a sense becomes the site of masochistic enjoyment, making good on the promise to enjoy violence that the masochist would otherwise have broken, and thus acting, we might say, as the mirror that lets the masochist glimpse herself in an image of unbroken desire. But since what the sadist enjoys *is* the failure of this desire and the interruption of this self ("You're not a masochist"), the sadist can no more experience the validation of masochism's Anything than the masochist can—the sadist, we might say, effects this validation while necessarily failing to recognize it. For whom, then, does the validation take place? In order to experience it at all, the masochist will have to gain access to a third perspective: a point from which I can regard my pain and enjoy it (as the sadist does) while at the same time confirming it *as mine*. Some mediation, some distance from the experience is necessary: not enough to alienate it completely but just enough to make it available for identification: while looking with the eyes of the aggressor, I also have to be able to find myself in the figure of the victim. And for Gaitskill, it is this possibility that the development of fantasy into written fiction enables.

Works of Fiction

We see, then, that masochistic fantasy includes an impulse to transcend not only whatever particular things might be happening but, more fundamentally, the perspective of the one suffering these things: masochism itself includes a movement toward the objectivity of a detached literary narrator. This idea is already familiar from Freud's 1919 article on patients who describe their fantasies in the impersonal phrase "a child is being beaten." The abstraction of this phrase is not just a ruse the patients are using to avoid being caught with their pants down but an accurate description of the way their fantasy offers itself to experience: by dislocating experience from the subject's own position. Kaja Silverman describes this process as a "heteropathic identification," producing pleasure through "the divestiture of 'self.'"⁵¹ For Freud's female patients in particular, this divestiture is never reversed: they can never consciously acknowledge that the child being beaten is a figure for themselves, but maintain their insistence that someone else is the victim, an insistence that leads Freud to characterize these fantasies as "apparently sadistic" even though masochism is the source of their pleasure.⁵²

It has often been observed that this "sadistic" version of masochism is spectatorial: "I am probably looking on," says the patient "in reply to pressing enquiries" as to where she is in the scene.⁵³ Less frequently discussed is Freud's emphasis on this mode of fantasy as an approach to authorial practice: the fantasies "almost rose to the level of a work of art" (*Dichtung*, also literary work); they constitute "an elaborate [*kunstvoller*, literally "artful"] superstructure"; Freud even tells us that they first arise when the child begins "to compete with … works of fiction [*Dichtungen*] by producing its own fantasies."⁵⁴ Indeed, Freud's decision to name the article after the patients' sentence also underscores the moment of verbalization, the importance of the fantasy's being put into words. The masochist *tells a story* in order to transcend her own position in that story; the story is thus always also a story of her escape from that position.

The "sadism" of Freud's girl is apparently very different from what we normally mean by that word, which is something more like Gaitskill's "he would beat her and fuck her mouth." But if we understand sadism as in fact the content of the masochist's Anything fantasy, then we can see how Freud's "sadistic" girl-becoming-author might be related to the standard sadist: in both cases, the sadist is the figure that preserves the possibility of pleasure by separating it from the body in pain and endowing pain *and* pleasure with the coherence of narrative. This is why it is Beth's lover whose formalizing triumph—"the mere contemplation of it gave him pleasure"—brings the story to a close. By aligning the narrative with his perspective in this final moment, Gaitskill suggests that the narrative discourse of masochism needs a sadist, a second person, to whom its narrative can pretend to belong.

Neither is it just Freud and Gaitskill who suggest this. In *Venus in Furs*, Sacher-Masoch's blissfully tormented hero Severin tells his story within a frame narrative in which he has now become a tyrant who enjoys terrorizing his pretty peasant maid with a knout.⁵⁵ In the anecdotal but now inescapable biographical gossip surrounding the once-anonymous *Story of O*, we learn that Dominique Aury wrote the book "for" her lover, lest he get bored and abandon her—a story in which something we might have imagined as her fantasy becomes, instead, somehow his, Aury serving merely as a kind of executor before the fact.⁵⁶ And then there is the remarkable twist in the tale of E. L. James, who after completing Ana's chirpy aria in the *Fifty Shades* trilogy began rewriting each of the three books from the point of view of the dominant Grey. What does this feat suggest if not an anxiety lest the fundamentally accessory nature of that figure stand revealed? Lest we see that sadism is just the *work of fiction* through which the masochist gets a grip on her own desire?

In this sense masochism *is* fundamentally romantic, reliant on the figure of the other, the sadist whose aesthetic purview will rescue me by sorting out the incoherence of my desire to desire and not to. The masochistic ego establishes itself through the pronoun "you," which is in turn mutually constitutive with that other pronoun, Anything: "Anything you do ..." The "you" addresses a subject, the sadist, who can wield the compositional mastery of the narrator. This means that a fundamental function of the sadist is to show the masochist what the masochist will have to become in order to maintain her masochism.

I've said both that the masochist needs to find herself as a subject of desire and that she needs to maintain the paradoxical structure that seems to make that self impossible. This is also to say that even before the shattering event of actual violence, the masochist finds herself split between her desire for that event and her awareness of what it will do to her desire, which imparts a distressing incoherence to fantasy itself. This suffering, rather than whatever the sadist actually does to her, is what teaches the masochist that pain and pleasure can coincide; so her identification with masochism—I am one who wants this—is an identification with the fracture. The disposition that can maintain this identification—needing to be the one who is not the thing she is, who does not have the experience she undergoes, and does not want the things she wants—is an aesthetic disposition, that is, a disposition that makes experience, including fantasmatic experience, available as fiction.

In Gaitskill, that means narrative fiction. As I noted above, "A Romantic Weekend" suggests that fantasy survives by undergoing a kind of intermedial shift, from the "manic and unpleasing revue" to the sequential organization particular to narrative ("then they would go back to her apartment"). Why this emphasis on narrative, as opposed to other forms of aesthetic coherence—why not stop, for instance, at the sequence of colorful, frozen images that come to Beth's lover in the sentence before? It seems to me that this is because narrative promises not just imaginary integrity but continuity across successive occurrences of suffering; it models the self that wants, that undergoes, and that will have undergone the unbearable event, and in so doing, provides the diachronic mirage of a perspective in which pleasure and unpleasure align. As Gaitskill's play with variable focalization emphasizes, narrative can navigate the gap between incommensurable positions without closing it, because its fiction takes place in and through the passage of time. Its itinerary logic is what the masochist needs in order to keep going—in order, that is, to keep wanting to get hurt.

The link between masochism and literature is quietly present in "A Child Is Being Beaten." In a much earlier, less frequently cited essay, however, Freud considers it explicitly and at length. "Psychopathic Characters on the Stage" begins by offering a simple theory of literary enjoyment: the common man is in fact "a 'poor wretch to whom nothing of importance can happen,'" but literature lets him "*identify himself* with a hero," producing a highly pleasurable sense of his own greatness.[57] Of course, Freud continues, "the spectator knows quite well that actual heroic conduct such as [the hero's] would be impossible for *him* without pains and sufferings and acute fears, which would almost cancel out the enjoyment."[58] Literary works deal with this potentially distressing implication in different ways: epic poetry minimizes it through uniformly triumphant portrayals of the hero; drama, however, wrests perverse pleasure from it by "depict[ing] the hero in his struggles, or rather (with masochistic satisfaction) in defeat."[59]

Freud is obviously not saying that such literature *produces* masochism. But neither does this account present masochism as a purely pregiven phenomenon that drama just happens to address. Wretches that we are, Freud suggests, it is ("almost") impossible for us to enjoy our own real-life suffering. Hence it's ("almost") only through the mediation of a fictional world that the experience our masochism craves can be had at all. Drama enables a mode of identification that lets me be *and not be* the one in pain: I submit to the fiction wherein I am the one who can do and suffer Anything, even as I "know quite well" that this is not true. Grammatically, this oscillation manifests in a strange ambiguity in Freud's sentence: in German as in English, it is impossible to be sure whether the phrase "with masochistic satisfaction" attributes pleasure to the defeated hero, to the spectator, or somehow to "Drama" itself.[60] This indeterminacy of person, this impropriety of pleasure, speaks to the way that, for Freud, plays make it possible to enjoy what I *know I would not enjoy*, where grazing that knowledge is part of the pleasure of reaching past it. When it is the analyst, moreover, who voices this knowledge on the subject's behalf—who reminds me that my enjoyment *would be impossible*—then he is speaking as the sadist from within my masochism, performing the figure through which I enjoy my noncoincidence with the suffering self; he *is*, in fact, the very interval of that noncoincidence. Perhaps we ought to see this masochistic sadism in all of Freud's deflationary moments, as we surely should in Gaitskill's: their "realism" *is* the perverse enjoyment they offer.

Freud's assignment of literature's masochistic affordance to drama, as distinct from other literary genres, will resonate with other readings that lie ahead in this book. Apropos of Gaitskill, however, it might give us pause: "A Romantic Weekend," I've been arguing, presents narrative fiction—not drama—as the best means of holding the fantasy-of-broken-fantasy that masochistic desire produces. This might just be a point on which Gaitskill and Freud think differently; but it might also be worth considering what "drama" actually means for Freud here. One answer would be that Freud seems to be thinking of drama mainly as tragedy, and of tragedy *as* a kind of narrative fiction, distinguished from epic by its affective content rather than its mimetic form: the difference made by theatrical performance barely enters Freud's reading at all. And if Freud can offer an account of drama that virtually erases performance from the scene, this is because drama itself—in the tradition of Aristotle, that is, in Freud's tradition—is the genre that is born *as literature* by striving toward that very erasure. When we regard tragedy, Aristotle says, we are meant to see through the performers—with their undignified gesticulations, their desperation to please—and grasp the poem as such; and even within the poem, we are to seize on the skeletal "soul" that is its plot. Indeed, the supreme importance of plot (he says) ultimately renders not just performers but even characters dispensable.[61] In this mode of artistic experience, the fleshly incoherence of bodies continually submits to being shaped by plot, becoming that which *could* always merely be told.

Theater, then, is the site where embodied experience continually tries to submit itself to the logic of narrative fiction. In drama, Freud writes, "the expectation of unhappiness"—the expectation that both threatens and constitutes masochistic desire—is "formed into pleasure" ("*das Drama [soll] … die Unglückserwartungen noch zum Genuß gestalten*").[62] And indeed, drama is the literary machine designed to subject the sensory panoply of performance to the dominating form that is plot. Plot is the switchpoint for narrative, the possibility of synopsis, as Aristotle reminds us, offering as his example: "A girl has been sacrificed and has disappeared."[63] Another example might be: A child is being beaten. Or: Anything you do will be all right.

"On the one hand, she was beside herself with bliss. On the other, she was scrutinizing him carefully from behind an opaque façade as he entered her pasteboard scene of flora and fauna. Could he function as a character in this landscape?"[64] It seems clear, based on every word of the story, that he can't; here, the sudden appearance of an explicitly theatrical register—pasteboard—seems to signify neither virtuosity nor imaginative control but rather the fragility of Beth's fantasy, its liability to collapse when the other enters for real. But then something shifts: "She imagined sitting across from him in a Japanese restaurant, *talking about any-thing*. He would look intently into her eyes."[65] What Beth sees—however fleetingly—is precisely the impossible masochistic self she seeks: a subject equal to the endeavor of "talking about anything," of subordinating mate-rial particularity to a narrative of pure syntax. This rare moment of purely pleasurable fantasy arises, Gaitskill suggests, from the previous moment in which Beth suddenly takes a kind of authorial responsibility, however self-deprecating, for her fantasy life: it is "*her* pasteboard scene." She is at once inside it and "behind" it, and then, with the restaurant fantasy, she's beyond it. If she's also "beside herself," this phrase of course means that she's carried away; but taken literally, against its own grain, it suggests that she's the one in the driver's seat—in the seat beside her self, the one occu-pied by her sadistic lover.

The Sadist Says "No": Deleuze and the Freudian Punch Line

The above discussion has produced some formulations that might help us get past a certain persistent theoretical disagreement: the disagreement about how (or whether) masochism relates to sadism. At the risk of over-simplifying, we might condense this thinking into two opposing camps: on the one hand, there are theorists who—drawing to different degrees on Freud's "A Child Is Being Beaten"—describe a structure they can call "sa-domasochism" because it assumes that masochism's drive to suffer can be redirected or extended toward others, whether through the "heteropathic identification" that makes masochistic experience always a relay with other bodies (Silverman), or by a masochist's learning to enjoy wielding the violence they originally enjoyed suffering (Sedgwick; see chapter 4). On the other hand, there are those who, following Deleuze's well-known rebuttal to Freud, insist that masochism and sadism are completely dis-tinct and incompatible perversions.[66] Does sadism arise from masochism, or are they fundamentally alien to each other? Our reading of "A Romantic Weekend" has suggested that, paradoxically, both must be true: a sadism alien to masochistic fantasy *is* what masochistic fantasy demands, and it's the destabilizing force of this fantasmatic requirement that launches the subject into literary production, precisely in order to surmount the in-surmountable difference. With this idea in mind, I'd like now to return to Deleuze's essay "Coldness and Cruelty," the work that most decisively es-tablished the critical impetus to keep the two perversions apart.

In this famous and sustained argument for sadism's thorough separa-tion from masochism, Deleuze elaborates a concept of each perversion based in his literary analysis of the work of Sacher-Masoch and the Mar-quis de Sade respectively. Against the psychoanalytic notion of a uniform erotic aggressiveness whose manifestations as masochism (wanting to be hurt) or sadism (wanting to hurt others) are just two sides of a coin, Deleuze presents two separate, self-sufficient erotic worlds, each with a unique sexual and aesthetic logic. His argument that there is no "sado-masochistic entity" contests both the developmental account wherein a subject's masochism can reverse into sadism (sadomasochism within the subject) and the relational—or, we might say, romantic—assumption that masochists and sadists are made for each other (sadomasochism between subjects).[67] Masochists and sadists want completely different things; their fantasies are incompatible, not complementary; a Sadean libertine could never be the object of a Masoch hero's desire, which demands a highly specific kind of lover, cold and cruel but also (shades of Grey!) nurturing. "We must not imagine that it is a matter of the masochist encountering a sadist by a stroke of luck," Deleuze cautions.[68] Instead, the masochist will need to "mold" his lover, "to educate and persuade" her until she treats him with the right kind of cruelty; independent sadistic designs on the lover's part would only interfere with this project, just as a partner who likes to be hurt would undermine the sadist's need to negate the other's pleasure.[69]

Deleuze makes this argument by enumerating the distinctive structures of each perversion, producing two vividly different portraits. By the end of the essay, the notion of an indifferently oriented "sadomasochism" has come to seem impoverished indeed, incapable of accommodating the richness and specificity Deleuze reveals in Masoch's and Sade's respective fantasmatic worlds. And yet it's surely remarkable—especially in a text first written as an introduction to *Venus in Furs*—that this demonstration of the two perversions' autonomy proceeds by bringing them back together at every turn. The following passage, on how language operates in Sade and Masoch, is typical:

> In Sade the imperative and descriptive function of language transcends itself toward a pure demonstrative, instituting function, and in Masoch toward a dialectical, mythical and persuasive function. These two transcendent functions essentially characterize the two perversions, they are *twin ways* in which the monstrous exhibits itself in reflection.[70]

The choice to examine sadism and masochism side by side makes sense, of course, given Deleuze's interest in disentangling them: to see all their differences from each other, you have to keep looking at both. It also makes sense that Deleuze would invoke sadism for the purpose of contrast, since he is writing amid a Sade-obsessed intellectual culture in which Sacher-Masoch (as he notes) is comparatively unknown. But as the surprising word "twin" in this passage suggests, the essay's constant invocation of

Sade and Masoch together creates a strange countercurrent to its own argument.

In each category of the analysis, that is, sadism turns out to be perfectly suited to highlight masochism's specificity, through contrastive pairings that irresistibly reestablish the sense of symmetry they are supposed to dispel. In a later passage, for instance, Deleuze reiterates that "sadism and masochism do not together constitute a single entity ... but each is complete in itself"—and then asserts in the very next sentence that "The masochist's experience is grounded in an alliance between the son and the oral mother; the sadist's in the alliance of father and daughter."[71] Even those of us most skeptical of family values can hardly help sensing, in this sentence, the presence of two halves that add up to a nuclear whole. Not all of the distinctions Deleuze draws are so perfectly symmetrical, but if each perversion is presented as "complete in itself," it is hard to escape the sense that Deleuze, like Gaitskill, needs the sadist in order to describe masochism. In other words, there may be no sadomasochistic "entity" within the psyche, and no prospect of a happy union between the two kinds of perverts; but there does seem to be a crucial relation between them at the level of representation. Sacher-Masoch's literary edifice may have no place for Sadean violence, but Deleuze's *Présentation de Sacher-Masoch*—the virtuosic critical effort through which he conducts us through masochism's pleasures—includes sadism as an ineliminable element of its adventure.

Deleuze argues in the essay that whereas the sadist pursues negation, masochism operates through disavowal.[72] What if what "Coldness and Cruelty" disavows is precisely its own masochistic relation to the sadist's negation? For Freud, disavowal is the structure that allows the subject both to know and not to know something; it is an oscillation between denial and acknowledgment, as when Deleuze calls sadism masochism's "twin" while supposedly demonstrating the two perversions' radical difference. Freud presents disavowal as one possible response to the horrifying discovery that the mother has no penis, that is, to the discovery of castration; Deleuze maintains this concept in his presentation of the masochist's ideal torturer as a phallic mother, though he also extends it, suggesting that masochistic disavowal takes hold of "the given" as such, and even "pleasure itself."[73] The pervert's response to castration, which Freud identifies as fetishism and which Deleuze, in turn, incorporates into masochism, is to erect a new fantasy structure that can contain or include the event that has injured him, while at the same time shielding him from full acceptance of it: the fetish disguises the loss of the penis, but it also *comprehends* that loss. In the analogy I am proposing, what Deleuze's theory of masochism disavows is not that the Oedipal subject is susceptible to castration but that the masochistic subject is fundamentally susceptible to the sadist—and not because the two might meet "by a stroke of luck," good or bad, but because masochism itself implies this bad meeting. Deleuze's response to this susceptibility is to include the sadist within his account of masochism, but in the "suspended, neutralized form" of a fetish: indispensable, but as it were encased in the claim of their mutual autonomy, the same claim that keeps bringing them together in Deleuze's argument.[74]

It's in terms of this perverse technique of inclusion that I think we ought to understand Deleuze's recitation of the "stupid joke" to which I referred in the introduction. Deleuze writes: "A popular joke tells of the meeting between a sadist and a masochist; the masochist says: 'Hurt me.' The sadist replies: 'No.' This is a particularly stupid joke, not only because it is unrealistic but because it foolishly claims competence to pass judgment on the world of perversions. It is unrealistic because a genuine sadist could never tolerate a masochistic victim.... Neither would the masochist tolerate a truly sadistic torturer."[75] The problem with Deleuze's rather blustery reaction to the joke is that his explanation of why it is "unrealistic" seems actually to affirm the opposite: wouldn't a sadist's inability to "tolerate a masochistic victim" mean that the sadist really *would* say no? Deleuze seems at once eager to negate the sadist's "No," and unable or unwilling to do so, offering a response that tends rather to affirm it. To understand this ambivalent response as a demonstration of disavowal, we might further consider that the sadist's "No," like the castration disavowed by Freud's fetishist, is a violent rebuke *aimed at desire*: in giving the masochist what she thought she wanted—in hurting her (by his rejection of her)—the sadist proves to her that she did not want what she thought she wanted after all. The sadist's "No" in the joke, I'm suggesting, is precisely analogous to Beth's lover's "You're not a masochist": it is exactly what the masochist doesn't want to hear, and thus it's *exactly what she does* want to hear. The joke, that is, shows that the question of the two perversions' compatibility versus their incompatibility is undecidable. Like "A Romantic Weekend" itself, the joke produces a harmony that occurs not as a compassionate relation between its characters but as it were synoptically, on the level of form. And in reciting the joke, Deleuze can't help but reproduce the satisfaction of its formal perfection.

This reading of Deleuze has a couple of implications that I now want to make explicit. The first is that, in using an element Deleuze finds in Sacher-Masoch (disavowal) to describe something that's happening in Deleuze's own text (its treatment of sadism), I'm suggesting that Deleuze's essay is caught up erotically in what is ostensibly its subject: that it is not just an essay about masochism but a piece of masochistic literature in itself. If this is right, then the type of distinction we began by questioning—between erotic texts that essentially just disseminate masochistic fantasy, and texts that, like Gaitskill's, bring an evidently critical eye to bear on it—is here undermined once again. This is not meant to elide the generic and disciplinary differences between "Coldness and Cruelty" and "A Romantic Weekend," but to suggest that in both texts, what appears to be a critical perspective on masochism turns out to be entailed in the erotic phenomenon it describes. Where masochism appears at the level of content, as it does in both Gaitskill and Deleuze, it reappears in the discourse about that content. Thus if the texts we are considering do not exactly suggest that all writers about masochism are (or become) masochists, they do suggest that writing about masochism may be the most characteristic thing a masochist can do. And writing about writing about masochism, as Deleuze does in his study of *Venus in Furs*, or writing about writing about writing about masochism, which I have been doing in discussing Deleuze, or writing about writing about writing about writing about masochism, as I am doing in this sentence, does not only interpose successive layers of critical distance between an author's subjectivity and the painful excitement of masochistic sexuality, but, by way of that distance, sustains the very structure that makes that sexuality possible.

The second implication of seeing in "Coldness and Cruelty" a masochistic disavowal of sadism (or more precisely, of masochism's dependence on sadism) is that this might offer a way to understand the essay's ambivalent challenge to psychoanalysis: after all, it's by contesting the psychoanalytic notion of a "sadomasochistic entity" that the essay conducts its revision of Freudian thought.[76] This ambivalence is evident, for instance, when Deleuze claims at the end of the essay that the "belief in a sadomasochistic entity is not really grounded in genuine psychoanalytic thinking but in pre-Freudian thinking which relied on hasty assimilations and faulty etiological interpretations that psychoanalysis merely helped to make more convincing, instead of questioning their reality."[77] The claim that "psychoanalysis" has not been "psychoanalytic" is not exactly self-contradictory—versions of this claim occur in virtually all post-Freudian thought—but this way of phrasing the critique does court a sense of paradox, as if to convey that Deleuze's own reading at once is and isn't beholden to psychoanalytic tradition. Deleuze conducts his reading in terms of Freudian concepts—ego and superego, death drive, etc.—to a degree that might well surprise readers of Deleuze's later, anti-Freudian work. "*It is not a child but a father that is being beaten*": in rewriting the Freudian formula for masochism, Deleuze negates it (*not* a child) even as he affirms and repeats Freud's own interpretive move of recasting the child's role.[78]

Again, there's not necessarily anything perverse about agreeing with some elements of a theory and challenging others. What I'm trying to set up, here, is a more specific relation between the role sadism plays in Deleuze's analysis of masochism, and the role Freud plays in it. *"It is not a child but a father that is being beaten"* marks a difference between Freud's vision of masochism and Deleuze's own, but it does so in terms that preserve and even insist on a kind of symmetry between the two, exactly as Deleuze also does each time he differentiates masochism from sadism. The two themes—sadism and psychoanalysis—are not merely parallel: they converge in Deleuze's discussion of the parental roles in masochism and sadism, which conveys that the Freudian account *does* have purchase *upon the latter*: "It is assumed that since the father-image is a determinant in sadism, this must also be true for masochism," Deleuze observes, questioning the inference (about masochism) but not its premise (about sadism); and his ensuing account confirms that indeed, psychoanalysis has gotten sadism right in this respect: "the paternal and patriarchal theme undoubtedly predominates in sadism."[79] If, for Deleuze, Freudian thought and practice have so much more purchase upon sadism than upon masochism, this discrepancy reflects not just a familiarity but an affinity between sadism and psychoanalysis—an affinity that Deleuze also gestures toward by including the "stupid joke," which gives the sadist the last word, as a popular emblem of what might be called psychoanalytic common sense.

The joke, you'll recall, is stupid "not only because it is unrealistic but because it foolishly claims competence to pass judgment on the world of perversions." Remarkably, Deleuze aims his ire not at the substance of the "judgment" the joke supposedly passes—say, that perverts are laughable and doomed—but at the "claim" of "competence" it implies, the assumption that everyone already knows enough about these things to joke about them. This assumption of general competence, or conversance, is exactly what Freud insists upon in "The Economic Problem of Masochism," in the passage I began this book by quoting. Perverse or "feminine" masochism, Freud writes, need not be described in detail. Among the forms of masochism that his article will consider, feminine masochism—the fantasies and sex acts of "masochistic perverts" who enjoy "being gagged, bound, painfully beaten, whipped, in some way maltreated, forced into unconditional obedience, dirtied and debased"—is "most accessible to our observation and least problematical, and it can be surveyed in all its relations.... It is unnecessary to quote cases to illustrate [it]; for the material is very uniform and is accessible to any observer, even to non-analysts."[80] Although Deleuze doesn't mention this passage, we might say that Freud's claim to be able to take masochism's phenomenal contours for granted is exactly where "Coldness and Cruelty" interposes its entire project, its excavation of masochism's far-from-obvious aesthetic and conceptual intricacies.

I'd like to suggest that part of what Deleuze is responding to here is *the sadistic bent of Freud's treatment of masochism*. The cruel timbre of Freud's remarks arises in part from his insistence that perverse masochism is already familiar to everyone, but also from the way he characterizes it, in passing, as theatrical: the masochist's sexual "performances" (*Veranstaltungen*), he remarks, "are, after all, only a carrying-out of the phantasies in play" (*nur die spielerische Ausführung der Phantasien*): even real-life masochistic sex is "only" a kind of representation.[81] This is cruel not only because it is dismissive but also because if perverse masochistic behavior is itself nothing but the reiteration of fantasy, then Freud's claim that since we have already seen it we *do not need to see it again* seems to threaten its very essence—since restaging is all it is.[82] "Masochistic tortures," Freud notes in a parenthetical, "rarely make such a serious impression as the cruelties of sadism, whether imagined or performed."[83] Whereas Freud finds sadism seriously impressive, his attitude toward perverse masochism seems concertedly belittling.

It's in the ensuing interpretation of this not-so-serious perversion, however, that Freud diminishes masochism most effectively, in a manner that ought now to remind us of Beth's lover in "A Romantic Weekend." Just as that sadistic character negates Beth's (and our) desire through his egregious fidelity to conventional (and conventionally racializing) gender norms, Freud rounds out his own brief consideration of perverse masochism by offering an utterly disappointing—that is, supremely unimaginative—interpretation of its details: "The obvious interpretation, and one easily arrived at, is that the masochist wants to be treated like a small and helpless child, but, particularly, like a naughty child.... But if one has an opportunity of studying cases in which the masochistic phantasies have been especially richly elaborated [*eine besonders reiche Verarbeitung erfahren haben*], one quickly discovers that they place the subject in a characteristically female situation; they signify, that is, being castrated, or copulated with, or giving birth to a baby."[84] What's disappointing here is not just that Freud has crammed the masochist's "richly elaborated" (and nonreproductive) fantasmatic plurality back into the impoverished terms of the gender binary but that this supposedly less obvious interpretation of masochistic sex turns out to be exactly the same as the stupidest, most popular fin de siècle account: the male masochist as a girly-man, whose kink is merely an "inversion of the healthy and natural relation between the sexes."[85] Freud's treatment of what he terms "feminine masochism" thus offers a kind of perfect negative precedent for Deleuze's rapt elaboration: hailing the phenomenon with an air of boredom (everyone already knows ...), Freud announces an interpretation of it which itself could hardly be more boring. But as Gaitskill shows, and as "Coldness and Cruelty," we might say, bears out, it's precisely this kind of bad sex that drives masochistic elaboration (Beth's, Deleuze's) onward.

And of course Freud does go on to say a great deal more about masochism in the "Economic Problem" article. Now that I've pointed up the sadistic valences of Freud's brusque account of "masochistic perverts"—an attitude that amounts, I've suggested, to something very much like the joke sadist's "No"—I'd like to consider the erotics of Freud's performance in the rest of that article, which goes on to produce a new figure: not the tie-me-up masochist but a determinedly indeterminate person whom Freud calls the moral masochist. Moral masochism is not exactly devoid of particularity—it manifests, as we saw in the introduction, in "many Russian character-types"[86]—but neither does it prompt imaginative detailing, even to the degree of the offhand list ("gagged, bound ...") Freud had rattled off above. The moral masochist does get his own list of symptoms, but compared to the other list *this* sequence is highly abstract: he "must do what is inexpedient, must act against his own interests, must ruin the prospects which open out to him in the real world and must, perhaps, destroy his own real existence."[87] Freud gives us nothing concrete to picture here, even as the passage summons a kind of thrilling sublimity, especially in contrast to the *spielerische* quality of "feminine" masochism. Moral masochism is tragic where perverse masochism, with its display of stock gags, comes off as farce. This analogy holds not only in the sense that moral masochism, like sadism, is described as more seriously harmful, but also in that Freud makes the story of the moral masochist compel our attention *without our having to "observe" its manifestations* through even cursory examples of what this might look like. Moral masochism's significance appears, that is, as independent from sensory or embodied representation. As we've already noted vis-à-vis Freud's earlier article on masochism and drama, Aristotle claims precisely this independence for tragedy, which is supposed to move us to pity and terror without any staging.

Where "feminine" or perverse masochism is merely common, then, moral masochism—like tragedy—approaches the universal, further illuminating the development of morality as such, which Freud had theorized in *The Ego and the Id*.[88] The "Economic Problem" article's progression from the mundane farce of perverse masochism to the tragic sublimity of moral masochism does not denote a developmental sequence: the two are separate pathologies, branching off from a common origin in erotogenic masochism, or pleasure in pain. The order in which Freud presents them, however, inscribes a trajectory of conceptual sublimation. Perverse masochism is the stagey, embodied phenomenon that we readers are to quickly re-view and then, as it were, transcend, a fleshy launchpad to the sublimated form of moral masochism, wherein masochism itself attains a kind of dignified abstractness even as its threat to the subject becomes more "real." This is also sublimation as Leo Bersani describes it: "a burning away of the occasion," an achievement of erotic independence from particular objects.[89] "All other masochistic sufferings carry with them the condition that they shall emanate from the loved person and shall be endured at his command," Freud writes. "This restriction has been dropped in moral masochism. The suffering itself is what matters.... It may even be caused by impersonal powers or by circumstances."[90] In progressing from the "feminine" to the moral masochist, Freud's article "burns away" not only the masochistic subject's particular erotic objects ("the loved person") but masochism's conceptual dependence on *any* embodied—or even fantasized—content at all.

But as we've seen, both in Gaitskill and in Freud's own "A Child Is Being Beaten," this kind of sublimating abstraction ("anything") is *exactly what the familiar masochistic pervert was already after*. When that pervert is not busy being bound and gagged or burned and bitten—or even when she is—she longs to find herself displaced in precisely this way, subjected to an abstraction that cancels her particular corporeal existence, fantasy sizzling in the light and heat of what Freud calls "real existence." In this respect, the theory of moral masochism is Freud's most elaborate way, in "The Economic Problem," of topping the masochistic pervert *just as the pervert would desire*, a revved-up sequel to the equally sadistic disappointment of Freud's "feminine" interpretation. In both of these facets of the article, it's as if the masochist had said "Imagine me!" and Freud—generously cruel—had replied, "No."

Freud thus theorizes masochism not by elaborating a network of fantasmatic details, as Deleuze does, but by negating such details in the skeletalizing pursuit of a universal truth. This is exactly how Deleuze describes sadism:

> In *The One Hundred and Twenty Days of Sodom* the libertine states that he finds excitement not in "what is here" but in "what is not here," the absent Object, "the idea of evil." The idea of that which is not, the idea of the No or of negation which is not given and cannot be given in experience must necessarily be the object of a demonstration (in the sense that a mathematical truth holds good even when we are asleep and even if it does not exist in nature).... The task of the libertine is to bridge the gulf between the two elements, the element at his actual disposal and the element in his mind, the derivative and the original, the personal and the impersonal.[91]

We might then understand both the account of "feminine masochism" and the account of "moral masochism," with their different approaches to negating empirical complexity, as sadistic theoretical performances on Freud's part. What Deleuze and Gaitskill both show, however, is that masochism is determined to take the sadist's joke: masochistic elaboration *sets itself up* for sadistic abstraction, the punch line that negates masochistic performance but, in doing so, obeys and develops the masochistic desire to be thus negated. This is because the sadist's "No" is not only a judgment upon the masochist issued from without; it also inheres, as we've seen, in the masochist's relation to her own desire.

Reading Deleuze through Gaitskill, however, also returns us to the question of gender raised in the introduction. How might the import of "Coldness and Cruelty" shift when we imagine the masochist as a woman? Deleuze does claim at one point that in masochism "a girl has no difficulty in assuming the role of the son" and that hence his version of masochism is, in principle, open to anyone; but this means, of course, anyone who finds no psychic barriers to identifying as a boy, a prerequisite that makes his democratizing gesture rather difficult to swallow.[92] I'd even suggest that "Coldness and Cruelty" exhibits a certain anxious machismo in its portrait of the sexually and aesthetically autonomous male masochist, which we might read as a reaction against the pervasive "feminine" conception of male masochism, or perhaps even against Freud's privileging of the female masochist in "A Child Is Being Beaten." Deleuze, recall, places "the daughter" on the side of sadism, which we might say gets the sexual *subject as feminine* out of his picture of masochistic experience, preventing any need for the male masochist to identify with her. But why exactly would this separation be so desirable?

Here we can observe a curious echo, in "Coldness and Cruelty," of a moment in Freud's "A Child Is Being Beaten." At one point Freud, commenting on the fact that a female patient's fantasies feature a boy being beaten, not a girl, writes puzzlingly that she thereby "*escapes* from the demands of erotic life altogether" (entläuft ... *dem Anspruch des Liebeslebens überhaupt*)—by which he seems to mean that she can find a sense of safety in referring her masochistic pleasure to someone else.[93] Subsequently Deleuze, writing of the female dominant in "Coldness and Cruelty," remarks that "the tortuless *escapes* from her own masochism by assuming an active role in the masochistic situation."[94] Deleuze thus reiterates Freud's notion of the masochistic girl as the subject who desires to "escape" her own desire; and, like Freud, Deleuze indicates that this escape is itself productive of further sexual fantasy. Neither Freud nor Deleuze finds it necessary to explain why the girl is so intent on escaping her desire while her male counterpart is apparently copacetic in his. Of course it is easy to think of reasons why acknowledging desire was and is more dangerous for women than for men, in Freud's time, Deleuze's time, and our own.[95] But these facts should not obscure the ideological implications of the move Freud and Deleuze both make here: they seize on the figure of the masochistic *woman* to embody masochism's constitutive negativity, as if to contain within this figure the self-sabotaging incoherence that always threatens masochistic desire.

When this incoherence manifests in Sacher-Masoch, it causes something like a stammer in Deleuze's account: this is how I would characterize Deleuze's discussion of the fact that Sacher-Masoch typically includes a sadistic male figure he calls "the Greek"—a figure that should, by Deleuze's own logic, have no place in the masochistic universe. Deleuze offers two incompatible explanations for this phenomenon. First, he argues that this character must be regarded as a hallucinatory "return of the real" that is absolutely *external* to fantasy or desire: "Far from being the truth behind masochism and the confirmation of its connection with sadism, the aggressive return of the father disrupts the masochistic situation; it represents the constant threat from the side of reality to the masochist's world."[96] We've observed in Gaitskill, however, that the "threat from the side of reality" is itself fundamental to masochistic fantasy, within which it operates as an ongoingly disruptive but generative force. And indeed, Deleuze himself concedes that his first explanation of the Greek is insufficient, asking: "But how shall we account for the fact that even in the contract [with the dominant woman] the masochist *requires* ... the Greek? Why should he so ardently *desire* this third party?"[97] He then proposes that the Greek "is never invited or sought after for its own sake, but to be neutralized" through association with the dominant "good mother"—and also that the Greek represents "the new man that will result from the masochistic experiment," that is, a version of the masochist himself.[98] It's as if Deleuze is working overtime to secure hetero masculinity for the masochist; to do this, he divides the figure of the Greek between an absolutely external "reality" that only ever "disrupts the masochistic situation," on the one hand, and ideally harmless instance meant to be "neutralized" within it, on the other. But this division itself neutralizes the truly perverse sense in which, as we've seen, masochistic fantasy seeks its own disruption, through a logic that makes it impossible to distinguish fantasy's failure from its success.

This is the incoherence Deleuze seems to me largely to occlude, the cost of his insistence that masochism is an aesthetically stable universe. "Symptomatology is always a question of art," he writes; "the clinical specificities of sadism and masochism are not separable from the literary values peculiar to Sade and Masoch."[99] I agree that it would be wrong to imagine a real-life sexuality that stands apart from, and has primacy over, the formal erotics of literature, especially in the case of masochism. But "Coldness and Cruelty" ends up producing its own kind of positivism. It is not only Masoch's scenes that "have of necessity a frozen quality, like statues or portraits"; Deleuze's own elaboration approaches a kind of frozen metaportrait that suspends the instability at the heart of masochism, refusing masochism's inability to stabilize itself within even the richest fantasy.[100]

Then again, our reading of "A Romantic Weekend" has already suggested that this is something a masochistic text might need to try to do. The masochistic movement of elaboration, in which the subject seeks "escape" from a relentlessly impossible desire by finding a position from which to write about it, may always mean setting one's sights on the kind of stabilizing reconstruction that Deleuze performs so gorgeously in "Coldness and Cruelty." To embrace the classically *feminine* version of this maneuver, however—as Deleuze perhaps knows—would mean never entirely achieving it. In Freud, the masochistic girl has honed her erotic daydream to the point that it "almost rose to the level of a work of art": *almost*. There is of course something unforgivable in that patronizing "almost," which keeps the patient—anecdotally Freud's own daughter—in her rightful subliterary place, even as it expresses a surprised admiration.[101] But the "almost" is also painfully precise: the masochist is one who *wants to be a writer*, that is, whose wanting is an approach to writing, and whose writing is not only the expression but the continued production of her desire. And this means that this masochistic writing cannot finally *be achieved*, both because that would imply the end of the desire that sustains the writing, and because the desire itself is inherently unsustainable, impossible.

In the next chapter we'll confront this paradoxical logic in stories about two more women who seem not to be authors, before passing in chapters 3 and 4 to texts in which authorship is at issue but never in question. Along the way, we'll encounter a few more cruel figures, some of whom will embody forms of violence unassimilable to the fantasy structures that nevertheless keep creeping up around them. To reaffirm that these forms of cruelty simply have no bearing on masochistic desire would be to underestimate the breadth, power, and ingenuity of that desire, its ability to build and sustain complex worlds while simultaneously unmaking them. So instead, we'll do our best to look out for the ways masochism cultivates whatever hurts most—which could, after all, be almost anything.

Cruel Theater

CHAPTER 2

Hedda Gabler and "Nona Vincent"

In chapter 1, our discussion of a short story by Mary Gaitskill brought us briefly to Freud's assertion, in "Psychopathic Characters on the Stage," that drama yields masochistic pleasure. I suggested that the special affordance Freud ascribes to this genre might have to do with the way that, for Aristotle, tragic drama is a machine for subjecting sensory materiality to the abstracting force of narrative—the same kind of abstraction that features prominently in the title of Freud's later and more famous essay on masochism, "A Child Is Being Beaten." The notion that, for Aristotle and his modern interpreters, dramatic writing summons the actual presence of particular bodies in order to negate their particular embodiment implies a fundamentally perverse understanding of Euro-normative models of theater; it's this perverseness that I want to pursue in the present chapter, through a reading of two texts contemporaneous with Freud's work: Henrik Ibsen's 1891 play *Hedda Gabler* and Henry James's 1892 story "Nona Vincent." These works both construct specifically feminine visions of masochism, in which what I called "masochism's constitutive negativity" gets assigned, again, to a female subject. And in both *Hedda* and "Nona," we'll see how this negativity produces feminine masochism as a model of artistic production: as the theatricalizing structure of authorship itself. I'll argue, then, that the practice and reception of an emergent "modern drama" around the turn of the twentieth century, emblematized by Ibsen's play and taken up by James's story, makes available a particular mode of sexualized authorship that we can call "dramaturgical masochism." This structure identifies pleasure with suffering and loss but also with a distinctive fantasy of aesthetic production that, in its attachment to femininity, challenges the dominant gender logic of authorship—a dominant logic that the texts themselves also inescapably register.

In this reading, "Nona Vincent" engages in a kind of dialogue with

Hedda Gabler, and with the uproar attending the latter's London premiere, which James reviewed the year before his story was published. Accordingly, the chapter will begin with a reading of Ibsen's play, which determinedly stages an excessive negativity internal to desire and pleasure, and conceives this bad enjoyment—Hedda's, and ours—as *theatrical* in particular ways. To articulate what the play is doing, I'll draw on the Lacanian account of the death drive presented in a work from the more recent turn of the century, a book that might seem an odd intertext for Ibsen, but whose appositeness I mean to make clear: Lee Edelman's *No Future.* I'll then turn from Edelman back to Freud, whose famous account of masochism in "A Child Is Being Beaten" resonates deeply with James's "Nona Vincent"; reading James with Freud, we'll discover the surprising contours of a theatrical desire that emerges between these two texts but finds its fullest expression in James. Finally, we'll examine the *Hedda*-saturated cultural context from which James's vision of theatrical masochism in "Nona Vincent" proceeds, to show how the theatrical landscape of the "woman's play" in James's London could have shaped this particular sexual disposition.

What can it mean to understand sexual desire as theatrical? We've already encountered one version of this notion in Freud's characterization of masochistic sexual "performances" (by men) as "*nur die spielerische Ausführung der Phantasien,*" the acting out or staging of scenes that originate in fantasy.[1] In psychoanalytic theory today, however, perhaps the most familiar concept of desire as theatrical derives from the work of Jean Laplanche and J. B. Pontalis, who describe fantasy as "the stage-setting of desire" in order to elucidate the way fantasizing subjects imaginatively occupy multiple positions within the erotic scenes they fantasize.[2] In this account desire is like drama: it distributes itself between multiple points of view, and its content demands a spatial rendering.[3] As Lauren Berlant notes, this idea "requires repositioning the desiring subject as a *spectator* as well as a participant in her scene of desire."[4] Freud's "A Child Is Being Beaten" is central to this theoretical tradition; as we noted earlier, Freud relates in the 1919 article that when he asks patients who report the eponymous fantasy—specifically, the women among them—where they "are" in the scene they imagine, they "only declare: 'I am probably looking on.'"[5]

These women's spectatorial relationship to their own enjoyment, and their refusal to identify themselves with any single character in their fantasy, make "A Child Is Being Beaten" a perfect parable of scenic desire. But to treat it as a paradigm for all fantasy, as Laplanche and Pontalis do, means eliding its singular constellation of violence and gender. In Freud's account, that is, the subject's simultaneous dispersal into and disappearance from the scene of her fantasy is specific to *women's masochism.* This specificity is interesting for two reasons. First, because the beating fantasy becomes the venue for a redefinition of sexual difference: women *have it* (the fantasy) *differently*, meaning that masochism makes gender itself available to experience in a particular way. In itself, perhaps, this is not surprising, given the widespread assumption—affirmed, as we saw, in Freud's own "Economic Problem" essay—that male masochism means wanting to be treated as a woman. As James will help us see, however, the concept of femininity that emerges vis-à-vis masochism in "A Child Is Being Beaten" is quite different from this conventional conflation of femininity with passivity.

Second, if we take up Freud's suggestion that the scenic mode of desire ("I am probably looking on") has a special relevance to *masochism*, we can pursue the implication that there is something pleasurably painful—that is, perverse—about scenic desire itself, in its very structure. And this, in turn, suggests a new way of pursuing the question of the relationship between desire and theater. Beyond affirming that desire or fantasy "is theatrical"—an affirmation that, as Lynda Hart has observed, too often relies on an unexamined reification of "conventional definition[s]" of theater—we might explore the possibility that actual practices of theater have given form to particular versions of sexuality.[6] And we might then look to theater itself, as a cultural endeavor, an imaginative site, and a locus of writing, to teach us more about how those particular sexualities operate. In this case, of course, the sexuality in question is a kind of masochism, one that bears a family resemblance to all those that show up across the texts this book considers.

Discussing Freud's "Psychopathic Characters on the Stage," we noted the difficulty of parsing out *whose* "masochistic satisfaction" the dramatic hero's suffering and defeat produce: is it only spectators who get off, or the hero too, or somehow "the drama" itself? The indeterminacy of who feels what in theater's masochism continues to resonate profoundly in "A Child Is Being Beaten," as it does in Ibsen's play, and especially in James. Taking a cue from Kaja Silverman's seminal analysis of masochism and the "authorial fantasmatic" in James and other male authors, I want to examine how James anticipates and develops a version of Freud's masochistic *girl* as the crucial figure of both painful pleasure and aesthetic creation.[7] As we will see, this fantasy refers irreducibly to theater—a medium with which James was, as we know, always desirously engaged.[8] Within that medium, the fantasy has a particular point of reference in the thrilling coldness and cruelty of modern drama's canonical antiheroine, Hedda.

In her pathbreaking reading of *Hedda Gabler*, Elin Diamond remarks upon the "power of ... imaginary identification" the London production seems to have enabled in female audiences, "opening access not only to masochistic satisfaction in Hedda's suffering and defeat, but also to the

more dangerous disturbance of counter-transference" and a kind of identificatory overinvestment in Hedda.[9] Diamond's analysis focuses more on
hysterical identification than on masochistic pleasure, but the play and its
reception lead her to wonder: "What happens when females occupy the
masochistic position? Is the quest for true interpretation deflected?"[10] Diamond insists that *Hedda Gabler* produces feminine versions of both pleasure and identification that are, in particular ways, *disturbing*—a claim
worth emphasizing since, as we know, pleasure and identification can also
be understood as profoundly stabilizing, ego-consolidating phenomena,
perhaps especially when they are shared by theatrical audiences. I'll suggest that the kind of pleasurable identification Hedda solicits is not exactly
"imaginary"—if this term refers to a psychic register in which subjects can
see themselves, in fantasy, as whole. On the contrary, *Hedda Gabler*'s offer
of identification follows a version of the paradoxical logic we have already
found in various instances of masochistic literature: just as the masochist wants what they don't want, the spectator of *Hedda Gabler* is invited to
identify with the unidentifiable, the unimaginable—and to identify *that*
identification, counterintuitively, with the making and watching of theater.

In psychoanalytic theory, one privileged term for this unimaginable is
"the death drive." Freud introduces this term in *Beyond the Pleasure Principle* as a name for the organism's drive to return (itself and others) to the
state of nonbeing. In order to account for its limited success in achieving
this, Freud posits a competing life drive; he calls the latter Eros. But its
wholesome bent on reproduction and survival has little in common with
sexuality as Freud had been theorizing it for decades; thus subsequent
thinkers—including Laplanche and, more famously, Jacques Lacan—
reformulate the death drive (or simply "the drive") as the impulsion toward jouissance that constitutes sexuality itself, conceiving it as at once
a structuring and a destructuring principle of the psyche. Elaborating
upon Lacan's distinction between drive and desire, Edelman writes that
whereas *desire* proceeds through "the successive displacement forward of
nodes of attachment as figures of meaning, points of intense metaphoric
investment, produced in the hope, however, vain, of filling the constitutive
gap in the subject," the *drive* "disarticulates the narrativity of desire" and
remains "intractable, unassimilable to the logic of interpretation or the demands of meaning-production"; the drive is "the inarticulable surplus that
dismantles the subject from within."[11]

What does this have to do with theater? For one thing, Diamond's
suggestion that a feminine theater spectator's masochistic investments
might "deflect" the "quest for true interpretation" obviously resonates
with Edelman's description of the drive as "unassimilable to the logic of
interpretation." Pursuing this resonance, I want to develop the notion that

Hedda Gabler sets up *as theater* a process of confronting and enjoying an ineliminable negativity or incoherence within psychic experience—the negativity that, for Edelman, denotes the drive. I realize, however, that to speak of "confronting and enjoying" the death drive might itself seem incoherent, since for theorists of the drive, the latter is prior to (and constitutive for) enjoyment or confrontation, or any other psychic event. As Freud writes, the drive is always "something in the background" that "escapes detection" except insofar as Eros drags its evidence into the light.[12] If you can't even detect it, how can you confront it? And if it is the condition of all enjoyment, how can the drive itself be something one enjoys? As I said a moment ago, it seems to me that the paradoxical logic of masochism—in which desire attaches to its own negation—offers a structure in which something that we know cannot appear within our fantasies nevertheless functions as those fantasies' referent; and that in theories of the death drive we might recognize a version of this masochistic something. This is not exactly the same as reiterating Freud's suggestion that masochism might be an "example" of the death drive at work: for the purposes of this chapter, I'm less interested in the death drive as an explanation for masochism than as one possible descriptive figure—and where *Hedda Gabler* is concerned, a remarkably precise figure—for the negativity that a masochistic imagination invokes and cathects.[13] Works like *Beyond the Pleasure Principle* or Edelman's *No Future*, in the course of theorizing the death drive, get some of us very excited about it, even as we know that what's turning us on in this particular way is the idea of the drive, rather than the drive "itself." Like these works, *Hedda Gabler* performs a theory of sexual subjectivity; like them, the play invites an erotic engagement with what it presents as the fundamentally destructive undercurrent of sexuality. Unlike them, however, it describes its own ability to do this to us as theater.

In one way, the notion of theater as a venue for encountering the death drive might be unsurprising: we're accustomed to the idea that theater makes us reckon with death, and an ongoing critical tradition has argued that live performance inherently holds mortality itself up to view.[14] This very lucidity, however, would seem to make it a particularly unpromising field in which to pursue the famously recessive death *drive*. *Hedda Gabler* approaches the question from a different angle: here theater offers a particular kind of access to a drive-infused erotics, not through its deathly spectacles but through its conflicted mediality, the uneasy conjunction of prescription and performance. It's precisely where theater offers its "live" present as the enactment of repetition and representation that *Hedda* invites us to inhabit—to feel, and enjoy—the temporality of the drive. As a staging of theater's drivelike structure, the play can help us further unfurl Freud's early claim that masochism has a distinctive relationship to drama.

For Edelman, approaching the death drive is not only a matter of enjoyment but an ethical imperative. Its stakes emerge with force in his *No Future*, published in 2004, which quickly became both seminal and controversial throughout queer theory and cultural studies. There Edelman describes a hegemonic social structure he calls "reproductive futurism," in which society fantasizes its perpetual self-identity through the figure of the child, while ensuring that the queer "figures ... the place of the social order's death drive."[15] But Edelman's aim is not simply to put an end to this distribution of values. "By denying our identification with the negativity of this drive, and hence our disidentification from the promise of futurity, those of us inhabiting the place of the queer may be able to cast off that queerness and enter the properly political sphere," he writes, "but only by shifting the figural burden of queerness to someone else. The *structural position* of queerness, after all, and the need to fill it remain."[16] In Edelman's Lacanian framework, the imposition of language enacts a painful discontinuity and insufficiency at the heart of the subject, incommensurable with any system of meaning, including politics; abjected figures like the queer offer a necessary alibi for that lack. So Edelman formulates a queer ethics as follows: queers should affirm their identification with the drive in order to proclaim the rift within society's (and subjects') fantasy of self-preservation. "Not that we are, or could ever be, outside the Symbolic ourselves; but we can, nonetheless, make the choice to accede to our cultural production as figures ... for the dismantling of such a logic and for the death drive it harbors within."[17] Willingly embodying the drive would not mean *achieving* the "dismantling" of reproductive futurism's violent exclusions because such violence, for Edelman, is structurally fundamental to any form of social life. But by choosing to figure the drive, queers can keep manifesting the disconcerting presence of that in the social order which perpetually undermines the social order; they can give the lie to the fantasmatic project of self-perpetuation and thereby denounce the violence it justifies.

The value of queerness in this argument resides in its negativity, the resistance it opposes to fictions of self-identity; thus Edelman writes that he is "proposing no platform or position from which queer sexuality or any queer subject might finally and truly become itself."[18] His call for a queerness that operates as a negation *of* rather than a program *for* the sociopolitical has been subject to widespread critique as "the statement of the entitled subject who can afford the simple negation."[19] But it seems to me that the queer identification with the death drive that Edelman advocates can also imply a complex practice of carrying on relations with the drive; more than a solitary, imperious demurral, this identification might be an ongoing and even collective process, lived out day to day in a shared world. The question is, how—and where—might this kind of ethical practice take place?

The queer figures Edelman analyzes in *No Future* are fictional characters from literature and film; they don't have to "make the choice to accede" to figuring the drive as queer because they simply *are* such figures. This is where the question of medium might begin to make a difference. Theater's figures are never fully given in advance; in theater, figuring or embodying is something people always have to figure out how to do. In fact, there are two stage figures who do receive passing consideration *No Future*: Antigone and—in a footnote—Kate from *The Taming of the Shrew*.[20] These characters' turns within *No Future* are anomalous, not only in that they come from plays but more strikingly in that they are the only female queers to appear in the book. I want to suggest that this conjunction of gender and genre opens onto dramatic theater as an oddly promising—and feminizing—mode of pursing Edelman's ethical project. This promise emerges when we bring a third theatrical femme into play and give her more stage time than her two predecessors get in *No Future*: I'm referring, of course, to Hedda Tesman née Gabler.

Hedda resonates in striking ways with Edelman's account of queer figures like Ebenezer Scrooge. Examining the ways in which she solicits identification with the death drive—that is, enacts something like an Edelmanian theory of queerness—might help begin to redress the infamously "narrow vision" of *No Future*'s "gay male archive," if only in relation to gender.[21] It is true that Hedda's emotional register seems largely to correspond with the "range of affective responses" identified with gay male canonicity, like boredom and irony—a fact that may help explain why Charles Ludlam was asked to play Hedda in the 1984 American Ibsen Theater production.[22] Nevertheless, the play's history of feminist (and outraged reactionary) reception suggests that its queerness cannot be divorced from its specifically feminist agency.[23] This means that thinking through *No Future*'s application to *Hedda Gabler* is one way to begin thinking through the former's relevance to feminist poetics. It is also a way to argue for theater's special relevance to the queer ethical problematic Edelman describes: in offering a vision of the stage as a place for engaging desirously—masochistically—with the death drive, *Hedda* helps us see what that paradoxical engagement might look like as a cultural practice.

Burning Your Child

Anyone who, through some accident of research or pedagogy, happens to look at *Hedda Gabler* and *No Future* in the same week will be struck by certain convergences. Hedda's climactic moment of wickedness comes when she burns the only copy of Thea and Løvborg's manuscript, a work that "deals with the civilising forces of the future" and about which we learn little else.[24] That the book's futurism is "reproductive" is something we are never allowed to forget. Books are first made to stand for babies in a comic dialogue between Hedda's husband Tesman and his aunt; Løvborg vaunts the manuscript as "the book I have put my true self into"; in his anguished confrontation with the devoted Thea after he believes he has lost the book, they both begin referring to it as their "child."[25] So it is precisely the child-future complex that Hedda tries to destroy, even as she regards her own pregnancy with unmitigated loathing. Her pregnancy operates from the first to shore up the coherence of her claustrophobic world. It makes Aunt Julle forgive her viciously insulting behavior; and later, when Tesman is upset with Hedda for burning the manuscript, Hedda's halting confession that she is with child—a sentence she can't even bear to finish—convinces him immediately that all is well.[26] Throughout the play, then, having children is not only the way we write the future; it is also the way we peremptorily suture even the most violent breaks in the status quo, convincing ourselves that things can keep going on as they are.

Hedda's rage in the face of this ubiquitous fantasy is one of the most powerful feelings the play offers. But the affect that links Hedda most markedly to Edelman's queer figures is her famous coldness, along with the peculiar pleasure it entails. "*Her complexion is pale and opaque*," Ibsen writes. "*Her steel-grey eyes express a cold, unruffled repose*."[27] Describing Scrooge before his Christmas redemption, Edelman writes: "The pleasure Scrooge takes, what turns *him* on, comes in part from refusing to ... drop acorns from the family tree. Indeed, his every enjoyment betrays the logic of such a refusal, the exquisite pain of a negation so great that he almost seems to rebuff the very warm-bloodedness of mammalian vitality, as if, like a textbook-perfect example of the death drive according to Freud, he aimed to return to the icy, inert immobility of a lifeless thing."[28] Hedda's own pronounced refusal of the "mammalian," her determined freezing of normative erotic currents, likewise offers a strange kind of sexual "pleasure." In light of Deleuze's account, we might hasten to describe our pleasure in Hedda's statuesque coldness as classically masochistic—and certainly, she enjoys controlling and hurting those around her. But to read Hedda as an icily voluptuous dominatrix—to see her, perhaps, the way Løvborg might—wouldn't really address the pleasure of her *self*-destruction. Immediately after her friend Judge Brack suggests that motherhood will soon fill the void in her life, the play rebounds into exactly this libidinal terrain. "Oh, be quiet, I tell you!" she responds, then: "I often think there is only one thing in the world I have any turn for." Brack, "drawing near to her," intones: "And what is that, if I may ask?" "Boring myself to death," Hedda replies.[29] This rejoinder thrills us not only with its deadly predictive force (she really will bore herself to death) but also with the shocking nullity of her response to the judge's, and our, curiosity—her interposition of the blank term "boring" where we expected to find her desire. Edelman's invitation to imagine the queer figure as a "textbook-perfect example of the death drive" implies just such a startling gap in erotic willfulness, the place where desire falters under its own force, marking the treacherous inconsistency of the subjectivity desire is supposed to sustain.[30]

Indeed, the drive's ongoing subversion of subjectivity produces the most challenging aspect of Edelman's argument, making it hard to imagine what "identifying with the drive" could even mean. As the function that lends the ego its fantasmatic consistency, identification is conservative and, indeed, reproductive—a concern that has haunted modern theater since Bertolt Brecht charged realist drama with naturalizing the social status quo.[31] But as we saw earlier in Diamond, another critical tradition has emphasized the destabilizing aspects of identification; in particular, feminist scholars like Diamond and, more recently, Shonni Enelow have explored the disruptive ramifications of identification in theater, the "abyssal psychic openness" it can wreak upon the performers who identify with characters onstage, and spectators who mirror this identification in spite of themselves.[32] A similar instability inheres in the societal dynamic of identification Edelman discusses: when society fashions the image of the queer as the container for its own death drive, it intends identification in the consolidating mode; but it opens itself to identification's destabilizing force by its very demonstration that this attempt at containment is necessary. And by taking over their own identification with the drive, queers—while necessarily failing simply to *be* the drive with which they identify—can enact the instability of identification, of identity, and hence of the social order itself.

In a frequently cited anecdote, the actress Elizabeth Robins relates an exchange she had with an audience member after playing Hedda in the play's English premiere: "One lady of our acquaintance, married and not noticeably unhappy, said laughing, 'Hedda is all of us.'"[33] The story, and the energy with which it has continued to circulate, suggests how powerfully the play positions its title character as a mirror: Hedda's claustrophobic fury stands for ours. For some critics, the Robins anecdote thus speaks to the play's potential for radical, politicizing feminist reception.[34] In a 2013 article, Toril Moi cites the anecdote to give point to her disappointment in recent *Hedda* productions that, she contends, attempted "to block identification" with the main character: "Missing in all these productions were the despair, the yearning for beauty, the depth of soul that give Ibsen's Hedda her complexity and grandeur," Moi writes.[35] These shows conceived the part with so little sympathy that it became impossible to identify with Hedda; the audience could neither "understand the play" nor "why Hedda kills herself."[36] But Edelman's reading of the queer figure paradoxically suggests that what "all of us" identify with in a character like Hedda might *be* the suspension of identifiable subjectivity. And this possibility depends on perceiving something in Hedda that is precisely not a "depth of soul" but a strange infectious pleasure in empty gestures—up to and including the unreasonable excess of her suicide.

Excessive, empty gestures are both a basic danger and a basic pleasure of theatrical performance, a fact to which *Hedda Gabler* is sharply attuned. In particular, the play eroticizes moments of noncoincidence between words and bodies, or between saying and doing, a disjunction whose possibility lies at the heart of theater, the medium of language enacted. Nowhere is this more flagrant than at the end of act three:

HEDDA: (*Throws one of the quires into the fire and whispers to herself.*) Now I am burning your child, Thea!—Burning it, curly-locks! (*Throwing one or two more quires into the stove.*) Your child and Eilert Løvborg's. (*Throws the rest in.*) I am burning—I am burning your child.[37]

Perhaps it is a stretch to hear in these words an eerie anticipation of the famous "Father, can't you see I'm burning"—the dream of Freud's patient that Lacan invokes as a paradigmatic return of the Real.[38] But the fact of Hedda's speech is also remarkable in its own context: the Tesman drawing room has not, up to this point, been a place where people soliloquize.[39] So when Hedda slips into verbalization in the burning scene, the effect is disturbing in a way that exceeds the murderous content of her action. The speech echoes as a drivelike excess, an empty letter, a histrionic moment that theater people might describe as outside-in. The more she describes her action, the less securely she seems to sit at the helm of it, her jouissance breaking with psychological consistency.

This moment has a precedent in Hedda's past relationship with Løvborg, which they recall together in act two. When she was young, he would call on her at her father's house and spend hours recounting the details of his debaucheries: "There I would sit and tell you of my escapades—my days and nights of devilment."[40] When Løvborg finally proposed that they embark on some escapades of their own, Hedda threatened to shoot him, and their relationship came to an end. Moi draws on this event in her helpful account of Hedda as a figure of "non-response"; any queer analysis of the play would have to agree with Moi's suggestion that what Hedda *didn't* do in that narrated moment—say, leap into Løvborg's arms—is at least as important as what she did.[41] But to understand this violent negation as a "refusal of sexuality itself," and to align this seamlessly with Hedda's "revolt against her pregnancy," is to suggest that "sexuality itself" must be continuous with the kind of act that makes babies.⁴² Such a reading suppresses the pleasure Hedda's reaction enables: a pleasure in the noncoincidence of words and deeds—racy stories told and *not* enacted—and in the interference that disrupts or splits desire.

To read this escape from normative sex as tragic would be to lag behind even Brack, who rallies in act four with a scheme of sexual blackmail, threatening to implicate Hedda in Løvborg's death. When she threatens suicide, he replies, "*smiling*," "People say such things—but they don't do them."⁴³ Of course it's reasonable to read in this line a patronizing (and predatory) complacency that will blow up in the judge's face when he's forced to echo these words in shock at the play's close. But if the divergence between saying and doing, or thinking and enacting, is indispensable to Hedda's pleasure, then we might also read the line as an erotic parry, an articulation of the logic by which they could have fun. Unlike anyone else in the play, Brack appreciates Hedda's negativity; the problem is that he assumes her "no" can be recuperated, housed within sex as he knows it: "(*Gently takes the pistol out of her hand.*) ... Ah—I know this pistol well!... (*Lays the pistol in [the case] and shuts it.*) Now we won't play at that game any more today."⁴⁴ Brack is not wrong to call Hedda's gunplay a "game"; he is only wrong to assume it will end with *da* and not *fort*.

Hedda's famous aestheticism, which culminates in her attempt to make Løvborg commit suicide "beautifully," thus operates in relation to what Edelman calls "the formalism of the drive."⁴⁵ Her own stagey suicide demonstrates a formalistic attachment to the noble or beautiful *as excess*, precisely where its demands exceed the parameters of what any subject can really intend to do.⁴⁶ A character who figured the death drive would be one whose motivations fell short of her movements—a signature risk, again, of theatrical performance. Hedda's mantric repetition of the phrase "vine leaves in his hair" enacts just this kind of emptiness: "Oh Hedda," Thea admonishes her, "you are just saying things you don't believe a bit."⁴⁷ Interestingly, this is just what Scrooge hears the first time he lets loose with *his* characteristic verbal tic, surely one of the most famous in modern literature. "'Christmas a humbug, uncle!' said Scrooge's nephew. 'You don't mean that, I am sure.'"⁴⁸ Like Hedda, Scrooge stands accused of histrionics, a classically feminizing charge.

"Try to—to Do It Beautifully"

If *Hedda Gabler* brings queer negativity more firmly into the orbit of femininity, its theatrics also diverge from the readily political notions of performance-as-defamiliarization that we customarily use to describe feminism in theater. One way to see this is to consider a contrast between *Hedda Gabler* and the play whose evil twin it sometimes seems to be: *A Doll's House*. Written eleven years earlier, *A Doll's House* is the story of a bourgeoise housewife who comes to recognize that her virtuosic femininity has been a command performance. If theater is able to "remind us," as Alisa Solomon writes, "of the disarming possibility that our own guarded identities, even those that feel as intimate as skin, must be aggressively and institutionally enforced if they are to be sustained," then *A Doll's House* is the Ibsen play most obviously situated to make good on this potential.[49] Theater's power to attack gender roles by exposing them *as* theater is one of the play's most appealing affordances; thus in the 2014 Young Vic production directed by Carrie Cracknell, Hattie Morahan's relentlessly heightened portrayal of Nora never let us forget this lesson for a second.[50]

As Solomon shows, the same tack can be taken with *Hedda Gabler*, so that we see Hedda fundamentally as someone who has been miscast in the domestic scene.[51] But whereas Nora leaves the stage in search of a self that might be more than an empty role, Hedda dies to protect the void at her center. *A Doll's House* offers the pleasure of watching Nora triumphantly shatter the mirror that no longer reflects her and go off in pursuit of another: "I shall never get to know myself—I shall never learn to face reality—unless I stand alone."[52] If Hedda undermines the performance of sexual difference, she does so less by claiming the right to perform otherwise than through a perverse intransigence that freezes the image of femininity and vitiates it from within.

Both plays thus play on the doubleness of the actor. But while Nora finds a possibility of liberation from that noncoincidence, Hedda grasps it as a source of pleasure in itself. The awareness that theatrical mimesis is unstable becomes, for Hedda and her audience, a creepy enjoyment of one's own replaceability. "Doesn't it seem strange to you, Thea? Here are you sitting with Tesman—just as you used to sit with Eilert Løvborg?" Hedda remarks shortly before her suicide, as Thea and Tesman labor together to reconstitute Løvborg's now-posthumous book.[53] Not only has Tesman replaced Løvborg as Thea's comrade, but, of course, Thea herself has replaced Hedda, whose own relationship with Løvborg consisted precisely of "sitting with" him. Perhaps the horror of this vision—or even just the tedium of endless musical chairs—is what drives Hedda to shoot herself. But with her death she also manages to *guarantee* her particular being as disposable, interchangeable, in the way people playing roles onstage always are.

Thomas Ostermeier's gelid 2006 German-language production, starring Katharina Schüttler, seized on this valence of Hedda's act; instead of discovering her corpse and reacting with *"confusion and cries"* as Ibsen stipulates, her friends laughed at the gunshot in the next room and continued contentedly working away.[54] Hedda's corpse—splayed at the foot of the wall in the study, below a vivid blood spatter—slowly wheeled past the audience on the revolving set. Her body cycled out of sight, replaced by the placid action in the main room, then was gradually revealed again. The sound system played the Beach Boys as the lights faded down: "God only knows what I'd be without you." The luxuriant cruelty of this ending caressed the structure of the theater event, the rotation of the stage simulating the daily round of the actor's day, her spectacular death appearing and receding with issueless regularity. As theatergoers, we can get the character back every time we lose her; like a kid playing with a spool, we take a pleasure in Hedda that accommodates her death. This is cruel of us, but she cues us to it: "Oh Hedda, Hedda," cries Løvborg, "how could you throw yourself away!"[55] The entire play is taken up with showing us how she could, showing us how it's done. Exploiting the theatrical condition of repetition, Hedda's nightly drop into nothingness dangles us over an empty place where subjectivity escapes and we aren't even nobody, then snaps us back up into everyday self-preservation for the curtain call.

Perhaps this sounds like the trick of any fictional death. But plays work differently from movies or novels in this regard because, in their indispensable reference to performance, there is the gristle of a trick we can never quite master ourselves. We don't simply decide when theater happens; it may need "all of us," but, unlike reading, it's mostly independent of me. Even to read a play *as a play* is to attend to its promise of a repetition that will negate the primacy of my desire. To like that about it—to finger the edge where my desire will end and something else will begin—is to stage a masochistic encounter with the drive.

This appreciation of theater's cruelty is what burns at the icy center of *Hedda Gabler*. Hedda is constantly both enacting and enjoying, and tempting us to enjoy, a theatrical attrition of the self. This attrition inheres in the beyond-pleasure principle that the show must go on, as in the peculiar hollowness of characters in plays. If Hedda "throws herself away," first in marriage and then in suicide, this exercise is patterned on the way the textual Hedda Gabler falls out and lets the actress perform in her place. One might object that this is an artificially dramatized account; after all, it's not as if there is a "real" Hedda whom the actress actually displaces. Yet the play itself stages the disappearance of its heroine, presenting her as lost from the front matter on; there is no Hedda Gabler in *Hedda Gabler*, as the dramatis personae reveals: "Jørgen Tesman, researcher in cultural history; Mrs. Hedda Tesman, his wife; Miss Juliane Tesman, his aunt."[56]

It is as if the requirement that Hedda be embodied—entered into the cast list—itself enacts her displacement. In Hedda's first exchange with Løvborg, they both dwell on this disappearance with what seems like perverse indulgence:

LØVBORG: (*Who has never taken his eyes of her, says softly and slowly.*) Hedda—
Gabler!
HEDDA: (*Glancing hastily at him.*) Ah! Hush!
LØVBORG: (*Repeats softly.*) Hedda Gabler!
HEDDA: (*Looking at the album.*) That was my name in the old days—when we two knew each other.
LØVBORG: And I must teach myself never to say Hedda Gabler again—never, as long as I live.
HEDDA: (*Still turning over the pages.*) Yes, you must. And I think you ought to practise in time. The sooner the better, I should say.[57]

Perversely, both Løvborg and Hedda talk of learning *not* to say her old name rather than of getting used to her new one. This choice emphasizes that Hedda is exactly not someone to build a future with; instead she offers herself as the site for a "practice" of deletion.

Her offer refers to dramatic theater's peculiar temporality. There is always an irreducible futurity to the written play as such; as Bert States puts it, "all dramatic texts are hypotheses, yearnings."[58] A play is always *to be performed*; in some cases we may experience this directive as ironical or utopian, but if we lose touch with it entirely, then we are no longer reading the play as a play. The same futurity also determines the horizon of doing or seeing plays; any performance of a play is just one iteration of something that can happen again. This sense that the play is necessarily still to come, in a future that will nonetheless reiterate what is already here, might seem to align theater with Edelman's "reproductive futurism": a "tenacious will to sameness ... endlessly protecting the fantasy space in which it is *always* there."[59] In one sense, Ostermeier's refashioning of Hedda's death scene indicts us for precisely this brutality of theater; like Antigone, Hedda might want to die, but we won't let her, trotting her out night after night to bolster our assurance that some things never change. Suspecting that Hedda might be pregnant, Aunt Julle drones: "Hedda is lovely— lovely—lovely" and "*takes her head between both hands*"; "Oh—! Let me go," Hedda begs.[60] Her queer voice breaks against theater's fantasy machine from inside it, registering the violence enacted by the wish for more of the same.

But Hedda's voice, too, belongs to theater. As powerful as our prescriptive fantasies may be, the seduction of theatrical repetition lies just as much in what will always exceed those fantasies: the unbridled contingency that threatens our best-laid plans *the same way every time* and *always differently*. The stage is a treacherous mirror; to subject our images of ourselves to nightly reenactment is nightly to open those images—those selves—to un-doing. "Throughout the last two acts of the play, Hedda has behaved like a producer and director trying desperately to stage a sublime idealist trag-edy entitled 'Løvborg's Death,'" Moi remarks.[61] For that matter, Hedda gives everyone directives on lighting and blocking from the moment she first appears—as when she "*forces Mrs. Elvsted to sit in the easy-chair be-side the stove*" in act one.[62] When Hedda tries to coach Løvborg in the sui-cide she wants to see, begging him to "try to—to do it beautifully," she lets herself in for utter devastation: he dies instead of an accidental bullet to the groin in a bordello skirmish, as Brack seems sadistically pleased to tell her. "Oh, the ridiculous and the low, it settles like a curse upon all that I touch," she replies.[63] As Moi points out, "'the ridiculous combined with the low'" is a classical genre formula for comedy or farce.[64] This means that Løvborg's farcical failure to enact his own death "beautifully" signals not the collapse of theater, but the working-out of a "curse" that afflicts theater from within—a curse, we might say, that theatrical authorship al-ways incurs, with its ever-present threat of the fall into the low.

In pointing up the cruelty of the fall and its inherence in theater, *Hedda Gabler* anticipates a theatrical vision notoriously at odds with Ibsen's real-ism: that of Antonin Artaud. "We are not free. And the sky can still fall on our heads," Artaud writes. "And the theater has been created to teach us that first of all."[65] But why, we might well wonder, do we need theater to teach us that when we've got real life? Guns going off in the wrong places are not unique to the stage; if only they were. Artaud also writes that "the theater is *the only place in the world* where a gesture, once made, can never be made the same way twice."[66] Again: why the *only* place? If contingency and ephemerality were all it took to make Cruelty, we wouldn't need the-ater; at best, we might explore them through a theater of improvisation. But as Jacques Derrida observes, improvisation is anathema to Artaud's theater, where everything must "be painstakingly determined in ad-vance ... *prescribed.*"[67] It seems to me that this is because theater's special, capital-C Cruelty arises from nourishing an outrageous criterion of repe-tition: a mercilessly rigorous formalism for which what would normally count as "the same" no longer qualifies. The attempt to reduce the irre-ducible interference of liveness to zero: this would be a way to define the death drive as Freud first formulates it in *Beyond the Pleasure Principle.*[68] It would also be a way to describe an essential impulse of *authoring* theater, a desire that only ever goes before a fall.

I think most of us who make theater would object, here, that the deadening tendency of repetition is something we try very hard to avoid; we want it to be different every night! But to try to get out ahead of theater's danger by embracing it, in practice or theory, is to disavow the violent negativity of live performance as Artaud speaks to it here. We lay ourselves open to whatever might fall on our heads each night, and we may try to master that contingency by commanding it to return, as if that were up to us; but every performance of a play is an experience of the way it is *not* up to us. No matter how loudly we celebrate the warm-blooded vitality of unpredictable copresence, something will be there that is alien to our intentions. Hedda's inability to make Løvborg die "beautifully" is the failure of every sex scene, which is to say, of every scene; it is the devastating impossibility of a jouissance that would really be what we wanted. Does *Hedda Gabler* mean simply to valorize or reconcile us to that futility? No: the play makes us want, like Hedda, to attack it, even though—and because—its resistance will hurt. In the friction of that brutal slapstick, we make theater: a masochistic attempt to body forth the negativity of the drive.[69]

Constantly planning for itself, theater can never relinquish the future; but in the midst of all this planning, we can feel ourselves suffer from— expose and enjoy—futurity *as cruelty*, as the necessary encounter with what *will refuse to* realize our fantasies. I don't believe this is simply one more variant of the futurist logic of deferral Edelman describes. Rather, it corresponds to an undertow that runs beneath and against the futuristic current, bearing nonsatisfaction *back* from the future and redeeming it as perverse enjoyment in the present. It is the future as radically discontinuous with our selves and our plans that we figure to ourselves in making theater—we figure, that is, not the future itself but its discontinuity with our own figuring.

Now, Edelman argues that *no* way of imagining the future can really break with reproductive logic, no matter how much allowance we try to make for the future's difference. That argument is the basis of his quarrel with Judith Butler's reading of *Antigone*, in which Antigone's unintelligibility figures "the social form of an aberrant, unprecedented future."[70] Citing Lacan, Edelman argues that the Symbolic always perpetuates itself through the appearance of change. "With this Antigone's 'aberrant ... future' proves orthodox after all," he writes: "Undermining its claim to be aberrant and unprecedented at once, it transmits, in the *requisite* aberrant form, as futurity *always* demands—in the form, that is, whose aberrant quality is therefore anything but and whose future repeats its precedents precisely by virtue of being 'unprecedented'—the Symbolic chain of discourse, in which, as everyone knows ... intelligibility must always take place."[71] It is, we might say, fundamental to the very concept of the future that it will be different from the present; in the most basic sense, this is what makes satisfaction seem to be worth waiting for. In this framework, "the future" just *is* the formula for conscripting into intelligibility, meaning, and desire everything "aberrant," everything that lies outside them now—thus neutralizing aberrancy in its own name.

What I am suggesting is that theater as described by *Hedda Gabler* activates a different function of the future, which "takes place" not as a progressive illumination of possibilities that now lie beyond the pale but as an encounter with that barrier as such. And not because the unthinkable beyond is not already with us (it is) but because the temporal division into *pre*scription and the performance *to come* sets up a space in which noncoincidence is not just an abiding fact of the psyche: in theater, noncoincidence is something that *happens* to us, takes us up and over, and hence actually interrupts our normal business of self-perpetuation. By engaging masochistically in this process, we train ourselves to enlist all of our energies in the perverse project of arranging for our desires to be overrun by what is alien to our strenuous intention. When Hedda burns the future, she sets up the future that burns her back. And in giving identification the chance to coalesce around something as sterile and empty as "boring myself to death," she offers us the theater as a site for rehearsing the disarticulation of pleasure from the structures through which we normally, violently, strive to secure it.

The "Added Intensity of Regret": James's Dramaturgical Masochism

I've argued that part of what Hedda gives us to enjoy is a painfully eroticized demonstration of theatrical authorship. Among the play's characters, however, it is of course not Hedda but Løvborg who is literally an author; indeed, Thea and even Tesman lead productive, recognizably literary lives, whereas, as we know, there's "only one thing" Hedda knows how to do: bore herself to death or, as Løvborg puts it, throw herself away. I hope, however, that we are coming to understand "throwing yourself away" as a formula for a certain kind of masochistic authorship, which may need and want to go misrecognized, and may even seek proximity to the obvious spectacle of masculine authorship for this very purpose.

In Henry James's "Nona Vincent," Mrs. Alsager also embodies this mode of enjoyment. Mrs. Alsager's erotic life, like Hedda's, plays out in an extramarital, unconsummated relation to a man who writes while she herself seems not to; and like Hedda's, Mrs. Alsager's story culminates in an elaborate act that thoroughly confounds authorial self-assertion with self-erasure. If James never gives us the cathartic finish that Hedda wrests from reality with her last formalizing coup, this may be because his erotic attachment to theater's repetitiveness is even more perversely profound than Hedda's—or because, more like "all of us" in this respect than like Ibsen, he can't finish letting Hedda go.

The obdurate quality of Jamesian passion will be familiar to readers acquainted with his unusually sturdy love triangles: triangles that refuse to collapse into dyads, even when resolution is apparently at hand.[72] In Jamesian conflicts there can be no clear winner, because to win in James is to lose, and to lose is to win—a logic that keeps animating a mutual reference between parties even after the competition has ended, even in death. This rule probably achieves its most perfect instance in *The Wings of the Dove*, but we can see it all over James's work. Critics have sometimes identified his characters' insistence on giving up the thing they want with an ethics of "renunciation," and as Kevin Ohi observes, this way of reading the stories has often been grounded in a sense of James's own life as one of sexual self-deprivation.[73] Whether lamenting or valorizing the way characters like Lewis Lambert Strether, Merton Densher, May Bartram, or Maisie always ultimately forgo the relations they seem most to desire, such a reading cannot but reiterate a commonsense notion of desire itself as a simple straining toward the object: a longing that would properly be satisfied by copulation or communion, were it not for the problem (social, ethical, or neurotic) that intervenes. The formula for Jamesian renunciation would then be: I want, but I must not have.

As Ohi and other readers have demonstrated, however, this reading obscures the erotic logic of both narrative and style in James, where enjoyment depends upon the subject's separation from what she desires. Silverman describes this as a "subject-position ... which is always set apart from genital sexuality, forever out of synchronization with the passion it witnesses"; Bersani, as a sensibility that consistently subordinates *doing* or *achieving* to the virtual and the hypothetical, with a stylistics devoted to weaseling out of "actual" experiences altogether.[74] Desire here is both self-referential and endlessly self-negating: in this formula, what I want *is* to want and not have. Oddly enough, then, the triangle—which would seem to epitomize narrative's most conventional sexual logic—can serve as a figure for what is most perverse in James, justifying the homonymy of the sexually "perverse" with any old tendency to act against your own best interests, as encapsulated in the "economic problem" known as masochism.

Other critics have already shown that reading James for his masochism needn't mean reducing his complex textuality to the familiarity of a symptom; the point, as with all these readings, is to reveal *this* masochism as a particular and surprising structure.[75] But even the most basic concept of masochism gets us out of the critical dilemma of either seeing his characters' suffering as a loss that happens *instead of* pleasure, or minimizing that suffering, as if the characters really didn't mind losing out after all.[76] Neither is right: the stories are painful, and the pain is pleasurable. If James's most beguiling characters are not always masochists, it seems clear that they at least perform a masochistic fantasy; Milly Theale herself may not exactly want to die betrayed by Merton Densher and Kate Croy, but the novel wants it for her, and makes it the substance, not just the price, of her triumph—a fact that constellates Milly, however oddly, with Hedda.

As we've already observed, Freud has a name for this kind of surrogation, in which a character becomes a bearer of a masochistic desire that originates elsewhere; in "A Child Is Being Beaten" this is what he calls *sadism*. This usage departs from the customary sexological notion—which Freud elsewhere retains—that sadism is the enjoyment of hurting others, and hence represents a *reversal* of masochism (or vice-versa); in "A Child," Freud uses the term "sadistic" to describe a particular *aspect* of women's masochistic desire. The fantasy named in the essay's title is sadistic, Freud suggests, insofar as its subject imagines a character other than herself as the victim of the beating, even though her enjoyment emanates from the victim's—not the aggressor's—place. "By what path," Freud inquires, "has the phantasy of strange and unknown boys being beaten (a phantasy which has by this time become *sadistic*) found its way into the permanent possession of the little girl's libidinal trends?"[77] Working backward from the conscious fantasy, Freud determines that it is in fact the third fantasy in a sequence of three: the first fantasy, of the father beating a rival child, was aggressive but "not clearly sexual"; the second, "the most important and the most momentous of all," is a masochistic (sexual) fantasy of being beaten by the father oneself, and can never be consciously remembered; this fantasy enters consciousness only by contorting itself into the fantasy that gives the essay its title, in which the subject appears neither as the victim nor as his persecutor or rival.[78] As noted above, the patients respond to Freud's "pressing enquiries" about where they themselves appear in the fantasy with the hesitant admission, "I am probably looking on."[79]

The titular fantasy thus seems to qualify as "sadistic" merely because the victim is someone else; but Freud continues to use this word even after he has revealed that the subject is unconsciously identified with the victim: "only the *form* of this phantasy is sadistic; the satisfaction which is derived from it is masochistic."[80] The "form" *is sadistic*, that is, even though the patient never appears, even falsely, as the aggressor: here sadism, a formal property that accompanies a masochistic content, consists precisely in installing a discrete character in the place of one's own pain/pleasure—or rather, in building a distance *into* pleasure itself, which becomes the space for another to step into.[81]

"Nona Vincent" identifies this space as the medium of theater. In James's vision, the formalizing movement through which masochism becomes "sadistic" stands revealed as the particular affordance of the theatrical art form, and of experiences of authorship that theater makes available: Freud's sadism is given the precise aesthetic contours of what I've proposed to call dramaturgical masochism. "Nona Vincent" is the tale of an aspiring playwright, Allan Wayworth, and his close friend, Mrs. Alsager, a married society matron who finds him "not only remarkably good-looking but altogether original."[82] After he reads his first play aloud to her in her "warm, golden drawing-room," Mrs. Alsager undertakes to help him get it produced, which turns out to be no small task.[83] When a company finally signs on and rehearsals begin, Wayworth's troubles only escalate: the play's heroine (and, presumably, title character) turns out to be a doozy of a role, and the young actress Violet Grey struggles with the part in spite of all the guidance Wayworth helpfully provides while falling in love with her. Opening night is a disaster: it becomes evident to everyone that Violet "has failed," and the next morning, the reviews all note an "odd want of correspondence between the heroine and her interpreter."[84] But at the second performance, a miraculous transformation occurs: Violet is a brilliant success as Nona. Afterward, she credits the change to Mrs. Alsager:

> "And how did Mrs. Alsager save you?"
> "By letting me look at her. By letting me hear her speak. By letting me know her.... Somehow she seemed to *give* it all to me.... For the first time, in the whole study of the part, I had my model—I could make my copy."[85]

The next day, Mrs. Alsager has left town for the season; the show is a hit, and Wayworth marries Violet, who then retires—gladly, we've been led to suppose—from acting; Wayworth's subsequent "plays sometimes succeed."[86] In the original serialized version of the story, the last line is brutally sardonic: "Mrs. Alsager continues to take boxes."[87] In the revised version, however, it becomes one of the most giddiness-inducing final sentences in all of James: "At these representations Mrs. Alsager continues frequently to be present."[88] Mrs. Alsager's continued attendance at the plays of the man whom she has given up, painfully and heroically, to Violet instances the masochism we've described as pervasive in James's work, which eroticizes the triangle from the loser's point of view. His narratives often endow this thrilling loss with a powerful finality—if not always, as in *The Wings of the Dove* or "The Beast in the Jungle," cementing it through death itself. "Nona Vincent," however, ends with an insistent, ongoing repetition.

It seems to me that what accounts for this difference—and perhaps even for the difference between Mrs. Alsager's fate and Milly's or Hedda's—is the central and literal presence in the story of actual theaters, which provide the characters of "Nona Vincent" with places built precisely for housing masochistic iteration. As Bersani argues in *The Freudian Body*, emplacement is always crucial to the fate of desire: all sexuality is violent, but "the catastrophe is produced when violence *stops*, when the dislocations produced by desire's mobility seek, as it were, to *take place*, to have a place, to become attached to particular objects and in so doing, to destroy them."[89] For Mrs. Alsager, we might say, theater absorbs and transmutes the taking-place of definitive endings, offering an alternative way for desire to territorialize itself. For the logic Bersani here describes is temporal as well as spatial: the violence that goes hurtling toward a target (the self or another) seeks the definitive moment of climactic closure, which is why Bersani associates this kind of violence with narrative. But the theater, to whose repetitions Mrs. Alsager can always return for a new jolt of pleasurable suffering, offers a temporality whose constitutive and obvious reliance on repetition undermines the fantasy of finality. Thus "Nona Vincent" does not quite end, even when *Nona Vincent* has closed after "two hundred nights."[90]

To understand the theatricalizing structure of Mrs. Alsager's painful enjoyment here—the "sadistic form," we might say, of her masochism—we have to consider the figure who most centrally mediates it, and who serves in Jamesian terms as the story's "center of consciousness": Wayworth. That Wayworth's experience as a playwright is fundamentally and classically masochistic is clear from the first.

> "Yes, indeed—to get it done!" Wayworth stared at the fire, slowly rolling up his type-copy. "But that's a totally different part of the business, and altogether secondary."
> "But of course you want to be acted?"
> "Of course I do—but it's a sudden descent. I want to intensely, but I'm sorry I want to." ... The roll of his copy, in his fist, was squeezed into the hollow of one of them....
> "Yes, the vulgarity will begin now," he presently added.
> "You'll suffer dreadfully."
> "I shall suffer in a good cause."[91]

To "want to be acted"—squeezing your rolled-up text in the hollow of your fist while you imagine longingly how you (and it) will "suffer" the "sudden descent" of enactment's vulgar blows—is what we might call the typically masculine posture of authorship-as-masochism in this text (we'll glimpse it again in Kennedy's Chris Aherne): the ego doesn't even bother to conceal its gratification, much less its identity as the blissfully passive object of violence.

This self-display is consistent—and here we begin thinking again about the difference made by (or as) gender—with Freud's observation that men who have the child-being-beaten fantasy can come to recognize themselves as the beaten child, whereas women never do. The masochistic fantasy "in which the boy's own self was retained as the person who was being beaten, differed from the second phase in girls in that it was able to become conscious," Freud writes; "the figure of the boy himself is not replaced," so the male masochist can enjoy the "familiar and conscious phantasy: 'I am being beaten by my mother.'"[92] This is not to say that the male masochist avoids repression altogether, since he too has an irreducibly unconscious fantasy at the root of the conscious one. Like the girl's, in fact, his desire is rooted in the unconscious form "I am being beaten by my father," which really means, "*I am loved by my father*," a formulation he cannot acknowledge because of its homosexuality.[93] He thus disguises father as mother in the conscious fantasy; but the male masochist—unlike the girl—still wants to see *himself* in the scene. And indeed, Wayworth himself ends up on display after the opening performance of *Nona Vincent*. At the curtain call, "some underling" calls him to take a bow: "'You're wanted, sir—you're wanted!' ... did he mean that he was wanted for execution? Some one else pressed him, almost pushed him, forward; he was already on the stage."[94] This is the culmination of the fantasy into which Mrs. Alsager has ushered Wayworth, the very thing he (is sorry he) wants: "to be acted," that is, to find himself in the grammatical position proper to the play itself, in the grips of an exposure that constitutes even as it endangers him: "wanted for execution."

In this respect, the logic of desire in "Nona Vincent" resonates with Deleuze's account of masochism—and sadism. As we observed in chapter 1, Deleuze emphasizes the *egoism* of the (male) masochist as, precisely, a specular technology of affirming the self: "in masochism the ego triumphs."[95] Deleuze's sadist, by contrast, "projects his dissolved ego outward and as a result experiences what is outside him as his only ego."[96] We can now recognize in this pair—which Deleuze insists is not a couple— the male and female patients, respectively, of "A Child Is Being Beaten": the "yes, it's me!" of the male masochist who lets himself be discovered in the fantasy scenario, and the "no, it's someone else!" of the girl who insists upon maintaining the distance of "sadistic form." Similarly, Mrs. Alsager's efforts are oriented toward procuring for someone else the passionate pain of being acted/executed/wanted, and thus enjoying that pain as his, not her own. "Her eyes were full of tears when he read her the last words of the finished work, and she murmured, divinely—'And now—to get it done, to get it done!'"[97] It is Mrs. Alsager who—with evident eroticism—conducts Wayworth into the maddening passivity of being a playwright, an act that would satisfy even conventional definitions of sadism. Wayworth *is* thus "wanted for execution" in much the same way Løvborg is: Mrs. Alsager and Hedda passionately desire these heroes to undergo the self-referential paroxysm of masochistic authorial performance *for* them, in masculine apotheoses that would at once constitute *and eclipse* the women's own authorship of these respective scenes. (It's in this sense that thinking of Hedda, too, as "sadistic" becomes richly descriptive, rather than just pathologizing.)

The spectatorial position—the female patient's "probably looking on"—is thus ineliminable from dramaturgical masochism, but what looks like reception is in fact a frenzy of production. At the end of "Nona Vincent" Mrs. Alsager might be mistaken for a mere spectator at Wayworth's plays, but the history of her varied "backstage" involvement with his career complicates this position.[98] At its most elaborate, this involvement incorporates her rival: the two women first meet when Mrs. Alsager tours a theater where Violet is performing, after which each reports to Wayworth that the other is in love with him.[99] The backstage is a space of both sheltering mediation and heightened exposure, in the traversal of which, we might say, each woman stages—in order to encounter it again later via the other two players—her own passion. In a turn of the screw past even hysterical identification, then, Mrs. Alsager goes to the theater not in order to see herself mirrored *in* the spectacle but to recognize herself *behind* it.

Theatrical three-dimensionality makes room for the spectator's painful desire not within but *on both sides* of the spectacle. This notion is, I think, slightly different from the scenic-desire account we discussed at the beginning of this chapter, which emphasizes the subject's unfixed position within fantasy, wherein "she identifies as the beater, the beaten, the spectator, the eavesdropper" all at once.[100] To take the theatrical situation seriously as an instigating model for fantasy here, as James does, we would have to add that the fantasizing subject can also—and even most powerfully—experience herself as "behind" this event, as having somehow authored it.

We noted in chapter 1 that "A Child Is Being Beaten" lends some surprising support to this idea, referring repeatedly to the high level of aesthetic elaboration that the female patients' beating fantasies display, and even describing their genesis as a kind of will-to-authorship: after reading stories featuring beating scenes, "the child began to compete with these works of fiction by producing its own phantasies."[101] Indeed, a few years after Freud's article was published, one of these girl-patients—Freud's daughter Anna—herself published an article expanding (in the third person) on her own case-history. Anna dwells, much longer than Sigmund had, on the "elaborate" quality of the fantasies, and goes on to reveal that at a certain point, "the girl suddenly made an attempt to write down [their] content. As a result she produced a sort of short story."[102] Noting the differences between the written story and the daydreams preceding it, Anna Freud theorizes that in the process of writing, "all regard for the dreamer's personal needs were replaced by consideration of the future readers of the story"; the girl "renounc[ed] her private pleasure in favour of the impression she could create in others," now deriving satisfaction from the latter prospect rather than from the events in the fantasy directly.[103] Anna Freud's evident approval of this apparently wholesome erotic turn toward "others" has struck some readers as lamentably normative.[104] It seems to me, however, that her account fundamentally extends a sadistic fantasy of authorship already found in the "private" fantasies themselves: the passion for "looking on" as others (now readers) undergo what might otherwise have been your own painful pleasure. Here as in "Nona Vincent," masochism operates through a relay in which the subject not only beholds the actions of others but also inscribes and registers her own creative presence behind the scene.

The question of Mrs. Alsager's authorship arises at the beginning of the story, in a passage that deceptively seems to deny its possibility:

> She loved the perfect work—she had the artistic chord. This chord could vibrate only to the touch of another, so that appreciation, in her spirit, had the added intensity of regret. She could understand the joy of creation, and she thought it scarcely enough to be told that she herself created happiness. She would have liked, at any rate, to choose her way; but it was just here that her liberty failed her. She had not the voice—she had only the vision. The only envy she was capable of was directed to those who, as she said, could do something.[105]

The story thus seems to be organized around the familiar gendered binary of artist/muse, the hero who can "do something" and the lady who will merely light his way by looking on. Indeed, the following paragraph dips into Wayworth's free indirect discourse to exacerbate the cliché, and within a few lines we find him bursting into her drawing room crying, "I've done it! I've done it!"—written the play.[106] Yet almost every supposed inability that occasions "regret" for Mrs. Alsager here will turn out to be equally true of Wayworth, whose "chord" turns out to need "the touch of another" just as surely as hers does, and whose "voice" proves not to carry beyond the drawing room where he reads his play to her—since someone else's touch and voice will be needed if the play is to be staged. Mrs. Alsager's cozy fireside is the nursery-space where this difficult reality is temporarily deferred, and he can execute his own performance: "Her eyes were full of tears when he read her the last words of the finished work."[107] But as we have seen, hers is also the "voice" that robs him of that illusion: "And now—to get it done, to get it done!"[108] Far from a world divided neatly into artists who "do something" and lady-friends who don't, we encounter the redistributive cruelty of a system in which having "done it" is always partial and provisional, returning the artist brutally (but "divinely," that is, pleasurably) to the fact of his own dependencies in the moment of his success.[109] Indeed, we might begin to suspect that the "real"—the male—author in the tale figures primarily in order to provide the mediation that will help Mrs. Alsager identify (with) herself in his position.

This twist anticipates the formalizing gesture that Freud ascribes to the female fantasist, who, you'll recall, "escapes from the demands of erotic life altogether" (*entläuft ... dem Anspruch des Liebeslebens überhaupt*) by substituting a boy's body for her own at the site of pain-pleasure.[110] And yet it may not be quite right to say that the woman "escapes ... altogether," just as it is rather evidently perverse of Freud to claim that the fantasy eludes or transcends sexuality; he has in fact already established that "the phantasy ... has strong and unambiguous sexual excitement attached to it, and so provides a means for masturbatory satisfaction."[111] From what, then, does the girl escape? The question is complicated further by Freud's assertion elsewhere in the article that the girl does *not* masturbate: "In two of my four female cases an elaborate [*kunstvoller*] superstructure of day-dreams, which was of great significance for the life of the person concerned, had grown up over the masochistic beating-phantasy," Freud writes. "The function of this superstructure was to make possible a feeling of satisfied excitation, even though the masturbatory act was abstained from."[112] In these cases, at least, the woman has escaped contact with her own body; but if this "elaborate"—literally, "artistic"—structure has taken on "great significance for [her] life," how can we doubt that the subject is acutely aware of her implication in this imaginative achievement? To say simply that the subject loses herself in fantasy is to ignore the way she reencounters herself across the space and time of the scene, a chiastic space where the authorship of fantasy is echoed and estranged in a fantasy of authorship.

It would be a misreading of "Nona Vincent," however, to claim that Mrs. Alsager is an author *only* of and in fantasy, that is, via her deployment of Wayworth—to assume that the narrator's initial account of her impotence holds true. The story's denouement gives her another path of access to the masochism of theatrical authorship ("being acted"), which is the specifically artistic work we must understand her to have performed in her visit to Violet. That is, we *could* infer that when Mrs. Alsager invites Violet to observe and "copy" her, she is simply acknowledging that she was Wayworth's model for Nona Vincent (which she had previously denied), and presenting herself in this light to Violet in an act of self-sacrifice that will make Mrs. Alsager herself superfluous to the story's erotic economy: "she seemed to *give* it all to me," Violet reports.[113] But the stress laid earlier on Mrs. Alsager's longing to "do something" artistic, and the lack of much impetus to imagine Wayworth himself as a great talent, invite a different reading of the interaction: Mrs. Alsager takes it upon herself to *invent* the true Nona Vincent, and performs the role so masterfully that Violet doesn't see it as a performance at all.

"You made her a little yourself," says Wayworth to Mrs. Alsager in their early conversation, though he continues rather deflatingly: "I've thought of her as looking like you."[114] The story's gambit is to literalize this pleasantry against its speaker's intentions. The same holds for another early conversation between the two friends, although this one remains (oddly but typically for James) hypothetical: if Mrs. Alsager had told Wayworth that she "would have liked to scribble," we read at the beginning, "he would have been in a perfect position for asking her why a woman whose face had so much expression should not have felt that she achieved. How in the world could she express better?"[115] In this exchange, Wayworth "would have" glossed over the devastating difference of agency between the two classically gendered modes of expression or achievement, a difference that nevertheless registers uncomfortably in the odd absence of the grammatical object: achieved, expressed *what?* But the cliché proves cannily rendered when Mrs. Alsager transcends it precisely by enacting it. In her visit to Violet, she must "express" Nona Vincent while seeming only to express herself; she must act as if she is doing nothing.[116] "I don't know what took place—she only sat there, and she held my hand and smiled at me," says Violet. "I kept her before me, I drank her in ... She kissed me when she went away—and you may guess if I kissed *her*."[117]

At the end of the story, then, we might say it is more fundamentally Mrs. Alsager than Wayworth who is "being acted." Violet teases Wayworth, and James teases us, with this glimpse of the erotic scene between the women, in which Mrs. Alsager surrenders to Violet's cannibalization, ecstatically erasing herself from Wayworth's life. But it is the remainder from this sacrifice—the part of Mrs. Alsager that survives having acted her own identity with/as Nona Vincent, having "done" or authored what Wayworth couldn't; the part that thus exceeds Violet's triumphant incorporation of her—to which James attaches the drivelike pleasure of theatrical repetition. What Mrs. Alsager feels in the dark at the theater, or what

Freud's lady sadist fingers in the rapt refusal of onanistic identification, is precisely that remainder, which hangs back from the plunge into character, into ego: the negative space of authorship, the enabling seat—the boney "box"—of other people's passions.

"A Woman's Play": James, Ibsen, and the Theater of Feminized Authorship

When she tells Wayworth about Mrs. Alsager's visit, Violet refers to it as a "miracle"; and indeed, the absolute efficacy of their session does seem, at least to this reader, somewhat improbable.[118] But what is strangest about this event is the way it seems to spawn a second version of itself, an echo which actually appears first in the narrative, though it turns out to have taken place at the same time as the women's colloquy. In this other scene, which has no effect on the plot, Wayworth is dozing dejectedly in his rooms when he receives a visitation from the fictional Nona Vincent herself:

> If she was so charming, in the red firelight, in her vague, clear-coloured garments, it was because he had made her so, and yet if the weight seemed lifted from his spirit it was because she drew it away.... From time to time she smiled and said: "I live—I live—I live." ... And as he slowly got out of his chair it was with a deep still joy—the joy of the artist—in the thought of how right he had been, how exactly like herself he had made her. She had come to show him that.[119]

The narrative excess of the scene—the way it falls outside the rule of dramatic unity by failing to make anything else happen—is itself doubled by the tautological language of Wayworth's encounter: "I live—I live—I live"; "how exactly like herself he had made her." This illogic, we might say, shows desire's excessiveness at its most naked: in the erotics of authorship.

At the same time, however, the narrative voice is remarkably tender here. Perhaps what is most moving is James's own heroism in being kindest to—identifying with—his character at the moment when Wayworth's narcissism is most blatantly exposed. But that is also, of course, *exactly what Mrs. Alsager does* throughout the story. And *this* identification—of Mrs. Alsager with James—suggests the real reason for giving Nona Vincent her own spectral body: it extricates Mrs. Alsager from the identity *with Nona* which the "real" scene might otherwise tempt us to ascribe to her. The spectral Nona "was not Violet Grey, she was not Mrs. Alsager"[120]: this means that not only Violet but also Nona "herself" can at last supplant Mrs. Alsager in Wayworth's affections. Mrs. Alsager can thus step away from the story's triangular structure without its collapsing into the

Wayworth-Violet dyad. The structure's ability to survive her absence is the very definition of authorial success, and it holds in relation not only to *Nona Vincent* but also to "Nona Vincent" itself.

Conferring the story's authorship on Mrs. Alsager, James makes his own authorial disappearance disappear into hers. In what remains of this chapter, I want to suggest a specific theatrical context for this feminizing escape: the scandal and excitement that greeted Ibsen's realist plays in London— including, of course, *Hedda Gabler*. The biographer Joanne Gates has proposed that "Nona Vincent" was inspired by James's friendship with Elizabeth Robins, the actress who played Hedda in the 1891 London premiere, and who Gates suggests was James's model for Violet Grey.[121] Robins and another friend, Marion Lea, had not only starred in *Hedda Gabler*; more remarkably, they had also retranslated the text (in collaboration with William Archer) and borrowed money to produce the show themselves after a series of theaters turned them down. Decades later, Robins recalls these conversations: "There's no part for *me!*" the male actor-managers complain; "this is a woman's play, and an uncommon bad one at that!"[122] This history of the resistance encountered by a "woman's play" in its path to the London stage—a play written by a man, but championed by women, and with a fictional woman at its center—certainly makes its way into "Nona Vincent," whose play's namesake even scans the same as Ibsen's.

The actor-managers were right to call *Hedda Gabler* a "woman's play," for several reasons. Most obvious is the way Hedda herself dominates the play, a fact not lost on James, who reviewed the London production in 1891. "*Hedda Gabler* is, in short, the study of an exasperated woman," James wrote; "if we ask for antecedents and explanations we must simply find them in her character."[123] James evinces both fascination and frustration with "the incalculable young woman into whom Miss Robins so artistically projects herself," and goes on to emphasize the "opportunity" Ibsen's roles offer to actresses.[124] Robins herself takes up this subject in a 1928 lecture, where she declares that "no dramatist has ever meant so much to the women of the stage as Henrik Ibsen."[125] As Solomon notes, Ibsen's plays fueled multiple female-driven theater ventures in this period.[126] Robins finds one reason for this in Ibsen's remarkable understanding of women's plight, exemplified in Hedda. She emphasizes the way this character provoked immediate identification from female audience members, while leaving male viewers puzzled: "any man except that wizard Ibsen really understand her? Of course not. That was the tremendous part of it."[127] This is another sense in which *Hedda Gabler* is a "woman's play"— one that, in speaking singularly to women, offers women a special opportunity to perform to and for each other.[128]

Robins ultimately suggests, however, that the plays' empowering effects had as much to do with form as with content:

> Ibsen was by training so intensely *un homme du theater* that, to an extent I know in no other dramatist, he saw where he could leave some of his greatest effects to be made by the actor, and so left them. It was as if he knew that only so could he get his effects—that is, by standing aside and watching his spell work not only through the actor, but *by* the actor as fellow-creator.... [Ibsen was] a poet who, with all his consummate craft, had taken Nature for his master-mistress.[129]

It is clear that Ibsen's invitation to "collaborate" has especially high stakes for performers whose gender would normally discredit them from a serious claim to authorship—the gender that inserts itself rather startlingly in the figure of Nature as "master-mistress." In fact, "mistress" here replaces the masculine "builder" in the title of another Ibsen play, *The Master Builder*, of which Robins remarks: "no other ever seemed *so much mine*."[130] Through this recasting, Robins—who of course did not play the builder Solness but his young temptress Hilda Wangel—appropriates Ibsen's oeuvre on behalf of "the women of the stage."

This feminizing appropriation echoes the accounts of London critics who saw these and other "women's" productions, accounts which themselves often devolved into descriptions of the women in the audience. As Susan Torrey Barstow shows in her reading of these write-ups, the plays seem to be swallowed up in an orgy of feminine objects: "Clad in beautiful clothes, ensconced in plushly upholstered seats, [the women] ate chocolate bon-bons and gazed adoringly ... at the 'hats' of other spectators and the actresses onstage."[131] Barstow demonstrates the intense oral erotics of these descriptions, in which women reportedly sat "with open mouths," "eagerly drinking in every word," even—in the later words of one of the spectators herself—"tasting blood."[132] Back on the Continent, the raging pundit Max Nordau went so far as to diagnose Ibsen's "unqualified approval of all feminine depravities" as literal masochism, picturing the writer as a "slave who rolls on the ground, compelled to obey the behests of his mistress" in "the inversion of the healthy and natural relation between the sexes" in which, naturally, men dominate women.[133] Nordau's conceptual grasp of masochism is unimpressive, but his portrait of Ibsen submitting to female depredation also shows a certain strange purchase on what was indeed happening around Ibsen's plays, whose "master-mistress" might be found in the female actor, producer, character, and/or spectator who "so artistically projects herself" (James) into and onto Ibsen's work. Amid the swells of discursive and theatrical production, Ibsen's masculine identity does threaten to disappear, his play to become a "woman's play," in all the ways we have just rehearsed.

James seems to sense this possibility—and its ramifications for his own writing—before he has even read or seen an Ibsen play. In an 1889 letter to Ibsen's translator Edmund Gosse, having "perused" Gosse's article on Ibsen, James writes: "You must tell me more about I. That is not in this case female-American for me."[134] One need not be an orthodox Freudian to read a kind of nervous reaction-formation in this joke—and another when James, in his review of *Hedda*, insists on seeing manliness behind I.'s emphatically domestic mise-en-scéne:

> the ugly interior ... which, to be honest, I like for the queer associations it has taught us to respect: the hideous carpet and wall-paper and curtains (one may answer for them), the conspicuous stove, the lonely centre-table, the "lamps with green shades," ... the very clothes, the inferior fashions, of the figures that move before us.... We feel that whereas, if Ibsen were weak or stupid or vulgar, this parochial or suburban stamp would only be a stick to beat him with, it acts, as the case stands, and in the light of his singular masculinity, as a sort of substitute—a little clumsy, if you like—for charm.[135]

The profusion of domestic objects that James observes in Ibsen is of course matched by James's own famously obsessive attention to furniture.[136] But James insists that this hyperbolic attention should *not* be read as a sign of the author's "inversion" (as Nordau would have it), each table-leg a "stick to beat him with": Ibsen's "singular masculinity," whatever that is, redeems these foibles and keeps him standing erect. James himself, however, could not maintain such equanimity for long: Robins recounts in her lecture that in 1893, after a dress rehearsal of *The Master Builder*, James "interrupted somebody's congratulations" to object to the shabbiness of Robins's costume: "'Yes, yes—but ...' he fixed me with his melancholy look, 'to-morrow a thousand eyes will be pecking at you—pecking at that'—he touched the collar." In another "inversion," the famous author frets about frippery, and it is the actress who "certainly was not going, on this last breathless evening, to worry about Hilda's collar."[137]

Theater's erotic logic ultimately renders any stable division of artistic labor impossible. "I'm glad to see Miss Grey is taking such pains with you," the theater manager tells Wayworth with a smile, upon catching writer and actress both near tears during rehearsal.[138] Wayworth laughs it off, but we know he is taken aback: he thought *he* had been taking pains with—forming or reforming—*her*. As a body that works for other people's pleasure, the actress seems an obvious candidate for passive conscription into the playwright's desire. But this reasoning cannot hold, because the playwright's own body, perilously extended in "the roll of his copy," is itself in play long before he is literally thrust onstage. There has always been someone else taking *her* pains with *him*—someone who finds him "remarkably good-looking," and takes pleasure in placing him in the position to "be acted." In this sense, the supposed femininity of male masochism reappears in a new position: not as a characteristic of the male subject but in the misadventure whereby his masochism is appropriated by a female subject's theatrical sadism, and subordinated to the fantasy machine of *her* desire.

The simplest way to articulate the parallel between the story of "Nona Vincent" and the story of the London *Hedda Gabler*, then, might just be to say that in both, *women do everything*; women and their fantasies are everywhere, taking over, as it were, the entire field of theatrical endeavor with the exception of that fragile point of perspective that is the authorial "I."—an I which itself threatens to dissolve into the "female-American" at any moment, as Robins and Lea feverishly retranslate the great man's text.[139] Fresh from his own engagement with Robins's scandalous productions, James imagines theater in "Nona Vincent" as a privileged mechanism for the defection—what Freud calls "escape"—*not* from sexuality but from the ego's presumptive masculinity, and the claims to agency and integrity the latter entails. That is to say: theater refigures authorship as the experience of one's own disappearance. And this disappearance is, specifically, a giving-way to the multiform expressions of femininity: women's curtains, collars, fireplaces, mouths.

As the apparent protagonist of "Nona Vincent," Wayworth embodies—and burlesques—the version of this desire that wants to suffer in its own person. James also, however, interposes Mrs. Alsager; and it is precisely by *keeping her experience at a distance* that he establishes her as the better figure of authorship, an authorship introduced under the sign of negation and protected, in the moment this denial proves most tenuous—the moment when she effectively authors the role of Nona—by a veritable flurry of supplementary negations, including (at one extreme) the narrative's insistence that her entire being can vanish, of an afternoon, into another's mimetic duplication, and (at the other) its forcible removal of her "to Torquay."[140]

In Freud, the sadistic girl's authorship is a vanishing act; this is true in James too, but then the theater brings her back. The pleasure of this disappearance is her province and her undoing; the theater exists so that she can return to glimpse that pleasure as hers *and* not hers. When the curtain falls on "Nona Vincent" it is Mrs. Alsager who finishes the story from the shadows. And when Hedda's dramaturgy finally prevails—when she plunges her play into the gap within desire—she takes "all of us" down with her, again and again. This is the sensorium of dramaturgical masochism, which confers authorship as the project of interposing form between yourself and enjoyment; which is also to say, between yourself and yourself, and at the very heart—the *breaking* heart—of pleasure. Its condition is theatrical, constituted across the radical interruption that is the intervening space of others' interests, submitted to the slapstick violence of contingency, the sky that keeps falling on our heads. Hedda gives this theater everything and nothing; and James insists that it is this predicament, this estrangement, that one can love.

"Caught Fire in My Mind"

CHAPTER 3

Adrienne Kennedy's Intimacies of Negation

In the introduction to this book, I quoted Hortense Spillers's warning that psychoanalysis, with its "universal sound," can "seduce us to want to concede, to 'give in' to its seeming naturalness." Spillers's point is that this kind of seduction must be resisted. And yet the figure of seduction itself implies a scenario in which a white universalism approaches the critical subject (who must not "give in") by activating her desire, making her "want to concede" to a body (of work) that enacts, through its denial of its own particularity *and hers*, a kind of violence against her. This way of framing the problem suggests, I said, that we might seek to confront universalism not only by persistently revealing its falseness and its complicity with structures of domination but also by inquiring into the ways it can awaken desire in different subjects. This chapter will pursue that inquiry through three plays by Adrienne Kennedy, who reckons with the devastating promise of the universal like no other author. Kennedy, that is, not only critiques white universalist culture but also scrutinizes its powers of seduction; she shows how, while serving the interests of domination, the falsehood of universalism can make an erotic appeal of its own. In Kennedy's plays—as, indeed, in the theoretical seduction scene we glimpse in Spillers—the subject always responds to this appeal *by writing*: even and especially at its most malign, Kennedy suggests, the violence of universalism can function as an engine of literary imagination for someone it was designed to erase.

In both Kennedy's 1964 play *Funnyhouse of a Negro* and her 1992 play *Ohio State Murders*, writing (and the reading that propels it) is the most fundamental means by which the protagonist, a Black woman, sustains a self; but reading and writing is also, simultaneously, a painful practice of intimate relation with the negativity at the heart of whiteness's presumptive universal, which constantly threatens that self with erasure. After examining these two plays to track the way this iterative intimacy works, I'll turn to Kennedy's 2018 play *He Brought Her Heart Back in a Box*, which asks more pointedly what kind of *difference* the passionate writing and re-writing of this violence might be able to make within a history of white supremacist domination, a system whose own apparently inexorable rep-etitions would destroy the Black female subject in order to prove its own rightness.

Should this complex concatenation of violence, suffering, desire, and writing be called "masochistic," in the sense the previous chapters have been elaborating? As Amber Jamilla Musser shows, and as we noted in the introduction, such a characterization would necessarily be perilous; and it would certainly be wrong if it implied that the complex response to anti-Blackness in Kennedy's work were somehow already contained or covered by any supposedly prior discourse on sexuality.[1] Fanon, Syl-via Wynter, and many other theorists have argued—so forcefully that it is by now a commonplace of intellectual culture—that every psychic struc-ture that confronts us today has been forged in the crucible of white su-premacy, whose status as a structure of modern experience always ought to be acknowledged as more foundational than any sexological or Freud-ian "constant," masochism certainly included.[2] Freud's mention of *Uncle Tom's Cabin* as a ubiquitous model for his patients' beating fantasies not only indexes the fact that psychoanalytic terms themselves emerge from a terrain always already laid out by the history of white supremacist domi-nation, and thus that theorizations of this domination and its effects must always (as it were) reach beneath psychoanalytic foundations, even when it also works through them; this moment in Freud also points to the kind of psychic appropriation that white fantasists like me have long been all too eager to perform, a tradition I am loath to continue here. I can't claim to be able to read Kennedy's work from any but my own perverse and white perspective; but the last thing I want to do is remake her protagonists' suf-fering in the image of my own prurient enthusiasms.

For these reasons, it seems important to be clear at the outset that when, in this chapter, I seek to enter insights from Kennedy's work into this book's larger discussion of *masochistic writing*, I don't mean—as I would in the case of James, Deleuze, or Gaitskill, or indeed Gary Fisher—that Ken-nedy's writing issues from and/or imagines subjects who want to be hurt.[3] I mean, instead, that Kennedy presents us with *writing understood as a technology for maintaining the possibility of desire in what, echoing Christina Sharpe, I call an "intimate" relation to a painful, historically determined ne-gation of the self*. Masochism finds its critical purchase here in the way that, for Kennedy, writing can engage society's systemic negation of desire and selfhood for Black women; writing drives the subject ever deeper into this negation, pursuing an experience in which the subject is taken up—and sometimes even seems to be taken in—by the negation, even as she also takes the negation itself as an object, making it submit to her own composition. Desire manifests in the ongoing pursuit, not of harm itself—which, for Kennedy's subjects, is always underway already—but of a relation with harm that would be lived as the painfully gratifying, iterative (re)constitution of the authorial self. Always registering pain in the lived experience of Blackness as the site of structural domination, Kennedy's writing fights to inscribe its own desire at the heart of that structure.

"White Page after White Page": Staging Authorhood in *Funnyhouse of a Negro*

The following passage is from Kennedy's first produced and probably most famous play, *Funnyhouse of a Negro*. It is spoken by the play's protagonist, "Negro-Sarah":

> As for myself I long to become even a more pallid Negro than I am now; pallid like Negroes on the covers of American Negro magazines; soulless, educated and irreligious. I want to possess no moral value, particularly as to my being. I want not to be. I ask nothing except anonymity.... I write poetry filling white page after white page with imitations of Edith Sitwell. It is my dream to live in rooms with European antiques and my Queen Victoria [statue], photographs of Roman ruins, walls of books, a piano, oriental carpets and to eat my meals on a white glass table. I will visit my friends' apartments which will contain books, photographs of Roman ruins, pianos and oriental carpets. My friends will be white.[4]

We might begin, once more, by noting the critique of universalism. In this passage, Kennedy works to expose the specific (white) racialization performed by the material trappings of a bourgeois everydayness that most often goes unmarked. The books, piano, carpet, etc. that furnish Sarah's fantasy are exactly like the objects named in the scene descriptions of so many realist plays, revealing as *white* those characteristic stage furnishings that theater history has typically conceived as simply "relatable" or normal. Indeed, Kennedy enacts a critique of realism itself as a genre here: not only does Sarah's imagined mise-en-scène satirize the universalism of the realist stage ("Hedda is all of us"), but in refusing to *realize* that stage except as words in a monologue, Kennedy literalizes the fact that the universalist impulse in realism is itself always fantasy, and in most cases a fantasy of whiteness *as* universal. For Sarah, however, the universal is also a fantasy in the sense that it is openly a matter of desire: "It is my dream," she says, in a phrase whose syntax (where Kennedy could have written, say. "My dream is" or "I dream of") emphasizes that society's fantasy, of a whiteness that could obliterate difference, is now also *hers*. This means that Sarah's critique of white universalism is also, however bitterly and ironically, an avowal.

From a pragmatic perspective, whiteness would grant Sarah access to the cultural, historical and artistic legitimacy she seeks as a writer—access to fields of power that society keeps out of Black women's reach, including the validation conferred by fame: magazine covers. But the fantasy of whiteness here is not exactly a fantasy of individual empowerment.[5] It's as if *some* whiteness—enough to become "even a more pallid Negro"—could raise Sarah to the cultural status of a representative image, while still preserving her individuality in some form. But Sarah's desire to whiten into an image intensifies beyond the craving for recognition, until the image itself bleaches into blankness: true whiteness would obliterate the very individual who had wanted it. At the limit, what Sarah wants from whiteness is a means "not to be": anonymity, amorality, "soulless" intellection. Sarah's "dream" is to attain a condition in which her life would be psychically empty and, as such, exactly *identical* to that of her white "friends"; a condition in which not only racial difference but difference as such—the distinctness of her own individual existence—would disappear. This is universality revealed in its negativity, stripped of its humanistic pretentions. And writing, page after page, appears here as a project of seizing this white universality in a drive toward willed self-erasure.

Onstage, this project is embodied by two characters called "Duchess of Hapsburg" and "Queen Victoria Regina," each of whom is also called "One of herselves," that is, one of Sarah's selves:

> *Both women are dressed in royal gowns of white, a white similar to the white of the Curtain, the material cheap satin.... From beneath both their headpieces springs a headful of wild kinky hair.... They look exactly alike and will wear masks or be made up to appear a whitish yellow. It is an alabaster face, the skin drawn tightly over the high cheekbones, great dark eyes that seem gouged out of the head, a high forehead, a full red mouth and a head of frizzy hair. If the characters do not wear a mask, then the face must be highly powdered and possess a hard expressionless quality and a stillness as in the face of death.*[6]

With "wild kinky hair" that "springs" from the "tight," "hard" confinement of white materials, these figures render Black women's bodies caught in a violent process of universalizing abstraction, bodies thrust halfway into the "stillness" and the mechanical reproducibility ("exactly alike") that characterize the "white page after white page" of text itself.

They are images of Sarah's own body rendering itself textually, as if writing were a process of submerging the self in a corrosive whiteness—and only thereby gaining access to the possibility of historical meaningfulness that these two white figures represent.

This suggestion that the very bodies of the "selves" onstage are *written*—that Sarah is not only their referent but their author—contributes to a broader sense that everything in the play, including Sarah, is caught up in her writing. Even in moments when Sarah's imagination seems to crack open and show us the real life beneath, textuality lays claim to the real too. Thus at the end we read: "*Another WALL drops. There is a white plaster statue of Queen Victoria which represents the NEGRO's room in the brownstone … a sitting figure, one of astonishing repulsive whiteness, suggested by dusty volumes of books and old yellowed walls.*"[7] In a kind of Wizard-of-Oz reveal, we now seem to see the real-life object behind the dream of Queen and Duchess— "real" in a densely impacted set of ways. First, the Victoria onstage is now a real plaster statue, not an actor dressed up in imitation of one. Second, we seem to have discovered a realistic space (the "brownstone") as opposed to a psychogeography (the funhouse, the palace). Third, the statue also points beyond the play into the real life of the author, referencing statues Kennedy actually saw and owned.[8] And yet even here, Kennedy's note that the statue's real whiteness is "*suggested by* dusty volumes of books and old yellowed walls" reintroduces a figurative register, in a curious phrase that gives rise to the question of what is a figure for what. Are the books and walls to be present onstage, or is this a simile meant to help us imagine the quality of the statue's whiteness—rescripting the actual object, in the very moment of its reveal, through the evocation of other, absent objects? Or if the books and walls are present onstage next to the statue, how exactly can they "suggest" its repulsive whiteness, except through a kind of metonymic relation more proper to words than to things? Either way, it's as if even in the moment of our literally seeing the statue, Kennedy wants us to access it primarily as a rhetorical figure. What is theatrically constituted as a moment of unmasking, a collapse into the real, immediately reasserts that real *as literary*, structured by a figurativeness itself figured by books and their constant but undecidable relation to the horror of white power.

In the next lines of the play, we see that Sarah has hanged herself. The persistence of the literary, however, seems to complicate this event too. At one level we might understand her death as the moral of the story, the inevitable end point of writing as self-erasure: white universalism finally finishes expunging Sarah's particular being, showing that for Black subjects, white culture—literature as instituted by white supremacist modernity—is a dead end. And yet throughout, Sarah's lethal attachment to white universalism is presented not only as a pathology or tragic *limit* of her imagination, but also as a feature that operates *within* her authorial fantasy, made explicit by her repeated "I want"; this self-destructive desire is also a generative principle. Sarah, that is, does not want to write like Edith Sitwell *although* doing so is killing her but *because* it is killing her; she is determined to be the author of—to write—her own disappearance or death. This intention is all the more remarkable because Sarah claims it on a stage and in a language that continually marks that desire as profoundly overdetermined by the historical reality of white supremacy as domination, which *wants her to want this*. Sarah is, and we are, constantly confronted with the ways in which domination has acted to produce the desire whose author she nevertheless demands to be.

I'm suggesting that in *Funnyhouse*, Kennedy constructs writing as the means or medium of owning an otherwise impossible desire. This desire is impossible not only in the sense we have already encountered in Hedda, Mrs. Alsager, or Beth—that is, in the sense that it entails a destruction of the desiring subject herself—but also in the quite different sense of that desire's so evidently issuing from the world outside the subject that it may well be nonsensical for her to claim it *as* hers. As an index of this difference, we might compare Sarah's suicide with Hedda's. Both plays end with other characters reacting to the discovery of the heroine's body; but whereas Judge Brack's response—"People don't do such things!"—emphasizes the utter incommensurability between Hedda and her world, Sarah's death prompts the following final scene:

(*Lights come on the laughing Landlady. And at the same time remain on the hanging figure of the Negro.*)
LANDLADY: The poor bitch has hung herself. (*Funnyman Raymond appears from his room at the commotion.*) The poor bitch has hung herself.
RAYMOND: (*Observing her hanging figure.*) She was a funny little liar.[9]

Whereas Hedda's suicide is so incomprehensible that her companions must literally deny it, Sarah's suicide is easily affirmed not once but twice. Her death creates no disruption at all; even the lighting is able to take in Sarah's death alongside the blasé response of those who survive it. In calling her "funny," her white lover Raymond claims Sarah as utterly continuous with the Funnyhouse world in which her body appears.[10] We might say that if Hedda's predicament is a nightmare of radical disjuncture between the world and the subject, such that her desires can find nothing adequate to them, Sarah's is a nightmare of tautology: even in death, her desires can only reinstantiate the logic of her world.

The play's last line, also spoken by Raymond, reaffirms this message. Throughout the play, Sarah and her selves have reiterated the story of her father's suicide; Raymond now denies it, rewriting her father's story in terms we have already encountered:

RAYMOND: Her father never hung himself in a Harlem hotel when Patrice Lumumba was murdered. I know the man. He is a doctor, married to a white whore. He lives in the city in rooms with European antiques, photographs of Roman ruins, walls of books and oriental carpets. Her father is a n—— who eats his meals on a white glass table.[11]

Bound up with this line's brutal racism is the horror of its suggestion that intergenerational repetition is inevitable: and not, as we might have expected, the tragic repetition of a father's suicide, but the hideously comedic ("funny") repetition of his inappropriate desire. According to Raymond, anyway, what Sarah has internalized and reiterated is not her father's death but his banal fantasy of whiteness—still marked *as* fantasy, even though the father seems to be living it, by the slur that sears the persistence of racial difference into our consciousness as the show comes to a close. A liar, after all, is a failed storyteller, someone whose fictions are not powerful enough to make us suspend disbelief. If Sarah dies a "funny little liar," then her project of authorhood is negated definitively at her death. Here again we seem to see something like the opposite of Ibsen: whereas Hedda's suicide was a radical gesture that finally secured her a kind of artistic autonomy, Sarah's seems to entail the relinquishment of any such claim.

But there's another way to read this moment, which is that Raymond's repetition of Sarah's words after her death—though he transposes their referent—actually extends the reach of her writing, as it were posthumously. This is also to point out that the repetition of text across bodies ends the piece with a gesture of formal closure that emphasizes the organizing consciousness of its writer—whom we now have to recognize not just as Sarah (who is dead) but as Kennedy. The devastating nature of this ending, which seems so ruthlessly to deny any possibility of authorial transcendence to Sarah, proves Kennedy's ability to give form *to* that negation of authorhood—more specifically, of Black women's authorhood—and thus a quite particular version of what Abdul R. JanMohamed, reading Richard Wright's novels, has called "negating the negation."[12] The demonstration of this scriptive power is the play's final and enduring gesture.

As we'll have occasion to observe again in reading Kennedy's work, however, the negation of a negation never just cancels the negative out. The ongoing dialectic of violence that *Funnyhouse* describes can't be buried beneath a redemptive interpretation in which, say, the play's characters only succumb to a lethal white universalism so that the author—and perhaps, by extension, the audience—can, in decrying it, defeat it. Instead, *Funnyhouse* offers a vision of writing as an ongoing process of seizing society's murderous desire for the Black subject's nonbeing, and subjecting that desire to form. This process entails maintaining a terrifying intimacy with that desire: staying with it, "white page after white page."

In a conversation published in a 1992 anthology of essays on and interviews with Kennedy, bell hooks discusses authorhood as a major theme in Kennedy's work. "Few writers have focused, as she has, on the place of black thinkers in a white world," hooks says, emphasizing the autobiographical strand of Kennedy's writing and noting that "Kennedy's work is as much about the development of a woman playwright as it is about a vast array of other concerns."[13] The conversation is at once a critical analysis and a ludic performance: framed as an interview of bell hooks by one Gloria Watkins, it is in fact—à la Kennedy—a dialogue between two "of herselves": "Gloria Watkins," as a footnote reveals, is bell hooks's own given name. "I dream of writing plays that are experimental, avant-garde in the contemporary sense," hooks says in the piece.[14] The implication, of course is that the "interview" itself might be one such experiment.

In some respects, the mimetic elements of hooks's essay seem to function as a kind of loving corrective. Where *Funnyhouse* articulates a "dream" of writing as, at one limit, a lethal dissolve into whiteness, hooks (who also quotes the "It is my dream" passage from the play at length) offers as her own counter-"dream" the vision of "experimental, avant-garde" writing that Kennedy was in fact doing, a writing that "charts new journeys for aspiring black women playwrights."[15] Later, hooks mentions a reference to Sylvia Plath in Kennedy's novella *Deadly Triplets*, and notes that "Plath's struggle to come to terms with marriage and motherhood was similar to Kennedy's" but that Kennedy, "unlike Plath, finds a way to unproblematically ascend her identity as a writer and clearly lets readers/audiences know that creating plays is life sustaining for her."[16] For hooks, Plath serves to embody the nexus of writing, whiteness, and self-destruction in a way that helps hooks separate this nexus conceptually from the more benevolent vision of writing she highlights in Kennedy's autobiographical work. "An interesting dimension of her/the work (which seems utterly *alien* to me) is the fascination and to some extent the love of white culture that she expresses in her work," hooks says of Kennedy.[17] Rendered "*alien*," that attachment to white culture registers in hooks's account as an intrusion from without, as something that doesn't properly belong to Kennedy's work, even though it appears there. In this sense, hooks's vision opposes itself diametrically to Sarah's "It is my dream."

But even as hooks attempts to parse the antiracist power of Kennedy's authorial success from a malignant engagement with whiteness and white universalism, the autointerview also self-consciously complicates this separation. Jumping repeatedly between the two topics with no obvious segues, the piece seems to enact an uneasy proximity between them.[18] By making an alter ego responsible for the structure of conversation, hooks suspends the need to produce the kind of continuous argument that might seek to resolve the relationship between the authorial Kennedy—who has, hooks notes, a "keen awareness of the politics of race and gender"—and the Kennedy gripped by a disturbing "fascination" with whiteness.[19] And yet the restlessness with which "Gloria Watkins" keeps bringing the critically aware Kennedy and the "fascinated" or, we might say, *alien*-ated Kennedy into proximity seems to suggest hooks's sense of the need for a form that can hold them together, even as it also tries to keep them apart.

As hooks's own production of herself as split subject here emphasizes—and as Elin Diamond argues explicitly in *Unmaking Mimesis*—Kennedy's work consistently makes it difficult to sustain the normative logic by which what is "alien" can be reliably distinguished from the self.[20] Instead, the self forms—tenuously but insistently—through what Darieck Scott, writing on texts by other authors, calls "pleasure in introjecting and assimilating the alien (perhaps, alienation itself), a sense of intimacy acquired even in situations of coerced pain, a transformation, through harm, of the foreign into one's own."[21] Again and again, the willful susceptibility to alterity proves fundamental to Kennedy's concept of writing. In itself, that might sound like a benign enough poststructuralism, but in *Funnyhouse*, the lure of the "alien" implies a thrall to white cultural hegemony; for Sarah, the will to write and the will to disappear into whiteness have become inextricable. Writing, here, at once insists on the self's desire and confounds it with society's desire for her nonbeing. Sarah's authorhood is also the passionate reinscription of her own erasure.

"The Violent Imagery in My Work": *Ohio State Murders*

Ohio State Murders premiered in 1992, around the chronological midpoint of Kennedy's career to date; its fictional protagonist, the well-known writer Suzanne Alexander, appears in several of Kennedy's writings from that time.[22] The play is set in the underground stacks of a university library, where Suzanne Alexander is "*rehearsing a talk*" she plans to give at the university, presumably the following day. "I was asked to talk about the violent imagery in my work," she begins, "bloodied heads, severed limbs, dead father, dead Nazis, dying Jesus. The chairman said, we do want to hear about your brief years here at Ohio State but we also want you to talk about violent imagery in your stories and plays."[23] As Suzanne recites the talk, its content is also enacted by performers playing young Suzanne and other characters from her story. Suzanne recounts her time at the school, a narrative not only punctuated by initially oblique references to "the murder," but rife with descriptions of segregation and institutional racism.

> I didn't know there were no "Negro" students in the English Department. It was thought that we were not able to master the program....
>
> Very few Negroes walked on High Street above the university. It wasn't that you were not allowed but you were discouraged from doing so. Above the university was a residential district encompassed by a steep ravine....
>
> A year and a half later one of my baby twin daughters would be found dead there. That was later.
>
> But in my freshman year the continuing happiness was Professor Hampshire's discussion of the Victorian novel.
>
> When he lectured, his small pale face was expressionless. Only his blue eyes conveyed anger, joy, vitality.[24]

The unadorned declarative style of Suzanne's lecture lays out the elements of her story in a kind of paratactical map: there is racism, there is the murder of her babies, there is English literature, with no explicit relation established between them.

True to the murder mystery genre that the play's title evokes, however, the elements soon begin to converge into causes and effects.[25] Professor Hampshire, whose physical whiteness ("pale face," "blue eyes") embodies the whiteness of the Victorian canon he teaches, becomes Suzanne's sole point of access to the "continuing happiness" of this literature: not in the familiar sense of a gifted teacher opening new vistas on the material but because of the grim reality of the school's racist policies, which make Hampshire's recognition of her talents her only source of hope that she might be allowed to pursue literary study. Institutional racism thus enforces the equation by which, for the young Suzanne, Hampshire—who will father and then murder Suzanne's twin babies—is "English literature." Literalizing this identification, Kennedy has Hampshire read aloud long passages from Thomas Hardy's *Tess of the d'Urbervilles* and, later, the medieval *Morte Arthure*, instances of the kind of intertextual collage that features in several of Kennedy's plays. The quotations continue well beyond what would be necessary to set the scene of Hampshire's lectures, or to emphasize particular moods and themes; what takes place here, it seems to me, is an invitation to engage the language of these canonical works directly, to let them fascinate us *even as* we come to understand their accessory function in maintaining a murderous system.

The play contains no amorous, or even faintly romantic, moments between Suzanne and Hampshire; indeed, their liaison is excluded from the narrative so fully that you might puzzle over when or how it has actually taken place. Their only pleasurable exchange in the play—besides the literary lectures themselves—takes place by way of writing on writing on writing, in a set of positive comments Hampshire has written on Suzanne's essay on Hardy:

SUZANNE (Present): Walking back in the darkness I remembered passages of my paper. And I remembered the comments Professor Hampshire had written on the margins.
SUZANNE (1949): "Paper conveys a profound feeling for the material."
    "Paper has unusual empathy for Tess."
    "The language of the paper seems an extension of Hardy's own language."
    (*She hears Hampshire's voice.*)
HAMPSHIRE: It's brilliant. It's brilliant.[26]

This iteratively mediated exchange of texts is the play's closest thing to a sex scene. It grants Suzanne and Hampshire a strange mimetic, even telepathic access to Tess, Hardy, and one another, and culminates in Hampshire's approbative ejaculation, which might be real or imagined by Suzanne, and might almost as easily refer to "Hardy's own language" as to Suzanne's paper. What seduces young Suzanne here is partly the possibility of establishing herself as a writer—proving that she *can* "master the program." At the same time, however, writing clearly also means submerging her difference in the general "brillian[ce]" of an unlocatable textual practice. The sequence of Hampshire's comments, from "feeling for the material" to "empathy for Tess" to the "extension of Hardy's own language," charts a procession from encounter with the object, through identification with the character, to a kind of merging with the author that occurs via the writing itself.

Kennedy's choice of this encounter's literary catalyst, *Tess of the D'Urbervilles*, is far from arbitrary. Like Suzanne (though, of course, differently), Tess is the victim of structural domination that manifests in a coercive sexual relation and produces an illegitimate, short-lived child. Unlike Kennedy, Hardy seems to agonize continually over whether his heroine is guilty of her own rape; Kennedy never introduces any parallel implication that young Suzanne could be morally responsible for what she suffers at the hands of the professor and the university.[27] What does seem parallel, however, is the presence in both texts of an erotic charge that exists in *excess* of the clear logic of domination.[28] For Suzanne, this charge seems to inhere not in her relation to Professor Hampshire himself but to the literary practice he embodies: an "English literature" that—imaged in "Funny-house" as an immobile plaster cast—now appears as a process of reading, writing, and citing through which Suzanne keeps dead and deadly texts alive by opening her own text to them. The cost of this erotic textuality in the narrative is undeniable: Hampshire sucks young Suzanne into a gothic slough of violation, death, and grief.

Suzanne survives with the help of her attentive husband-to-be, David Alexander, "*an extraordinarily handsome young black man [who] looks like Frantz Fanon, whose biography he will one day write.*"[29] The Manichaean contrast between David Alexander and Professor Hampshire is obvi-ous; most importantly, David signals the possibility of a literary practice that, while still driven by mimetic attachment (here to Fanon), consti-tutes a properly Black textual exchange instead of a deadly engagement with whiteness. David is first introduced via a photograph, which Suzanne shows the imagined audience early in her talk: "This is a picture of my husband, David, who, as you know, is a writer, political activist, and bi-ographer of Frantz Fanon ... running the 100-yard dash at Ohio State's spring track meet. I knew he was a state champion." Young Suzanne first sees the picture because the owner of her boarding-house has "hung [it] in her hallway. She loved David Alexander."[30] The photograph conveys not only David's vitality and physical prowess but the stability of his iden-tity, which can be captured and proudly displayed; it seems his identifica-tion with Fanon—framed as a kind of successful mirroring—can only re-affirm this stable identity. In contrast to this image of loving and lovable Black authorhood, Professor Hampshire embodies a perverse textuality that obviously tends toward violent erasure. This tendency ultimately con-sumes Hampshire's own body too: Suzanne recounts that when she last saw him—before he murdered their second baby, then killed himself— "He seemed far paler and smaller than I remembered. He didn't seem like anyone I had known."[31] In this scene, Hampshire gives a lecture on King Arthur and "the abyss," which is both a reference to the ravine where (Su-zanne will later discover) Hampshire has drowned the first of their twin babies, and a reminder that his version of the literary, the version that had so thrilled her, always converges on nonbeing.[32]

Like *Funnyhouse*, then, *Ohio State Murders* seems to outline a clear moral logic, condemning the canon-bound literary practice through which the Black female subject succumbs to her own negation. And yet the play also takes pains to reiterate that practice; its long literary quotations threaten to proliferate Suzanne's unwholesome attachment by inviting audiences to share her fascination, the fascination hooks calls "alien." Meanwhile David Alexander, exemplary though he may be, appears just once in the play and never speaks. In two of the other Kennedy plays that feature David and Suzanne, *She Talks to Beethoven* and *Dramatic Circle*, David does speak; but in those stories he is either distressingly absent or, following a political imprisonment for his work with and on (or as?) Fanon, appears so "changed" that his family can "hardly recognize" him.[33] David's decline, horrifyingly enough, echoes Hampshire's; and Hampshire's decline echoes the second passage that Hampshire reads from Hardy, in which Tess herself, having finally committed murder, appears as an unrecognizable shadow: "It was not until she was quite close that he could believe her to be Tess.... She was so pale, so breathless, so quivering in every muscle."[34] This collapse of David-as-Fanon into Hampshire-as-Tess suggests that—as Diamond also shows in her reading of intertextual identifications throughout the Alexander Plays—a distinction between a mimetic practice that repairs and sustains the Black subject, and one that negates and destroys her, cannot finally be preserved.[35] From Sarah's Edith Sitwell to Suzanne's (Hampshire's [Hardy's]) Tess, the "white glass" of the *writing* table always threatens to submerge and corrupt the particularity and integrity of the Black writer's image.

Ohio State Murders, more explicitly than *Funnyhouse*, is a story of surviving this threat by continuing to subject it to new forms. After she finishes the horrifying story of the second baby's murder, Suzanne ends the play with a stunning punch line: "And that is the main source of the violent imagery in my work. Thank you."[36] The line resounds with irony, emphasizing the absurdity of a question about violent imagery from an institution that has perpetuated ongoing, actual violence. But Suzanne's last words also pointedly reiterate her hard-fought identity as a writer, funneling the story's maelstrom of violence and grief into the precise end point of "my work." Suzanne is now a successful author; she has returned triumphant to the site of her negation—and she has objectified that negation in a new poetics. More unsettlingly, however, the play's final direction—"*Lights bright on hundreds of books in stacks and on the window, falling snow*"—reminds us that after all of this, Suzanne is still in the library, suggesting that her story remains inextricable from the tradition that came close to destroying her.[37] Reanimating the "*dusty volumes of books and old yellowed walls*" that signified "*astonishing repulsive whiteness*" in *Funnyhouse*, the books of the Ohio State library preside over this play's ending, ominous as the final shot of a horror movie. But at the same time, by making us linger in this silent, eerie space for a moment after the narrative has come to a close, *Ohio State Murders* also seems once again to assert the literary as a force in *excess* of the play's narrative and moral logic, "bright" with a libidinal charge; a source of dangers and pleasures that will keep calling for more new forms, will keep the subject writing painfully about writing.

Monstrous Repetitions: Adrienne Kennedy with Christina Sharpe

In *Monstrous Intimacies: Making Post-Slavery Subjects*, Christina Sharpe reads works of Black diasporan literature, film, and visual art to trace "the monstrous internalization and perpetuation of [slavery's] violence in various forms of power and desire among the formerly enslaved and those who claimed ownership over them."[38] Sharpe attends to "the ways that desires that are congruent with the law of the master are interpellated by the enslaved, remembered, and passed on to the [subsequent] generations as their own."[39] She thus argues for the relevance of the erotic in conjunctures where the force of structural white supremacist violence might seem to preclude it, insisting that this domination, whose ongoing social, economic, and psychic legacies we readily acknowledge, also perpetuates itself at the sexual core of modern subjectivity. In tracing the libidinal afterlives of slavery, Sharpe is consistently attuned to the danger of conflating forced submission with desire, and follows Saidiya Hartman's lead in tracking down "master narratives of violence and forced submission that are read or reinscribed as consent and affection."[40] At the same time, Sharpe also questions critical efforts to purge Black sexual desire of its own relation to the history of enslavement and domination, positing "the fear for some that there may well be a point where the black (female) subject's horror" upon confronting this history "slips into pleasure."[41] "It is a statement that would be true historically as well as psychoanalytically: one cannot cleanse one's fantasies of the other, of slavery, of the gaze," Sharpe writes, "and there is no fantasy without the other."[42] One implication of this double approach is that while we must insist on separating the terms that racist and misogynist ideology conflates—rigorously distinguishing, for example, between passionate consent and forced submission—this ethical clarity will be compromised if it depends upon disavowing the different ways sexuality, fantasy, or desire might be entwined with both phenomena.[43]

Sharpe's work thus offers a model for how to think about what can look like a desire, in works of Black expression like Kennedy's, to reinscribe the negation of self that society has already performed upon Black subjects. Because of this, Sharpe's work seems to me to illuminate the "alien" attachments to whiteness as negation that haunt the act of writing in Kennedy's plays. As we've seen, Kennedy's work is specifically concerned with the fate of writing under white supremacist patriarchy; writing here is never simply the self-assertion of a subject who fights to find her voice in spite of these structures but always also enacts a recursive, reiterative *intimacy* with the domination exerted in and through canonical writings. The aesthetic power of these older writings is complicit in—and may ultimately be inseparable from—the structures of domination. What is "monstrous," as Sharpe shows throughout her book, is not just the ongoing history of violation and harm but also desire *trained on* this history; in Kennedy, this desire coincides with the desire for writing. The violence is "in my work," not just in the sense of a sublimating representation of the horrors that haunt the subject but in the ineradicable further sense that the work itself, its very text-ure, *is* the continuing iteration of this monstrous intimacy.

In *Funnyhouse of a Negro* and still more markedly in *Ohio State Murders*, this textual intimacy with historical violence is forged specifically through the relation with "English literature." Both plays present writing as a fundamentally intertextual endeavor, produced through a powerful identification or obsession with the white canonical texts that Sarah and young Suzanne are reading. Elsewhere, Kennedy also offers more benign images of intense relations with canonical objects; these include the 1987 autobiography *People Who Led to My Plays*, which presents, as Diamond puts it, "a subject … who sees herself and enriches herself in her objects…. Who, instead of being lacerated by remembered objects (as her protagonists so often are), simply shows them."[44] It seems to me, however, that the plays we've been looking at work to lay bare a kind of degree-zero threat lurking in these literary attachments, which we can't then un-see. As hooks writes, these attachments are "constructed as problematic" in Kennedy's work; and yet in these plays it almost seems as if authorhood cannot proceed without them.[45] Writing in these plays means returning, again and again, to a site of pain and negation: the "white glass table," the "Vale of Blackmoor," the university library.[46] It seems it's only in this recursive movement back toward what has denied and threatened the self that something like self-expression becomes possible.

In the more recent Kennedy play to which I now want to turn, *He Brought Her Heart Back in a Box*, this is still true; its two main characters spend most of the play writing each other letters in which they keep revisiting the racist violence that has haunted their young lives. While literature is displaced from the central position it occupies in the earlier plays, writing remains central, still a process of painful recollection and return. Yet because this play's writing occurs within the framework of a fictional narrative, writing is now relativized (as it were) by the story that frames it: in *Heart*, writing occurs as an *event within* a story of a deadly intergenerational violence, which the play frames clearly as the violence of American history itself. The play thus poses as a new question the relationship between, on the one hand, the iterative practice of writing, and on the other, the deadly fixity of a history that reproduces domination, operating directly and violently upon raced bodies. The play asks: can writing's painful repetition be *different* from, and make a difference within, history's? And as such, might writing open a different space for desire?

He Brought Her Heart Back in a Box premiered in Brooklyn in 2018. It takes place in 1941, in the fictional town of Montefiore, Georgia, and between Georgia and New York; it revolves around two seventeen-year-olds, Kay and Chris, who want to get married. Kay is Black, and orphaned; her white father, Charles, who never acknowledged her, was suspected of having murdered her Black teenage mother, Mary, shortly after Kay was born. When the play begins, Kay is a student at the town's boarding school for "colored" children; later, she begins attending Atlanta University.[47] Chris, white, is the only legitimate son of the "landowner and businessman" Harrison Aherne, "architect of the town's segregation," who is also "one of the founders of the school" Kay attends at the start.[48] Chris's father—a good friend of Kay's father—has also fathered several children with Black women; those children attend his school, and their mothers are buried in a cemetery that Harrison designed for this purpose. Chris has been helping out in the office of the school; the play begins on the day of Chris's mother's funeral, when Chris comes looking for Kay to ask her to marry him after he moves to New York City; she agrees. After this scene, most of the play consists of the letters they write to each other; at the very end, they finally—wordlessly—meet in New York, only to be "shot dead" by an unseen figure whom we assume to be Chris's father Harrison.[49] Throughout, almost all of their lines—their conversation as well as their letters—consist of long recollections, as Kay tries to make sense of everything she has been told about her mother's death, and Chris tries to make sense of his father's disturbing deeds.

He Brought Her Heart Back in a Box was inspired by Kennedy's memories of her childhood summers in Montezuma, Georgia, during the same period in which the play is set. "I've never been able to unravel that town, and all those relationships.... I always try to unravel those things," she said in a 2017 interview.[50] In *People Who Led to My Plays*, she recalls her early impression "that the South was a strange mesh of dark kinship between the races."[51] Kennedy's description of the play as her attempt to "unravel" that "mesh" also describes the writing that Kay and Chris do over the course of the story. Their complex implication in "dark kinship" returns us to Sharpe, where it resonates in particular with Sharpe's reading of Gayl Jones's 1975 novel *Corregidora*. Reading Jones, Sharpe defines the "Corregidora complex," an "Oedipus Complex for the New World": here, as in Freud, incestuous desire links a parent and child; but here they are also, respectively, enslaver and enslaved.[52] Sharpe sources the formula for this relation from the proslavery politician Henry Hughes's outraged and apparently counterintuitive declamation that "amalgamation [of the races] is incest."[53] In the Americas, this equation was often factually true, given the strategic—and, Sharpe suggests, psychically paradigmatic—

practice wherein white masters fathered successive generations of "property" by raping their own enslaved daughters.[54] *He Brought Her Heart*, set in 1941, contains no overt references to slavery, but it centers around the geography and history of the Georgia town's segregation, and the open secret of powerful white men fathering Black children there. As Kennedy writes in the play's headnotes: "People see each other constantly on Main Street. / The people are all somehow connected."[55] The play is set, that is, in a landscape defined by both the most rigid institutional separation between races, and the "constant" intercourse that takes place across and—as also in *Ohio State Murders*—via this segregation.[56]

Indeed, the sense that incest haunts the main characters' attachment to each other goes beyond the general sense that the town is a web of unacknowledged relation. Kennedy informs us in the headnotes that "Chris and Kay have known each other all their lives"; while Kay's dead father, Charles, was "a white writer of history and mystery" who was close with Chris's father Harrison, the play places Kay in a kind of filial relation to Harrison too, by repeatedly emphasizing that the school she attends is a site for housing and displaying Harrison's children.[57] The play also refers to Charles's and Harrison's routine abuse of Black women as a kind of undifferentiated mutual habit, rather than a discrete series of actions: "Your father and Harrison Aherne did just as they pleased with colored women. People were afraid of them," Kay remembers a family friend telling her.[58] And while the language of the play refers to two white fathers, only one (Harrison) appears onstage, which also tends to collapse Kay's and Chris's lineages. Intertextually, incest also haunts Kay's name: she shares it with Kay the Sister Rat in Kennedy's 1967 play *A Rat's Mass*, a nightmare landscape (set, like *Heart*, during World War II) in which two "pale Negro" siblings have had sex with each other at the command of a white playmate.[59]

All this would seem to cast Kay's relationship with Chris as fraternal rather than parent-child incest; but Kennedy also undermines that distinction by stipulating that Chris's father Harrison is "played by the same actor as Chris."[60] This generational indeterminacy itself resonates with the particular monstrousness of Sharpe's "Corregidora Complex," a mode of reproduction that creates parents who are also their children's (half-)siblings. The end of the play identifies Harrison/Chris even more strongly with Kay's father, Charles: Kay and Chris "are shot dead," presumably by the unseen Harrison, an act that decisively elides any remaining distinction between the fathers.[61] "I believe [your father] killed her and he might kill you," Kay's grandmother had said to her.[62] In realizing this prediction, Harrison/Chris now assumes the murderous paternal function in relation to Kay: Harrison, who shares a body with Chris, becomes Kay's father in the act of killing her. Killing Chris at the same time, he also kills off the version of himself that had hoped for a nonmonstrous mode of interracial relation.

This ending accords a terrible power to history as a force of repetition. Asked how *Heart* "emerged," Kennedy says: "I got angry—I was angry at my grandson's high school in Virginia. It so reminded me of Ohio State in the fifties ... I just couldn't believe that [the Black kids] were going through the same thing, basically, that I went through at Ohio State."[63] The play is correspondingly relentless in its portrayal of history's compulsive repetition, the violent destruction that meets any attempt to forge a new logic of living; it's as if Kay cannot *not* repeat her mother's fate. "There is no doubt that they are quite drawn to each other," the stage directions in the first scene read; the phrase denotes mutual desire but also suggests subjection to a kind of compulsion.[64] The more we learn about Kay and Chris's histories, the harder it is not to feel that their attraction occurs not in spite of these histories but because of them. They may be star-crossed—and the staging of their first encounter, with Kay at the top of the stairs and Chris at the bottom looking up at her, does recall Shakespeare's balcony scene— but the same stars that cross them also guide them to each other in the first place: their "amalgamation" has the awful inevitability of an intergenerational mandate. Rather than the familiar story of two young lovers who have to fight against the limitations of the identities history would impose on them, that is, we have a pair who seem to be born(e) toward each other through the channels history—embodied in Harrison Aherne—has carved out. This sense of naked fatality is underscored by the fact that the play contains very little language that could be considered romantic; in their letters, Kay and Chris rarely acknowledge each other at all. It's almost as if their relation is pure structure.

The jarringly unromantic portrayal of their relationship resonates with the critique Sharpe adopts from Hartman: a warning against "the elaboration of a racial and sexual fantasy in which domination is transposed into the bonds of mutual affection."[65] Psychologically and affectively, Kay's disposition toward Chris remains opaque. We do not learn what she feels from what she says; in the premiere, the actress Juliana Canfield preserved this opacity beautifully, performing with a luminous, quiet intensity never quite readable as either desire or fear. The question whether their relation can be anything other than a repetition of coercion and murder—that is, whether it can *be* a relation at all—is never affirmatively settled. Kennedy is careful to foreground the asymmetry between their positions from the start; to their first spoken lines—"Good evening, Kay." "Evening, Mr. Chris."—she adds the stage direction: "He is white. She is not. He is still, in 1941, addressed with 'Mr.'"[66] And yet the play also seems to propose a kind of likeness between the two characters: in the murder at the end that, even as it repeats the murder of Kay's mother, also pointedly contrasts with it (and, we might observe, with the ending of *Funnyhouse of a Negro*) by leaving Kay *and* Chris dead; and formally, in the alternation between Kay's and Chris's epistolary monologues, which creates a rhythm of verbal balance throughout.

This coexistence in the play of both an irreducible positional difference *and* a kind of mirroring between the characters—a combination that, again, reiterates the logic of Sharpe's "Corregidora Complex"—unfolds in the play's only obviously romantic exchange:

CHRIS: I came here because I wanted to see you. I want to write to you. I want
    to marry you. We could run away and live in Paris after the war.
KAY: Just like in *Bitter Sweet*.
CHRIS: Yes.
KAY: Yes, I'll marry you, Chris.[67]

Chris's anaphoric repetition of "I want" here might seem simply to reflect the fact that as the white man in the scene, his and only his desire is operative. Chris is socially positioned to *get* whatever he wants, like his father(s) before him; especially, the play has already established, if what he wants is access to a Black woman. The dialogue underscores this asymmetry by contrasting Chris's emphatic announcement of his desire with Kay's brief acceptance. Chris's series of "I wants" also, however, echoes Sarah's repetition of that phrase in *Funnyhouse of a Negro*; and as in *Funnyhouse*, the repetition here suggests a speaker struggling to *claim* a desire as their own. Like Sarah's desires, though for very different reasons, Chris's desires here are overdetermined: the world may want this for me, but no, it is *I* who want it. But for Chris, white, male and wealthy, this *act of claiming desire* is also *itself* the societally mandated act. His position as the paradigmatic subject of desire means that in desiring, he can only ever comply with the social mandate (that he desire). Chris's desire for Kay is mired in a paradox wherein the more actively he claims and differentiates it from society's desire, the more obedient to society's logic it becomes: his activity *is* passivity. As his double-casting with his own father emphasizes, there is no chance of his emerging as a fully agential subject, precisely because doing so could only be his privileged inheritance, never his choice. This means that in spite of his absolute advantage over Kay, the power differential that has held her in her place her entire life also holds him in his.

For Sharpe, as we saw in the introduction, the phenomenon of monstrous intimacy becomes constitutive for modern subjectivity—for white as well as Black "post-slavery subjects," albeit, of course, differently.[68]

Heart seems to me to echo this claim, elaborating two characters who are both (differently) subject to the same structure, and who cannot *not* repeat the violence of history. Through the text that passes between these subjects, the play poses the question whether, under conditions of domination, writing *or* desire can emerge as anything but the compulsion to repeat.[69]

"An Opening That Leads to the Stage"

There is also another system of repetition at work in *Heart*: theater itself, which becomes more central here than in any of Kennedy's previous plays.[70] *Heart* begins with a school performance of Christopher Marlowe's *The Massacre at Paris*, a political drama about the 1572 slaughter of Huguenots, which is being put on by some of the other students as Kay watches from behind the auditorium: "*Kay is at the top of the stairwell and can see through to the stage, hear clearly, see vague motion.*" The first words we hear are ten lines of a soliloquy from Marlowe, in which the villainous Duke of Guise expounds his ambition to take over France in the bloodiest and most ruthless manner possible, though Kennedy tells us the words are "*barely understandable.*"[71] After Chris enters and the dialogue begins, "*muffled lines*" from Marlowe are heard intermittently throughout their scene.[72] Harrison Aherne—who, we are told at the outset, has chosen *The Massacre at Paris* as the school play "*for unknown reasons*"—reads aloud from its text himself at the end of Kennedy's play, just before the murder; these lines, in which two different characters vow bloody revenge on their political enemies, are the last words spoken live in *Heart*.[73]

Then there is Chris's budding career as an actor, which seems to get underway immediately upon his arrival in New York; he writes to Kay from the dressing room at the "small theater" where he works, and we also see him rehearse or perform on its stage.[74] Curiously, the show he's in is none other than Noel Coward's *Bitter Sweet*, whose movie version he and Kay had both seen in their town's segregated theater, and to which she had referred when accepting his proposal: "Just like in *Bitter Sweet*." "Yes." (It might also be worth noting that the tragic ending of *Bitter Sweet* itself revolves around the production of an operetta; that its protagonists cross lines of class and nationality, though not, of course, race, to elope; and that its hero is stabbed to death by a predatory Austrian military officer, a plot point echoed, perhaps, in the revelation of Harrison Aherne's ties to Nazis.[75]) The play's two theaters—which is to say, Harrison's boarding-school theater of *The Massacre*, and Chris's aspirational theater of *Bitter Sweet*—converge at the end, when Harrison—who has followed Kay to New York—

shoots the lovers just after "*Kay ascends the stairs to the stage*" and "*Chris goes to her. They meet.*"[76] The murder itself is preceded by the wordless image of "*Darkness, then a very, very bright stage.*"[77]

Why does Kennedy choose to tell the story of Chris and Kay as a story about theater? Reading *Hedda Gabler*, I suggested that dramatic theater might offer a privileged kind of access to our own repetition compulsion; that theater can help us grapple with, and indeed eroticize, repetition's dominating psychic force. From the beginning of *Heart*, however, theatrical repetition serves a domination that is not only psychic: Black children are literally forced to perform before their white father, enacting the script he has prescribed. In this context, Chris's desire to "go on the stage" reads most obviously as a fantasy of standing in for the Black children who occupy his father's gaze—a wish that might remind us of the fantasmatic restagings of *Uncle Tom's Cabin* among Freud's patients. We might even imagine Chris's death at the end of the play as a culmination of this fantasy: my father is finally beating (loving, watching, killing) *me*. As this suggests, the play conceives theater as a machine that realizes fantasies—or confounds the boundaries that ordinarily separate fantasy from reality—*for certain subjects*, by reiterating the real subjugation of others.

This critique seems to resonate with Kennedy's own expression of frustration with experiences she has had working in theater.[78] And yet in having the lovers die at the very point where Kay *would have reached* the stage, the play also seems to gesture toward an unrealized theater that would be something else if it could occur—perhaps something like happiness. The image of the "*very, very bright stage*" that precedes this event seems to encapsulate this ambivalence. On the one hand, it recalls the "*Lights bright on hundreds of books*" at the end of *Ohio State Murders* (which itself recalls the deadly illuminated ending of *Funnyhouse*); it invests the theater, like the university library, with a kind of frightening power to contain and compel, a power that operates as social domination, in which aesthetic pleasure colludes. On the other hand, the image of the empty stage that momentarily suspends the play's climactic sequence also seems to signal a space of unfulfilled possibility, an *open* space in which something other than the relentless return of domination *could* happen. Is this space of possibility completely closed by the violent denouement that follows it, if it is not already foreclosed by the logic of domination that maintains the theater as an institutional space? Or might this instant offer a glimpse of the stage as a site—and an interval—that the deadly repetition of domination never quite contains?

That this question arises at all points to another way that *Heart* organizes itself around theater: more than any of Kennedy's other plays, this one is constructed as a *drama*. By this I mean—following genre theorist

Peter Szondi—that in *Heart* Kennedy constructs both (1) a fictional story (the story of Kay and Chris's romance) that is enacted rather than told, and that accordingly seems to take place in the present, that is, "happens before our eyes" as if for the first time, rather than being recounted as something that has, in its entirety, already occurred; and (2) an event constituted in dialogue and interaction between characters, that is, in interpersonal relation.[79] As we've seen, Kennedy's plays typically flout both of these norms: her protagonists tend (1) to speak mainly of past events in the past tense (*Ohio State Murders*) and/or in an atemporal mode of self-description (*Funnyhouse*), and (2) their words rarely seem to be responsive to, or directed toward, others.[80] Writing on Kennedy's subversion of dramatic norms, Elinor Fuchs describes her 1976 play *A Movie Star Has to Star in Black and White* as "a text composed of writings derived from other writings, some of which are derived from still other writings. This writing is always reminding us that it comes from a finished past—old diaries, old movies. Its present life is not the interaction of 'living' characters uttering seemingly spontaneous speech, but a life of texts refracted through each other to produce an eerie interaction of genres."[81] There is a sense in which this still holds true for *Heart*: Kay and Chris spend almost the entire play separately thinking and writing through the mysteries of their own pasts, rarely responding to anything the other has said. And yet it would not be quite right to say that *Heart* foregoes "the interaction of 'living' characters" in favor of "a life of texts," or even that the present disappears into the "finished past" that is the object of Kay and Chris's writings. Writing here is still largely about the past, but it is also something that *happens* in the play's discernible present, within its fiction; it is something the characters *do*.

To be sure, taken from context, most of the play's language could easily be the text of diary entries; but instead, the play frames this text—dramatically—as a series of letters that Kay and Chris write to each other (and before that, as a series of things they say to each other) as the event of their elopement nears. This means that unlike *Movie Star*, *Funnyhouse* or *Ohio State Murders*, *Heart* invites us to invest our desires in not one but two central characters and their relation to one another; and it establishes writing as that relation's medium. This also means that within the fiction the play establishes, this writing is *not* "finished," so that up until the end we can wonder—as Kennedy's other plays do not really invite us to wonder—what its issue will be.

It seems to me crucial that this play, while its attention remains largely riveted to questions about the past, constructs these questions in a dramatic frame that implies the possibility that something new could happen to or with these questions in the present; and that although its language is fundamentally monologic, these monologues are *occasioned* by the premise of correspondence, that is, of relation. Solitary, reflective discourse may be a constant feature of Kennedy's poetics, but the dramatic frame of this play invites us to encounter that characteristic mode of prose more naively: not as a formal strategy of the author's but as something that the characters are "really" doing as part of the event unfolding between them. Without this framing, we might interpret their letters as another instance of what Fuchs calls Kennedy's "eerie interaction of genres"— nondramatic discourse superimposed on a dialogic scene, like the lines spoken by Queen Victoria and the Duchess of Hapsburg in *Funnyhouse*.[82] But it seems to me that *Heart*'s repeated references to these texts *as* letters function to justify their lengthy, self-referential musing without that kind of extradiegetic explanation—that is, without negating the dramatic fiction that a relation is unfolding now, between characters. The fact that Chris and Kay launch into accounts of their family traumas within moments of first speaking to each other might be played for formal alienation, but it might also suggest the particular way in which these two young people are "drawn to each other." If this is right, then what the play stages is not a relation subsumed by nonrelational writing but a relation whose uncanny intimacy unleashes that mode of writing and sustains it. This is not to say that Kay's and Chris's speeches and letters don't strain the dramatic norms of presentness and interpersonal motivation—they do, and it is hard to imagine a performance of this play that would not create some discomfort around genre. But the sense that Kay and Chris are somehow catalyzing each other's projects of recollection, and thus producing each other as writers, seems to me to open this play to the unfinishedness of a dramatic present in a way Kennedy's previous works tend to avoid.

I'm suggesting that in *Heart*, Kennedy turns toward theater both to reckon with its complicity in domination *and* to allow its influence to operate on her own playwriting, at the level of genre. Setting *Heart* at the theater, she also writes something surprisingly akin to a "normal play": a text that solicits us to imagine that what we see and hear is happening now, anew, for the first time. We have come to expect that theater—in the dominant, dramatic tradition that comprehends, for instance, both Marlowe and Coward—will work to support this fantasy of nonrepetition, even as we also know that repetition is theater's most fundamental premise. And it seems to me that by framing *Heart*'s story through both theatrical performance and this dramatic norm, Kennedy asks whether this paradox in theater might speak to what the individual can do with (her) history in writing it: asking whether, in the fantasy of new possibility that dramatic theater sustains *despite and through* its determined repetition, we might find a model of how a writer painfully gripped by repetition can open a

nonrepetitive possibility *in the very act of reiterating* the history that bru-
talizes her.

Here I find it helpful to turn to the Lacanian theorist Joan Copjec,
whose work Sharpe also engages, more critically, in her discussion of Kara
Walker in *Monstrous Intimacies*.[83] Copjec's own essay on Walker elucidates
what Copjec calls "the Freudian thesis on history," a vision of history as
having no outside—no transcendental, eternal beyond that would mark
the limit of what can be called historical.[84] In order for history to comprehend everything but also to proceed contingently, as this thesis demands,
there must be "an internal limit" *within* history that resists its smoothly de-
terministic functioning, by displacing the historical from itself: this split-
ting is the site of ghosts and other "uncanny repetitions" that haunt the
historical field, which Copjec identifies with the Lacanian Real.[85] In individual psychic development, Copjec argues, this structure means that
when a subject is compelled to give up her mother—as she always is, in the
Freudian narrative—there is no beyond or elsewhere to which the mother
can safely be banished. Instead, the subject retains a remainder from/of
the mother, a "part object," which remains in the psychic field as excess,
and thus "gives body to" the uncanny split in history: the subject "is de-
completed by the addition of a surplus object that interrupts or blocks the
formation of a whole, the One, of her being."[86] This disruption of whole-
ness in the subject mirrors the disrupted totalization of history.

What Copjec's analysis helps me see in *Heart* is how the play's search-
ing question about the violence of history—the question of how this violence works, and whether, in love or/as writing, there can be anything like
an escape from it—finds a kind of answer in the node of pain and desire
that is the play's titular image.

> My great-aunt, my grandmother's sister, talks all the time about the green
> box, all the time. "Your mother did not kill herself," she says. "She was
> killed and Maggie knows it. It was in the winter. I saw him with my own two
> eyes. Your father returned from up North with a green box—everybody
> saw it; it was a long glass box. Everybody said it had your mother's heart
> in it. We all saw it. He sat it in the center of the colored garden, the Aherne
> Garden.
>
> "We all knew it was Mary's heart. Then it disappeared. Your father
> brought your mother's heart back in a box."[87]

This tale literalizes Copjec's Lacanian part object as the mother's heart,
placing it "in the center" of the play as an excessive remainder of the
lost mother, a remainder that disrupts any possibility of closure for—
decompletes—Kay, the town, and indeed the play itself. Returning to

the naive reading of Kay and Chris's exchanges that I proposed above, in which the charge of their encounter actually provokes them both to launch into monologues, we might say that for Kay, the prospect of a sexual relation with Chris immediately prompts an obsessive return to this narrative, as if her mother's heart is the dominant organ of her own desire, and as if the opportunity of reencountering it is the thing she most wants from Chris. His inherited proximity to the scene of this partial truth—"the Aherne Garden," which bears his name, and where his own father's Black victims are buried—must contribute to the force whereby Kay is "drawn to" Chris. "I wonder what really happened to my mother," Kay says in her last speech of the play.[88] This same desire to approach the unbearable revelation, and the sense that Chris appears as a route of access to it, also manifest early on, when Kay asks Chris to tell her what is in the school's storeroom, an impacted trove of town history that houses Aherne's scale model of the segregation system. The storeroom is later illuminated in the play's final image, as if to suggest that the heart Kay seeks is (really or figuratively) buried there.[89]

Robbed of the possibility of ever knowing her mother, Kay bears a loss that starkly echoes the "enforced state of breach," as Spillers puts it, that systematically dispossesses the Black mother of her child, and vice-versa, in slavery and its modern continuations.[90] "Kay will never know whether her mother shot herself in the head or whether she was found stabbed to death in the freight elevator": this is the last line attributed to Chris in the play—or more exactly, to "Chris's Voice," presumably because it is spoken when the double-cast actor is already onstage as Harrison, suggesting that the line might be recorded or otherwise deflected from the actor's body so that we can *hear* Chris while *seeing* his father.[91] This staging of the line, together with the fact that it is the only line Chris speaks that could not, grammatically, be addressed to Kay, suggests a sinister dissolve of his resistance to identifying with his/the father, as if he has finally become a Raymond figure, the impersonal white *monteur* that knows and sees all.[92] But while Kay's familial and epistemological loss, her "never," is undeniable, both Spillers and Copjec offer support for resisting this declaration of loss or lack as the last word on Kay's subjectivity. Citing the principle of American slave law that "the condition of the slave mother is 'forever entailed on all her remotest posterity,'" Spillers asks: "But what is the 'condition' of the mother? Is it the 'condition' of enslavement the writer means, or does he mean the 'mark' and the 'knowledge' of the *mother* upon the child that here translates into the culturally forbidden and impure?"[93] As Spillers points out, a fundamental ambiguity here renders undecidable the alternative between "enslaved" and "mother" in this phrase, and thus collapses the two. She goes on to argue that per this cultural logic, the descendant of enslaved people will always be "touched" not only by slavery but thus also "by the *mother, handed* by her in ways that he cannot escape."[94] In this sense, the "breach" in Black maternity must be understood not only as an *absence* ("Kay will never know") but also as a maternal *presence* at once constitutive and perpetually disturbing.

Copjec's claim that the trace of the lost mother remains present to the subject as a part object, or body part—a claim that also seems to me to resonate with Spillers's "*handed*"—helps us to refocus our gaze on the heart that *is there* at the center of the play's narrative, in its title, and in the claim of the Black townspeople in Montefiore, while it is left out of the white voices' accounts, just as it has "disappeared" from the Aherne Garden. Copjec's analysis suggests that the insistence of the mother's heart *as excess* rather than absence might be precisely what interferes with any logic of totalization, the logic that would identify history entirely with the smooth, unceasing operation of power, manifested in *Heart* as relentless genocide and war. This latter, totalizing version of history is voiced in Marlowe's *Massacre at Paris*, the play Harrison Aherne forces his Black children to perform, and from which he reads aloud just before murdering Kay and Chris. Given the way Marlowe's text begins and ends the play, we might say that this version of history—as the absolute, unremitting working-out of the wills of the powerful—is the play within and against which Kennedy's play, and the acts of writing inside it, take place, and from which they must somehow make a difference. Kay's mother's heart is the organ of this difference, precisely because it is the unassimilated remainder that prevents the story of these events, and of Kay's brief life, from being finished or settled. The heart, in other words—not the murder itself, nor the loss it entails, but the exuberant *excess* of the organ's uncanny return—embodies the drive that compels the play's writing.

Its title, after all, proclaims this: as a full sentence, "*He Brought Her Heart Back in a Box*" signals (as we have also noted about one of Freud's essays) the significance of the statement itself as an act of language, emphasizing that it is always through someone's *telling* the story of the heart that we encounter it. The title also, of course, conveys that the violent, excessive return of the heart is what the play is most centrally about; it thus disrupts the otherwise impressively balanced weight the play distributes between Kay's and Chris's respective narratives, a tip-off that the scale of our attention should be tipped in Kay's favor. In this sense, Kay's "I wonder what really happened to my mother" might almost serve as a synopsis for the play. Whereas Chris asks himself questions (about his father) whose unbearable answers he basically already knows, Kay's wondering about her mother remarks something really (Copjec might say, Real-ly) unknown and unknowable.[95] The play takes pains to maintain this indeterminacy: thus while the title, as we've observed, seems to enshrine one version of the story, the play's headnotes say that Kay's mother "shot herself in the head when Kay was a baby."[96] Normally, I think, we would take such a statement in the headnotes as definitive, since it seems to come directly from the author, but here the rest of the play, including the ending, makes the veracity of the headnote hard to accept. Not only have different people told different stories about Mary's death, which Kay repeats, but at different points Kay cites the same family friend telling both versions.[97]

Why this relentless contradiction? In *People Who Led to My Plays*, Kennedy recalls the influence of overhearing her parents' gossip: "Often they'd say, 'No one really knows the truth, but people say …' Contradictory voices, different versions of a story as a way of penetrating to the truth of things, would become important in my work."[98] This approach to narrative suggests not only that both sides of a story can be true, or that truth is multifaceted—a principle that might be served simply by attributing different opinions to different characters—but rather that there is something else to which one "penetrat[es]" *by way of* these contradictions, a singular "truth" that the "contradictory voices" help us encounter. In this play, that something else is the heart in the box: the object that compels narrative, compels speech and writing, precisely because no stable knowledge, no systematic statement of its presence (or absence) is possible.

This is also a way to understand the play's relation to *Snow White*, the classic heart-in-a-box fairytale its own story of the heart transfigures. In fact, *Snow White* appears prominently in *People Who Led to My Plays* as well. The memoir is formatted as a kind of scrapbook, its text interspersed with images of many of the "people" whose formative influence on her Kennedy recounts, and the first chapter includes an especially large image from the Disney *Snow White*, in which the evil queen stares angrily at her magic mirror. "I often thought, why did Snow White's stepmother want her killed in the woods and to have her heart brought back in a box? To be the 'fairest' in the kingdom must be very important."[99] A few pages later, Kennedy returns to this theme: "After seeing the Disney movie, I'd think of Snow White in her casket in the woods. Why did Snow White have to die, even though her Prince's kiss would later awaken her? Why did she have to 'sleep' in the casket in the woods?"[100] There is something heartbreaking in the child's wondering and protesting at the violence of power; even more so when we consider that *Heart* identifies the embalmed fairytale heroine as a figure for the lost mother. The "green glass box" in Kay's great-aunt's story is not only a version of the corresponding box in the Disney movie—which gets filled with a pig's heart instead of Snow White's own—but also, perhaps, a miniature of Snow White's iconic glass "casket in the woods," gone green instead of clear because in Kennedy's version, no one can see what's inside. Kennedy's play reprises the image of the evil queen in the figure of Kay's white grandmother, who—Kay's Black grandmother tells her—"would look at [Kay] like she was going to kill [her] right there on Main Street."[101] As in *Snow White*, it's Kay's "fair" looks—"she is pretty, fragile, pale"—that presumably mark Kay out for this murderous rage, by marking her as her white father's daughter.[102] Indeed, we can't know whether Kay is finally killed more for that pallor (that is, to prevent an incestuous alliance with Chris) or for its opposite (to prevent interracial marriage); Sharpe's "Corregidora complex" helps us see how these two alternatives may themselves be structurally undecidable.

Of all these echoes, though, it is the heart that most strongly binds the play to *Snow White*, and it does so in a doubled negative of an event in the original tale. In *Snow White*, the wicked queen orders a woodsman to bring the girl's heart back in a box, but he doesn't—the girl is too "fair" to kill. In Kennedy's version of this story, fifteen-year-old Mary's white rapist *doesn't not* execute this imperative; he *fails to fail to* act in accord with power; he does kill. We might say this is a story of what happens in America to the girl who is *not* snow white, the disavowed (and constitutive) shadow of the Disney fairytale. There is no reprieve; her heart does get brought back in the box. And yet I think the play complicates this perfect reversal. Not not brought back: as Kennedy's discussion of gossip shows, she rejects the logic of noncontradiction, and as we noted earlier in reading *Funnyhouse*, a double negative in Kennedy is never exactly an affirmation. Instead, I'd suggest that the "not not" buried in *Heart*'s title is an instance of precisely the kind of uncanny doubling that Copjec describes as the site of resistance to history within history. The heart which is *not not there* embodies the space in which the subject's fate could be something more than what historical power determines, even as she is also subjected by that power. Love, the would-be transcendent truth of the fairytale, is not totally negated by historical truth but remains to haunt a history that is thus relativized, put into play, *occupied* by this negative doubling. In this process, devastation opens onto the uncanny possibility of the heart—the mother—being "brought back" not only by the murderous white father but *again, differently* by Kay's questioning, and by the play itself.[103]

This possibility, Kennedy suggests, is precisely what theater is for. When theater first appears among her recollections in *People Who Led to My Plays*, she notes that seeing Tennessee Williams's *The Glass Menagerie* in high school provoked in her a very specific desire: "it was that summer evening when the idea of being a writer and seeing my own family onstage caught fire in my mind."[104] Of her early playwriting efforts, she writes: "I still didn't really understand how intensely I wanted my family on the stage (like the family in *Our Town*)."[105] Of course this refers in part to the overwhelming whiteness of midcentury American family drama, which the casts of Williams and Thornton Wilder emblematize. But Kennedy twice mentions wanting to see "*my* family," rather than, say, "families like mine," onstage, positing a personal, autobiographical impulse at the heart of her work, and casting this tendency as a kind of drive: "how intensely I wanted"; "caught fire in my mind." She suggests that her writing is fundamentally a desirous project of staging her family: doubling them as text so that they can appear again—and again, and again—on the stage. This doubling is always also a reinvention: they return here as sites for Kennedy's imagination to occupy, to transpose and transform.

These recollections speak to a fundamental relation between writing and theater in Kennedy's work—a relation that is not only causal or instrumental (texts are written to be staged) but also figurative, driven by the ways text and performance double each other. In writing, the writer perpetually reopens the personae of her imagination to new embodiments, new forms; theatrical performance reembodies this process of reembodiment.[106] In a way that *shows* what writing is always doing, theater is designed to keep bringing the same people (characters) back differently (performers, performances). Theater thus enacts the same kind of reanimation that drives Kennedy's own emphatically iterative practice of writing—where a character named "Kay," for example, turns up as a dead child with a rat's head in *A Rat's Mass*, as a New York intellectual in "Sisters Etta and Ella" and *Etta and Ella on the Upper West Side*, and again as the protagonist of *Heart*.[107] Theater's ability to keep enacting its own version of this reanimation—the promise that each time *Heart* is staged, Kay will be there again, in a different body—is fundamental to our recognition of dramatic theater as a cultural practice, to our sense of what we are seeing. This is to say that Kennedy's writing is always asking us to see writing as theater.

This analogy between writing and theater also offers a way to think about the crucial role of movies throughout Kennedy's work—most obvious in *Movie Star*, but also, more subtly, in *Heart*. Kennedy loves movies, a fact evident throughout her interviews as well as her texts; and writing and theater both offer her the means of repeating filmic material, that is, of *doubling* an object that—precisely because a movie is understood to be the same thing across each reproduction of it—would not in itself allow for the *difference*, the event, of reanimation. We can see this in the trajectory of Coward's *Bitter Sweet* that runs through *He Brought Her Heart Back*: it is referred to first as a movie, which Kay and Chris have both seen in the theater; then as Kay's fantasy of what their own life together might be like "after the war"; and then as the stage play that Chris stars in. This reversal of *Bitter Sweet*'s real-life stage-to-film trajectory suggests that theater is not only—as we said earlier—a machine for executing dominant subjects' fantasies but also a machine for appropriating objects from dominant culture, subjecting them to the fold of a passionate repetition that opens them to the difference of other subjects' writing.[108]

Adrienne Kennedy's Sadistic Form

You've probably noticed that "Kay," this name that returns throughout Kennedy's work, is also the initial of the playwright's own surname. But there are two writers in *Heart*; and if Kay's textual drive can stand, in some ways, for Kennedy's—and if her story is, as I believe it is, the "heart" of the play—then how should we understand the role Chris's writing plays here, in an allotment of stage time to a white guy that has no precedent in Kennedy's work?

Reading *Funnyhouse*, I suggested that when Sarah's white tormentor/lover Raymond gets the play's last word, his speech emphasizes Kennedy's own act of composition and, as such, both repeats *and negates* society's negation of Black women's authorhood. In this sense, Raymond's cruelty is one more "white page" for Kennedy to fill. But this does not seem to me like an adequate description of Chris's role throughout *Heart*, nor does the violent literary mimetism embodied in Professor Hampshire seem to offer a model for what Chris is doing here. In *Heart* it is Harrison, not Chris, who figures and performs white supremacist negation; and while their shared body makes Chris's implication in this violence obvious, the time and care the play takes in presenting Chris's experience alongside Kay's makes it hard to characterize him purely as an instrument of her destruction.

I want to propose that Kay and Chris, spatially separated through most of the play, enact something like a classificatory distinction between two differently raced and gendered *modes* of writing; and that this distinction echoes, but also significantly revises, the Freudian difference between male and female masochists, a difference whose implications for authorship we explored in chapter 2 by way of Henry James. There is an analogy to be drawn between the way *Heart* stages Chris's writing and the way "Nona Vincent" stages Wayworth's, as well as a dissymmetry. Like "Nona Vincent," *Heart* figures a heroic, white, masculine mode of writing in a character who takes the stage and performs writing *for* a female authorial counterpart, whose own writing is thus positioned in shadow. In James as in Freud, this positioning offers the female subject a kind of "escape" from sexualized embodiment. But *Heart* shows that when this subject is a Black woman, such "escape" may be impossible; her racialized embodiment marks her out for violence—enfleshes her, to recur to Spillers—more radically and indelibly than the Jamesian/Freudian authoress.[109]

Like *Heart*, you'll recall, "Nona Vincent" places two writers before us. Wayworth appears to be the writer in the story, as well as its center of consciousness; but the story shows us that this very impulse to *appear as* writer—to perform that role in his own person—ultimately disqualifies Wayworth from being the true subject of Jamesian authorial fantasy. The better figure for that subject, I argued, is Mrs. Alsager, who sits in the dark and lets Wayworth perform "his" authorhood for her: "He was already on the stage." This positioning corresponds to the perverse theory of sexual difference that Freud presents in "A Child Is Being Beaten," in which the male patient more or less eagerly casts *himself* as the masochistic victim in fantasy, while the girl keeps herself out of the picture by installing a boy in her place, and by means of this substitutive evasion, embarks on the path to authorhood.

I have already suggested that Chris's will to "go on the stage" fits Freud's analysis of the masochistic male, whose performance in fantasy puts him in the position of being hurt by his father, a transposition of the love he craves. For Chris, the desire to be an actor would be imbued with the fantasy of being watched the way his father watches his captive Black children at the school, a coercive voyeurism that his mother has taught him to recognize as love: "She used to say, 'Christopher, your father loves those nigra children more than he does us.'"[110] Like Freud's patients' incorporation of *Uncle Tom's Cabin* (and indeed like that novel itself), this desire on Chris's part would be an instance of the constitutive psychic behavior Sharpe calls "entering into black bodies for enjoyment."[111] Eager to claim this imagined pleasure, Chris proclaims his desire to act and his desire to write in the same utterance: "I want to go on the stage. I came here because I wanted to see you. I want to write to you."[112] This straightforward assertion makes acting, writing, and desire continuous, assimilating all three in the same bravura performance, just as Chris will hop back and forth from the dressing room, where he writes, up onto the stage, where he performs a love song.

Kay, however, has stepped out of the way, stepped off the white father's stage of compulsory Black performance, leaving a space that Chris will eagerly step in to fill. Instead of performing for the murderous white father, that is, Kay/K. has Chris perform for him *for* her. Like Freud's masochistic girl, Kay thus sidesteps "the demands of erotic life"—but in this case, the stakes of the escape are much higher, since the "erotic life" in question is an anti-Black sexuality murderously instituted by the father; it is a "life" of racial subordination, and its "demands" comprehend her rape and death. So where the Freudian girl avails herself of binary sexual difference to install a *boy* in the fantasy as the most effective guarantee of her own absence there, *Heart* more than redoubles this negative move, by finding Kay's boy performer directly across the fault line of a more profound antagonism; finding him, indeed, in the very same body as white supremacy itself. Chris's exuberant self-expression takes the stage so that Kay can write, as it were, through him. That is: if history has determined that Chris, not Kay, should be the one who initiates their conversation and correspondence, his doing so also functions as a literal pre-text for her own writing, her writing of the mother's heart. "Kay, we buried my mother today," Chris says at the start of his first monologue. "My mother is dead too," Kay begins two pages later, as if she had been waiting for her turn to seize this opening.[113] Within the dramatic frame Chris's will-to-performance opens, Kay attempts to write her own desire: her relation to a mother who is always present as lost, always brought back in a terrible incompleteness, in part.

Where *Funnyhouse*, and to some extent also *Ohio State Murders*, constructs a Black female writer-protagonist who writes through an attachment to deadly self-negation, *He Brought Her Heart Back* uses self-negation in an attempt to displace, not destroy, the writing self—uses it, indeed, as something like a means for desire's survival. And yet Kay doesn't survive: the frame, the drama, collapses with painful abruptness before she can finish.[114] After all, given the seemingly interminable violence of a history of white supremacy, what hope can there have been for escaping it? There has been no "after the war," no time outside domination. When Kay and Chris fall from the stage, their death seems less like a defeat, more like a revelation that their fate has been sealed all along. And—the play insists—this is something we knew going in, because it's a play.

Heart thus avows and emphasizes theater's subjection to repetition, just as it avows the relentless insistence of historical domination. And yet in the course of this repetition, the play has made a space for something else to come back too: the heart, the thing that keeps on doubling the negative, never erasing but—by repeating—troubling the real, historical negation of the mother's and the daughter's being. What thus returns is the interval of writerly inquiry, a weird, passionate obtrusion that cannot cancel this destruction or redeem its cruelty, but prevents its ever coming smoothly to its logical close. The possibility that the same might come back different if we (re)turn to writing it would be a way to describe the poetics, and ethics, of Kennedy's writing. It is also, I think, the clearest reason why that writing keeps directing itself to the stage.

This *theatrical* understanding of both history and aesthetic production corresponds not only with Copjec's reading of Freud but also with certain remarks Sharpe makes in her reading of Isaac Julien's 1993 film *The Attendant*, which stages scenes of interracial, sadomasochistic desire at a London museum dedicated to commemorating slavery. By elaborating "connections between daily life and libidinal excess," Sharpe writes, "Julien explodes calcified modes of seeing and understanding. These connections are not, however, even collectively an end in themselves; rather they create an opening with which an as yet undetermined something else can emerge."[115] Sharpe observes that Julien "is not attempting to install an alternative *history* of chattel slavery but to hold a space open, to imagine a gap in signification itself."[116] As I understand Sharpe, this kind of "opening" appears where the historical givens of a modernity built on slavery are revealed as a structure that subjects, including Black subjects, inhabit in the full complexity and contingency of a psychic life, including enjoyment; and where enjoyment can emerge in intimate proximity to this painful history, neither as proscribed nor as prescribed by it but as a faculty for living with it that exceeds its determinations.[117]

In Kennedy's plays, this faculty is the essence of writing. We might cautiously cast this writing as masochistic insofar as it always conjoins desire with pain and negation, and works by reiterating itself, again and again, in and as the elaboration of this conjunction; or, if we maintain that the conceptual history of masochism will always remain too beholden to a discourse of white subjectivity to define what Kennedy does with these terms, we can adapt Scott's strategy and pronounce masochism an "analogy," rather than a name, for the structure Kennedy elaborates. But either way, it seems to me, that structure in Kennedy cannot but inform this book's most intimately held endeavor: to offer an account of how writers have imagined writing as a technology of wanting—more specifically, a technology for wanting precisely where cruelty threatens to obliterate desire and with it, the consistency of the subject herself. This is not the masochism of a subject who, secure in her world and in her person, rehearses suffering "in play" (Freud) from a space safe in the real.[118] But neither is it, in Kennedy, a straightforwardly redemptive project of redress or repair. Instead, writing becomes the tortuous endeavor of continually doubling—repeating—the negation that threatens the subject, who would thus "*take*" (Scott) that negation inside as her own, and thereby make herself impossibly—monstrously—its author. Writing thus becomes the organ of survival, but also of a fierce, upsetting pleasure. It is a heart that beats back, bloody and insistent.

"With Both Hands"

CHAPTER 4

Autotheory's
Masochistic Theater

Adrienne Kennedy's *Funnyhouse of a Negro* envisions authorship as a deadly dialectic. In this vision, writing is a way to seize control of the negation that society wreaks upon Black female subjects, and it is also a tautological or excessive reiteration of that negation; authorship arises as a resistant project of self-empowerment that may be ultimately indissociable from a compliant project of self-erasure. The autobiographical element that runs prominently throughout Kennedy's work, and has come into focus for bell hooks and many of Kennedy's other readers, makes clear not only the degree to which the self is always at stake in Kennedy's writing but also the way that writing is at once dangerous and indispensable to the erotic sustenance of that self.

Whereas I have hesitated—following arguments by Hortense Spillers, Darieck Scott, and Amber Jamilla Musser—in naming this structure in Kennedy's work an instance of masochism, I'll now pursue the theme of writing as desirous self-making and self-negating in work that does explicitly invite masochism as a discursive frame. Eve Kosofsky Sedgwick's 1987 essay "A Poem Is Being Written" is a paradigmatic example of the genre now commonly called *autotheory*; before turning to Sedgwick, I'll also consider Paul B. Preciado's 2008 *Testo Yonqui* (*Testo Junkie*), a text that helped usher the term "autotheory" itself into widespread use. Toward the end of the chapter, I'll make a brief excursus on a story by Gary Fisher, a student and friend of Sedgwick's whose work she edited posthumously. To ask what the writing of self does in Sedgwick and Preciado, in the wake of what we have seen it doing in Kennedy (and what we'll glimpse in Fisher, also a Black writer), is inevitably to recognize stark differences in the kinds of domination, violence, and negation the white writers' selves (don't) encounter in the course of their literary self-constructions. But this sequence of readings will also bring out certain continuities between these bodies of work. Among them is the fact that Sedgwick's essay, like Kennedy's plays and Fisher's story, elaborates a fantasy of how writing might overtake and contain, but simultaneously reactivate, a negation that threatens to unmake the subject.

As we'll see, Sedgwick both describes and demonstrates her own remarkable command of this dialectic, which she (auto)theorizes explicitly as "sadomasochistic." Indeed, the "auto" of autotheory here might seem to rhyme literary self-mastery with erotic self-sufficiency, or auto-eroticism: to autotheorize would mean subjecting oneself to the kind of painful-pleasurable objectification that might otherwise depend upon the violent agency of another—spanking oneself, as it were. We would thus seem to be approaching yet another "version of masochism that does not require a sadist to achieve its effects," as Tim Dean writes of Leo Bersani's *The Freudian Body*.[1] The self-inflicted rigors of autotheory would afford an independence from the kind of unpredictable parental intervention that had inaugurated masochistic enjoyment, replicating this enjoyment in the writer's own ability to take herself critically in hand. This is not exactly the argument I want to make, however. While I'll take Preciado's work as an opportunity to consider the autotheorist's identification with sadistic mastery (and with Sade), I'll end up emphasizing the ways Preciado's work and especially Sedgwick's in fact rely upon, and perpetually reactivate, the potential devastations of an exteriority they cannot control or master. The masochism of this work plays out in autotheory's recurrent return to this unpredictable relation, pleasurably reiterating both the insufficiency and the precariousness of its "auto-."[2]

This erotic reliance upon a danger that comes from without brings us back to the terrain of chapter 1. In Gaitskill's "A Romantic Weekend," you'll recall, the sadist proves crucial to masochism—precisely because he negates its fantasy through behavior so bad it makes masochistic desire itself impossible to sustain. In Gaitskill's rendering, that is, masochism entails actively seeking out someone who will not only hurt you, but hurt you in the wrong way, their desire obeying a fantasmatic logic that is "incompatible" with your own. For Lauren Berlant, reading another Gaitskill text—in a chapter of *Cruel Optimism* that is also, like the chapter you're reading now, a reading of Sedgwick—the prospect of this kind of wrongness may always structure sexual encounter. In the passage that furnished my first chapter's epigraph, Berlant writes:

> Even though I wish to remain myself, I may want also to experience the discomposure of intimate relationality, yet want only the discomposure I can imagine, plus a little of the right kind extra, and how can I bear the risk of experiencing the anything that might be beyond? How can I bear

not seeking it? What's the relation between the contingency I'm used to, the kind I seek in relation, and the unbearable kind, since the pressures of proximity to the unbearable might be the motive for my attachment-seeking in the first place? These questions of the seeming and being of exposure and instability are central to the erotics of, the attachments and aversions to, the scene of sex in practice. Both confirming and interfering with patterns of self-intelligibility, sex's threat is objectively indistinguishable from its capacity to confirm. How do you know whether a change is the kind of change that involves a welcome loss of sovereignty?[3]

Berlant suggests, here, that the main appeal of sex in general—not just sex that is overtly perverse—might just *be* its offer to upset and unmake us; and not only in the ways that accord with our fantasies ("the discomposure I can imagine") but also "a little of the right kind extra," that is, in a way we could *not* have imagined or desired but that will somehow turn out to have been "right" nevertheless. Berlant is building on Bersani's famous proposal that "sexuality be thought of as a tautology for masochism," an argument that, as we saw, casts actual S&M as merely a "melodramatic" rendering of what is always going on in desire and pleasure anyway.[4] But even if the pursuit of disrupted fantasy is so broadly constitutive of sex that it cannot distinguish masochism as a particular kind of sexual disposition, there may yet be specifically masochistic ways of attending to the conundrum Berlant describes. That specificity might consist in a masochist's characteristic attempt to eliminate the optimistic assessment that the "little … extra," the disturbance whose qualitative dimensions she knows she cannot imagine, will be "right"; and to shift that *wrong* "extra" from the periphery of her fantasy to its center, as if to organize her erotic life around whatever might disorganize it. One way of doing this is through a version of the process we've described as masochistic elaboration: writing about, beholding, encompassing and reiterating the limit where desire becomes unpleasure, each time that limit reappears. Precisely because this elaboration always threatens to neutralize threat by encompassing it within the imagination, however, the masochist may continually find herself relying upon a sadistic other: someone whose own pleasure will be organized around causing her the pain she doesn't want, and who will thus keep renewing the threat of the unbearable. Of course, any particular sadist may get subsumed in an aestheticizing or fictionalizing (dramaturgical) process that tends toward a moment of autonomy for the masochist; but this does not mean that the sadist could always have been dispensed with, that they could have been anyone, or that the writer will not need a sadist again.

Autotheoretical writing may or may not feature sadistic figures. More crucially, the genre can work to assign a sadistic function to exteriority as such—invoking a sadistic reality that interposes itself violently against the writing subject. The world manifests a causality that is incommensurable with the writer's own desire, a vector of hurt that runs violently athwart the subject's own violent fantasies. The readings in this chapter will suggest that autotheory's masochistic desire is attached to its own heteronomy: even as it labors toward creating autonomous formal totalities, it feeds on the awareness that it is *also in the world*, a world that is shared and unpredictable, and (like the sadist who sometimes embodies this heteronomy) more than likely to fuck you up.

As will be equally evident, however, autotheoretical writing also offers the masochist a means of vaulting into a sadistic, formalizing perspective on the self, subjecting the self-as-material to the pitiless glare of universalizing abstractions (the "theory" part of autotheory) and the rigors of expository composition. Repeatedly enacting the particularized self's submission to abstraction, we might say that this masochistic movement executes an erotic restaging of the dynamic Michael Warner (in an essay dedicated to Berlant) theorizes as constituting modernity's "public subject" through the "normalizing [of] a public print discourse":

> In the bourgeois public sphere, which was brought into being by publication in this sense, a principle of negativity was axiomatic: the validity of what you say in public bears a negative relation to your person. What you say will carry force not because of who you are but despite who you are. Implicit in this principle is a utopian universality that would allow people to transcend the given realities of their bodies and their status. But the rhetorical strategy of personal abstraction is both the utopian moment of the public sphere and a major source of domination. For the ability to abstract oneself in public discussion has always been an unequally available resource.[5]

Warner's essay "The Mass Public and the Mass Subject" emphasizes two problems with the abstraction that produces the public subject as the modern subject of reason: first, that it necessarily and deceptively implies this subjectivity is available to anyone, whereas in fact it can only be fully accessed from within the "unmarked" identity of a white man, and never by individuals always already "marked" by race and/or gender; second, that even the "privileged subjects" of "self-abstraction" are required to negate their particular embodiment each time they access this subjectivity, producing an irreconcilable conflict between "positivity and self-abstraction" even for socially dominant subjects.[6] We might imagine autotheory as a genre that, by moving concertedly back and forth between the abstract and the particular in its approach to "public discussion," attempts to reconcile this conflict. In the following readings, however, autotheory will rather heighten the inevitable *failure* of any such sublimating resolution, seeking painful pleasure in critical discourse's "negative relation to your person" by pursuing a form that can continually summon both the personal and its negation. That the particular self ("your person") is, in autotheory, also always avowed as the one appropriating this negativity—the one doing the abstracting, the theorizing—means that any enjoyment thus produced is not only masochistic but also sadistic, as Warner's account of the public subject's "violently desirous" appetite for spectacular disaster similarly suggests.[7]

Autotheory thus enacts masochism as a dialectic: in one movement, the particular self is written in order to be overwritten by theoretical truth, with which the writer will also attempt (sadistically) to identify; in another movement, the writing self establishes itself and its work—including this work of self-abstraction—in perpetual relation to an outside that always has the power to hurt it worse than its own abstractions can. It might be tempting to call this dialectic "sadomasochistic"; and yet this term seems to me to elide the incommensurability that is fundamental to the second movement of desire here: the irreducible difference from masochistic fantasy that a violently contingent exteriority brings to bear. As Sedgwick's work in particular shows, the writerly resourcefulness of masochistic fantasy can be deployed not only to manage the precariousness of desire but also to exacerbate it, repeatedly invoking an excess beyond what the work can compose. While writing in any genre can enact this, I want to argue for the special aptness of the genre we now call autotheory for staging this perverse venture.

The term "autotheory," as Lauren Fournier explains,

> refers to the integration of theory and philosophy with autobiography, the body, and other so-called personal and explicitly subjective modes. It is a term that describes a self-conscious way of engaging with theory ... alongside lived experience and subjective embodiment, something very much in the *Zeitgeist* of cultural production today—especially in feminist, queer, and BIPOC ... spaces that live on the edges of art and academia.... [The term] autotheory points to modes of working that integrate the personal and the conceptual, the theoretical and the autobiographical, the creative and the critical, in ways attuned to interdisciplinary, feminist histories.[8]

As Fournier notes, Maggie Nelson's 2015 book *The Argonauts* often stands as a paradigmatic example of autotheory; the very prominence of this book, which opens with a joyous passage in which "you fuck me in the ass, my face smashed against the cement floor," is liable to make any announcement of autotheory's masochism patently unsurprising.[9] I won't focus on *The Argonauts* here, though I will be reading two earlier autotheoretical texts that belong to its literary-theoretical landscape: Sedgwick's "A Poem Is Being Written," itself one of the most important late-twentieth-century texts on masochism, and Preciado's *Testo Yonqui*. As Fournier reminds us, however, although autotheory's recognition as a "new" literary genre is often associated with this white queer work, the practice was already central to twentieth-century Black and Chicana feminist writing—including work by Audre Lorde, Gloria Anzaldúa, Cherríe Moraga, and others—as well as a range of other intermedial artistic experiments and a long history of other philosophical practice including, as Carolyn Laubender has pointed out, Freudian theory itself.[10]

The strategy of grounding theoretical work explicitly in the writer's "lived experience and subjective embodiment" has often emerged as a way to counter the erasures enacted by the putative neutrality of theoretical abstraction (erasures Warner's account of public subjectivity also emphasizes), and to articulate how unremarked norms of critical discourse, which have themselves emerged from particular, embodied positions—dominant ones—can be destructive in theorizing other subjects' realities. Thus one fundamental impulse to autotheory manifests as an act of claiming discursive space on behalf of a larger group to whom such space has traditionally been denied. By staking this claim in the first-person singular, writers can offer the facts of their own lives as empirical evidence for their arguments, while also avoiding the pitfalls of seeming to essentialize the position from which they speak. Making the politics of personal experience legible, these particular authorial selves can become flashpoints for solidarity, as Fournier suggests, and as earlier accounts of feminist writing also insisted.[11] Understood in this way, autotheory functions as a politicizing insistence on existing discursively, an assertion of the minoritarian writer's *I* in the face of a disciplinary consciousness whose dominant logic wants that *I*—as Kennedy puts it in *Funnyhouse of a Negro*—"not to be."

The prominence of autotheory in today's literary landscape, then, is if anything overdetermined; it doesn't seem to require further explanation, especially when we recognize its emergence as a vital technique of twentieth-century Black and Indigenous feminist critical practice, and acknowledge continuities between this practice and its emergence in subsequent queer white and nonwhite texts, as well as its continuation in twenty-first-century Black and Indigenous feminist works, such as Saidiya Hartman's crucial *Lose Your Mother*.[12] To speak an experience that has been systematically marginalized is a risky endeavor in all sorts of ways;

but it can also be politically lucid, socially progressive, and rational, a refusal to disappear that could in no sense be called perverse. In fact, both "A Poem Is Being Written" and *Testo Yonqui* use autotheory in politically strategic ways too. These white authors' assertions of self and claims to truth cannot have the same stakes as those of writers of color, whose power to represent philosophical truth has been more systematically refused; but both Sedgwick and Preciado—and, for that matter, Nelson—do speak from positions that they, at least, perceive as effectively occluded by dominant discourse: female anality and transgender identification (Sedgwick), transmasculinity and medical noncompliance (Preciado), queer pregnancy and queer motherhood (Nelson). Alongside these relatively wholesome representational aims, however, Sedgwick and Preciado also manage to suggest that autotheoretical writing—the explicit introduction of the particular, embodied authorial subject into the field of their own theorizing—may always harbor a perverse affordance in addition to the progressive one.

Indeed, Sedgwick argued explicitly for the cultivation of modes of writing whose political affordances would be inseparable from their erotic ones. In "Queer and Now," the opening essay of her 1993 collection *Tendencies*, she discusses her sense of the need, in a murderously homophobic culture systematically neglecting "the AIDS emergency," for readers and writers to make nonnormative forms of desire appear.[13] Part of this task, she subsequently notes, is to reopen the question of "what *critical* writing can effect (promising? smuggling?); anything that offers to make this genre more acute and experimental, less numb to itself, is a welcome prospect."[14] The autotheoretical and openly autoerotic experiment of "A Poem Is Being Written" seems to me one of the most striking examples, in *Tendencies* or almost anywhere, of the critical practice of theorizing deviant sex in a way that also imbues that theorizing with "pleasure ... not only taken but openly displayed."[15] For Sedgwick, in other words, the contagious performance of perverse enjoyment—eroticizing the site where critical-theoretical and personal "tendencies" cross—can sometimes not only lubricate but *be* a text's politics; this would be another way to think about autotheory's multiple reasons for being.

In terms especially resonant for my own approach, Berlant writes that for Sedgwick, "any writer's task ... would be to track desire's itinerary, not on behalf of confirming its hidden or suppressed Truths or Harms but to *elaborate* its variety of attachments as sexuality, as lived life, and, most importantly, as an unfinished history that confounds the hurts and the pleasures."[16] The suggestion that the kind of elaboration performed by such writing might be a system for keeping hurt intermingled with pleasure, and that there are high stakes for ensuring that the performance itself remain "unfinished," is an insight upon which this chapter will try to elaborate.

Testo Yonqui and Demonstrative Sadism

If autotheory has come to seem strangely contagious—if reading it has made an embarrassing number of us try to write it—this is no doubt because, perhaps more overtly than any other genre, it conveys an erotics not only of writing but of living as a writer: it registers the charged periodicity of disappearing into, and reemerging from, the content of one's work. Perhaps all writing testifies to this process in some way, but autotheory tends to present it with a focus and clarity verging on that of the how-to. It is both a theory and a story of its own writing, whatever else it is about. Its name, after all, harbors a semantic ambiguity: "auto-" might refer to the self, the person of the writer (as in "autobiography"), but it might also work like a reflexive pronoun to name theory theorizing itself (as in "automobile"). This ambiguity is resolved, and autotheory emerges as a coherent concept, where the two meanings intersect: autotheory is theory about the theory itself, the work itself, *as* produced by the self who makes it, while it is about that self *as*—most fundamentally—the writer of that work.

This means that a work of autotheory has to account for its own emergence, and it often does so by looking back toward other times, scenes we understand as moments of its germination. These narrative returns are always defamiliarized: because of the ongoing movement between self-revelation and the production of theoretical meaning, when the writer conveys us to a moment from their childhood, say, we know not only that we will be whisked away again soon, but that the memory is being made to mean something specific in the perspective of the theoretical project. This need not feel instrumentalizing; indeed, rather than dissolving the sensory qualities of the recollection by prompting us to boil it down to meaning, our awareness of the project's theoretical commitment tends to heighten our sensitivity to qualitative detail in its capacity to resist synopsis. The abstracting drive of theory makes us *more* aware that we are visiting an irreducibly particular moment, and we perceive the poetic effort that has brought us there. If the content of such scenes exposes the author-as-person, that is, their relation to the theoretical text exposes the compositional project of the author-as-writer. And where such scenes convey us to an earlier time in the writer's past, they thereby assert authorship as a diachronic pursuit; they construct the writer as one who records what befalls them so that later they can make sense of it, theorize it, *hold* it in a composition, even if—and here Hartman's *Lose Your Mother* is exemplary—it is to be held there as a painful aporia.

Autotheory is thus *demonstrative* in both senses of the word: "tending to show feelings, especially of affection, openly" and "serving as conclusive evidence of something; giving proof."[17] The first of these definitions speaks to autotheory's confessional, affective dimension; the second to its propositional claim, which marks it *as* "-theory," a discourse that can be evaluated in terms of its philosophical truth. You might assume that the genre's postmodern bent implies a renunciation of such distinctions, but before you've even started reading *Testo Yonqui*, the Espasa edition confronts you with jacket flaps that couch the book in no uncertain terms as a work of serious philosophy: the author photograph shows a bespectacled Preciado apparently giving a lecture, and the bio presents his impressive academic pedigree after stating definitively that he "is a philosopher."[18] And while Preciado quickly acknowledges that the work is "a fiction," he also emphasizes its status as a "corporeal experiment" or "protocol," an emphasis that—among its other discursive effects—locates the book's significance in an objective, *wissenschaftlich* realm.[19]

The "serving as conclusive evidence" sense of "demonstrative"—the one that corresponds to philosophy, not sentimentality—is the one Deleuze invokes when he uses the word *démonstrative* to characterize language in the writing of Sade.[20] As is often the case in "Coldness and Cruelty," Deleuze develops this characterization both to establish a common ground between sadism and masochism and to stage, on that ground, their diametrical opposition. Thus while sadistic language and masochistic language both exhibit a "transcendence of the imperative and the descriptive"—that is, of the pornographic—"toward a higher function," which in both cases we might call the theoretical, Deleuze also rigorously distinguishes between their respective ways of doing so.[21] Whereas masochistic language attempts to affect its recipient through "persuasion and education," he writes, "nothing is in fact more alien to the sadist" than this wish: when the Sadean libertine holds forth in philosophical speeches, it is in order "to demonstrate that reasoning itself is a form of violence, and that he is on the side of violence.... He is not even attempting to prove anything to anyone, but to perform a demonstration related essentially to the solitude and omnipotence of its author."[22] We might point out, however, that the rift cannot be as absolute as Deleuze claims: the Sadean demonstration of "solitude and omnipotence," what we might call its passion for nonrelation, can itself be powerfully persuasive—that is, seductive—even if persuasion (which Deleuze associates with masochism) is never sadism's avowed intent. We may rarely see rhetorical persuasion operating as such between the characters of Sade's texts, since his libertines prefer coercion to consent; but it would be hard to deny that Sade's language operates as a potentially seductive exchange between writer and reader. In that exchange, Sade's writing offers itself not only as a model for sexual fantasy but as a literary model. This version of the Sadean text's "demonstrative function" would inhere in the text's offer to instruct us, not how to fuck or what to think (which, for Deleuze, would be the purview of masochistic pedagogy) but how to *be* a writer, how to enact one's sexual subjectivity in writing.[23]

Preciado takes up this offer in *Testo Yonqui*, one of the first works to conceive itself explicitly as *una autoteoría*; Nelson has remarked that she "flat out stole" the term from Preciado, a confession that locates *Testo Yonqui* at the origin of the genre's recent institutionalization as such.[24] I want to suggest that if *Testo Yonqui* marks a moment at which autotheory needs to name itself as a distinct genre—even though, as noted, the genre's roots are much more complicated—this impetus comes about at least in part through Preciado's untimely and processual identification with Sade: a certain sadism thus catalyzes the book's, and the genre's, self-conscious project of self-inscription.

By Preciado's "identification with Sade" I'm referring to explicit as well as structural elements of the 2008 text. Explicit: in the last chapter, Preciado recalls a conversation with the late writer Guillaume Dustan in which Dustan tells Preciado that he masturbated while reading Preciado's first book. "Me dices: 'Hueles bien. Tu libro es lo mejor que he leído in filosofía después de Sade,' me dices ... Me dices que este tipo de inteligencia te la pone dura." (You tell me, "You smell good. Your book is the best philosophy book that I've read since Sade." You tell me that this kind of intelligence makes you hard.)[25] Dustan is the addressee of *Testo Yonqui*, the "you" whose death begins the book and who returns to haunt its autobiographical sections throughout. "Tú eres el único que podría leer este libro" (You're the only one who could read this book), Preciado writes.[26] On the day he learns of Dustan's death, Preciado videotapes himself applying testosterone gel, shaving himself, and fucking himself with dildos; addressing Dustan, he says to the camera: "Esta testosterona es para ti, este placer es para ti" (This testosterone is for you, this pleasure is for you).[27] Both the book itself (*"este libro"*) and the process it documents (*"Esta testosterona"*) are thus dedicated to the one person who has been able to recognize Preciado explicitly as Sade's analog; if Dustan is Preciado's only possible reader, the text suggests that this is because he is the one who has found the Sade in Preciado. This recognition identifies and enacts the proper response to Preciado's Sadean poetics of demonstration, registering its sexualization of the theoretical by getting hard in response to its intelligence.[28]

Structural: "getting hard" could also name what both the Sadean text and *Testo Yonqui* perform at the level of composition, in that *Testo Yonqui* alternates between sexy narrative and philosophical treatise in much the way Sade's novels do. A reader of *Testo Yonqui* might find herself tempted to skip over the "hard" parts exactly as she might in reading Sade; and also as in Sade, a tautological bent to the theory sections underscores the rhetorical nature of their demonstration. I don't mean that Preciado isn't serious about, or doesn't really mean, his theoretical claims in *Testo Yonqui*, but that their import in the text is heavily weighted toward what they might be able to do to readers, writers, and thinkers. "A esto se reduce hoy la filosofía del siglo XXI, a un gigantesco y goteante Butt plug. Frente a este estado de cosas, la filosofía de esta alta modernidad punk solo puede ser autoteoría, experimentación de sí, autopenetración, pornología." (The philosophy of the pharmacopornographic regime has been reduced to an enormous, dripping butt-plug camera. In such circumstances, the philosophy of such high-punk modernity can only be autotheory, autoexperimentation, auto-techno-penetration, pornology.)[29] Throughout the book, Preciado's theorization of contemporary society as *el capitalismo farmacopornográfico* seems fundamentally to operate by eroticizing an account of global capitalism that—as his network of citations suggests—will already be largely familiar to most of his readers; his main intervention is to insist on the crucial role of corporeal pleasure throughout this system.[30] A reader's uptake of, or susceptibility to, this argumentation will thus depend at least in part on whether this claim of pleasure's importance is itself seductive to her as she reads, that is, on whether Preciado can make her feel it. Addressing his readers (as *vosotros* rather than, as when he addresses Dustan, *tú*) Preciado writes: "aspiro a convenceros de que vosotros sois en realidad como yo" (My ambition is to convince you that you are like me).[31] The universalizing drive of this aspiration echoes Sade's attempt to prove that sexual cruelty is everywhere, in everyone, including you, even if Sade never acknowledges his universalism as aspirational.

I think *Testo Yonqui*'s Sadeanism indexes the text's attempt to open itself to what Deleuze calls sadistic negation. Preciado articulates this intention in the book's opening salvo: "No me interesan aquí mis sentimientos, en tanto que míos.... No me interesa lo que de individual hay en ellos. Sino cómo son atravesados por lo que no es mío." (I'm not interested in my emotions insomuch as their being mine, belonging only, uniquely, to me. I'm not interested in their individual aspects, only in how they are traversed by what isn't mine.)[32] The translator Bruce Benderson renders *atravesado* as "traversed," a term familiar to English-language readers of French theory; other possible translations might be "crossed," "broken through," or "pierced." The phrase figures autotheory as a desire to position the self and its feelings as objects of violation, if not actually to violate them—though the double penetration Preciado performs upon himself on video in the subsequent pages makes the image of literal self-violation hard to shake. The "hard parts" reiterate this traversedness at the level of the book's theoretical claims, arguing repeatedly that subjects are produced and manipulated by capitalist systems of corporeality that act upon us from within.[33] Presumably, Preciado makes this argument not only because this vision "interests" him, but because it is (I think most of his readers would agree) pretty clearly true. But the confessional and explicitly erotic moments that frame these theoretical claims, including Preciado's espousal here of "interest" in whatever can break through his own feelings, prepare us to experience the theory sections not only as *claiming* that what we feel is always already "traversed" by systems that are "not ours" but also as *enacting* the prurient interest of a subject who wants to feel the negation whereby this always-already breaks through what they might otherwise innocently consider their own experience; who wants, as it were, to undergo theoretical abstraction *as* a violence that will relocate "my" desire to a structural zone—call it "pharmacopornographic capitalism"—in which, much like Warner's public subjectivity, it no longer seems to be anyone's in particular, and thus no longer seems to be mine.

Testo Yonqui demonstrates that the manifest presence of an authorial self in the theoretical text can be wrested into a passive function: the text stages the writer's body, his particular adventures in pleasure and pain, in order then to enact the theoretical leap that betrays this embodiment by opening a perspective that—all the more so because, like Sade's philosophy, this perspective *comprehends* embodiment, pain and pleasure—makes itself imaginatively independent of that particular body, which it relativizes as an effect of the system to which it now lays epistemic claim. This movement should remind us of the way dramaturgical masochism withdraws from its own performance to seek "sadistic form"—except that in autotheory, this *negation* of the self is always also reclaimed as the *performance* of the self, which constitutes that self as author. Were we to swap in the gendered terms Freud applies to these two poles, we would have to say that the girl masochist ("I'm not there") is reconstituted in autotheory *as* a boy masochist ("here I am!"), and vice-versa. As we've seen, however, the possibility of such dialectical reversal was fundamental to the Freudian girl's gendering from the start: like the pretransition Preciado of *Testo Yonqui* who still uses assigned pronouns and name, Freud's masochistic girl keeps "her" femininity in play only as a basis for negation, for disidentification, for non-self-coincidence. "La subjetividad política emerge precisamente cuando el cuerpo/la subjetividad no se reconoce en el espejo.... Es fundamental no reconocerse." (Political subjectivity emerges precisely when the subject does not recognize itself in its representation. It is fundamental not to recognize oneself.)[34] If this "no" to the self produces what Preciado calls "political subjectivity," then the political here is also another name for the authorial, the project of imaginative and intellectual re-form that occurs in, and maintains, the space of this negation. The event of this *no reconocerse*, furthermore, takes place not only *within* the origin scene Preciado describes but also in the way Preciado constitutes the scene itself. In the formulation I just quoted, that is, Preciado produces a generalization at the site of what is in fact a quite specifically embodied trans experience; by way of this abstraction, he theorizes a condition of alienation-as-political-consciousness that could presumably arise for *any* "body/subjectivity," not just a transmasculine one. He is, we might say, refusing to recognize *himself* as the particular subject of the scene, either in the mirror or in front of it: "No me interesa lo que de individual hay."

This refusal might well be an instance of what the critic Grace Lavery has named "egg theory." For Lavery, egg theory is a mode of queer theory that uses abstraction and generalization to make the recognition of actual, concrete gender transition appear impossible. "Egg" is a term for the protototrans subject (Lavery begins her essay with a reference to her younger self "in boy drag") who has yet to recognize the real prospect of transition. As Lavery explains with exquisite irony, egg theory's prohibition against transition

is not generally ethical, but technical. One simply cannot. Which among us, given the chance, would not? But of course it is not so simple; indeed, the categories at issue are endlessly complicated, existing on different ontological orders (sex and gender, for example), and battened by chaotic forces so powerful and incoherent (desire, say, or sexuality, or "socialization") that to attempt something like a sex change would not so much be malicious as it would be gauche.

The second step of egg theory is its abstraction, via a curious and ambivalent universalism, into a set of general observations about a system in which the desire is found aerosolized into a fine spray. Here is egg theory at its purest, a medium of thought form and desire, a desire with no object and with, perhaps, not even a subject to speak of; here, at last, is the compensatory hallucination of a system of delight and foreclosure. We may have different names for this system—we may call it "affect," we may call it "queer," we may call it "aesthetic"; there are plenty of other names—all that is required is its ontology be both virtual and plastic.[35]

Preciado is not mentioned in the article, whose primary object of critique is, as it happens, Sedgwick. Sedgwick wrote several times about her own gay male identification, but Lavery points out that this identification always "remains psychic or notional" for Sedgwick; its problematic implication is that critically minded queers shouldn't take gender identifications too literally, which in turn bolsters "the voice that harasses trans people for the force of our identifications in the name and voice of queer theory."[36] In *Testo Yonqui*, Preciado explicitly rejects the diagnosis of "gender dysphoria," and mostly conceives his recourse to masculinizing technologies, including testosterone and drag workshops, as "experiments" in political resistance rather than as expressions of his real gender identity.[37] The book would seem to be an obvious example of the kind of theory Lavery is critiquing; indeed, the claim for *Testo Yonqui*'s "egg" status might be strengthened by Preciado's subsequent real-life transition.

In the egg-theoretical perspective that Lavery is characterizing, the trans subject—the one who does actually "attempt something like a sex change"—looks "gauche," both self-indulgent and haplessly literal. Watching the trans subject *claim* their gender identification *as real*, the egg theorist is seized by an envy that is also a judgment of that other subject as impossibly misguided: "Which among us, given the chance, would not?"—as if the trans subject had made a category mistake, like a child crying out to characters on TV. Here the egg theorist supposes—in effect, insists—that the trans subject has simply failed to grasp gender's impersonality, an impersonality which, once grasped, should make it impossible to take gender so personally: gender is a cultural code to which we more or less conform; if I find I can't recognize myself in the gender assigned me, what I have come up against is the universally alienating nature of the gender system, not a deep-seated truth of my individual nature. Against this complacent common sense, Lavery has elsewhere argued for a "*trans realism* ... responsive to the ontologies of trans life"; refusing to "reduce such ontologies to intellectual or aesthetic patterns," Lavery grounds these ontologies in the trans subject's "overwhelming feeling that one's body is not sexed adequately and that one's claim on the world depends on a self-shattering acknowledgment of that fact," and notes that "the method by which [this fact] is accessed is not experimentation but submission, not appropriation but surrender."[38] In the face of this determining and shatteringly experienced reality, egg theory's insistence that gender be regarded as an abstract system rather than as an individual truth disavows the particular, brutal intensity of force that the identification with a gender exerts on some subjects, psychically and corporeally.

What I want to suggest here is merely that the egg theorist's impulse to universalize trans desire and thereby erase the particular needs of trans people—which is also to say, that theorist's impulse to universalize *their own* trans desire into something that could really only be addressed at the level of entire systems, thereby disavowing the particularity of their own drive to undergo a more than "notional" sexual reassignment themself—might be something else besides an attempt to protect themself against a "self-shattering acknowledgment" of their own inadequate sexuation. It might be that at least some of these theorizing subjects (call them masochists) have attached the possibility of survival to a different mode of self-shattering acknowledgment, in which what is acknowledged—what one submits to—is an overwhelming sense of the body as wrong *just because it is this particular body*, a sense of a wrongness that might later resolve into the wrongness of one's assigned sex but also might not. Until such resolution takes place, abstraction may furnish the only perspective in which the acknowledgment of wrongness is possible, since abstraction is what affords a subjective position not subsumed by the unbearableness of being embodied. By claiming the perspective of abstraction, I can fantasize the total negation of the body I hate being, and thereby access both pleasure and a way of living on. For such subjects, abstraction is also a mode—perhaps *the* mode—of enjoying having a body.

To voice one's desire by choosing the negative universalizing formulation "which among us … would not?" over the formulation "I would" or "I will" (or "I will not"), then, might itself express the urgency of an identification with abstraction, through which I might survive the recognition that my body—my genitals, ass, mouth, feet, belly, nose, hair, skin, larynx, breath, blood, what Warner calls "the humiliating positivity of the particular"—is so inherently foul that it will never otherwise be a site of pleasure.[39] Renouncing this body's claims by subsuming them into a universalization may function socially as bullying self-aggrandizement, but psychically it may also entail a longing to shatter the self, to make what I feel count for nothing. Giving into this longing, I try to forestall *any* reconsolidation of my self as a real subject with a "claim on the world," whether or not I sense that I must thereby renounce trans realism's different shattering.

This kind of sexualized recourse to abstraction bears an obvious resemblance, again, to structures we have described both as "dramaturgical masochism" and as the accession to "sadistic form." By these lights, the cruel negation that founds the generality of theory appears as a textual act of yielding to jouissance.[40] But if—for *some* among us—such performative self-cancellations in and as the writing of theory have become erotically indispensable, how can we pursue them without dragging other subjects—specifically, in this instance, the real, particular subjects of trans realism—into the gears of this negation?

This is where, it seems to me, *Testo Yonqui*'s autotheoretical return to Sade—its development of autotheory as, specifically, Sadean—might be useful. When the attempt to articulate "a desire … with, perhaps, not even a subject to speak of" (Lavery) occurs within autotheory, it shows up more clearly as a libidinal project of self-cancelling enunciation. In this way, universalizing abstraction stands revealed as a discourse that speaks, for pleasure, for no one, and hence as a discourse that cannot be taken to override the realism of any subject's claim. Sade's erotic investment in universalization returns, in Preciado's autotheory, as the insight that by universalizing gender trouble, a theorist may be desirously inviting philosophical truth to shatter the theorist's own particularity above all.

Lavery's "Which among us … would not?" finds its mirroring reversal in Preciado's "aspiro a convenceros de que vosotros sois en realidad como yo," but it would work even better as a tag line for Sade—whose books, as we noted, insist that their heroes' sexual cruelty are *what everyone, everywhere, ever would like to do*. In Sade's fantasy, anyone who accesses personal power will immediately use it to torture and rape: who among us would not? To state the obvious, I don't think we can really believe this assertion, or even believe that we are meant to believe it. (It's true that some philosophical and psychoanalytic positions one might find compelling can look like versions of Sade's claim—for example, Freud's suggestion in *Beyond the Pleasure Principle* that aggression is the origin of any interpersonal sexuality.[41] But these theories allow for violence to abide in an unconscious, which Sade's does not permit.) We don't need to believe these universalizations; instead, we are asked to see how good they can feel. Sade thus stages an experience of abstractive theory as pornography that can help some of us come without ever supposing or demanding anyone's agreement, or chastening anyone's exception, to the "general observations" (Lavery) it enounces.

What this theory invites us to enjoy, I think, is the sexualized abandon offered in structural claims, even as it remains evident that no one's reality is being adequately represented by them. When Sade writes, for example, that "A child breaks its rattle, bites its wet nurse's nipple, and strangles its pet bird, long before it reaches the age of reason," he is producing universality *as* irresponsibility *as* pleasure.[42] No wonder "a child" is being beaten! The putative neutrality of that indefinite noun, its ability to stand in for *anyone*, is false on its face: not only because there must be children who would not do these things but because, as Sade and his reader know, most children have neither a pet bird nor a wet nurse. The fact of class difference invoked by these terms necessarily evacuates the universal cruel subject whose universality is precisely what Sade appears to be arguing. The point is not that Sade is qualifying the objectivity of his own argument by explicitly avowing his positional perspective, as we are often reminded to do today. Rather he *demonstrates* the pleasure that can be taken in a claim to total objectivity whose spuriousness he does not bother to conceal, and collocates that claim precisely with the pleasure of cruelty. (In a similar way, Warner suggests that the filmmaker John Waters's avowed delight in anonymized scenes of mass disaster constitutes a "delirious perverseness in spelling out [the] link" between sexual enjoyment, violence, and bourgeois disembodiment, which in turn "helps him to violate" the very logic of abstraction *by* openly enjoying it.[43])

Between Sade's "a child" and Freud's, we can read a continuous sadistic project of negating the personal origin of ideation, letting abstraction take confession's place. Here abstraction *is* the enjoyment toward which desire impels the theorizing subject, the hardness on which the subject shatters. So I want to ask: precisely because Sade's way of doing philosophy makes the irresponsibility of its own universalizing gesture so flagrant, might it offer a model for a responsible deployment of egg theory—a way of continuing to submit the ontologies of sexed being to the abstraction and generalization that alone make sexual life bearable for some of us, without actually harming those who are more powerfully driven to inhabit those ontologies? Could we be more frank about the sadism, the turn-on, of our own impulse to install structures and systems of negation in the place of real, particular, livable possibilities? Could we avow the prurience of the move to produce, in their place, lives that are no one's?

Preciado's announced intention to write his own feelings only as "atravesados por lo que no es mío" speaks, I've suggested, to the masochistic resonance of this sadism; it flags the way autotheory offers to wreak this aggression directly upon the writing self, laying the self down in the path of structure, as it were. Indeed, in saying that what I feel isn't what's important here, this autotheoretical mode may be producing the only kind of self some writing subjects can bear to have at all. Recall Gaitskill's Beth, imagining that her lover "would crush her like an insect, and then they would talk about life and art": the crushing (shattering) and the talking are sequenced as two separate events in Beth's fantasy, but their ironic juxtaposition expresses a longing for abstract theoretical discourse ("talk about life and art"—or, as Gaitskill has it later in the story, "about anything") *as* the horizon of the self's obliteration: the dissolve into theory is the province of the crushed subject; Beth's ideal submission to violence would be both of these things at once. Autotheory like Preciado's can similarly position abstract intellection as something that violently befalls the subject, summoning the confessional, particular *yo* of the auto- so that we can see and feel it getting overrun by a discourse of systems.

Since in autotheory the personal "self" *is also* the writer who is deploying abstract discourse, however, it might seem obvious that the masochistic submission to abstraction is always immediately recouped as sadistic domination via the abstract mode, producing a closed system of erotic self-sufficiency.[44] As I wrote at the start of this chapter, I want to suggest something else, which is here indicated by the way Preciado's "you"—his *tú*, not his *vosotros*—places his autotheoretical text in the world. In *Testo Yonqui*, we've noted, Guillaume Dustan is both the addressee and the figure who embodies Preciado's link to Sade: the dead friend who had, as it were, conferred sadism upon Preciado. Dustan is also the figure in the book who enrages Preciado by misgendering him as a "lesbian."[45] In this respect, we might imagine that Preciado's literary absorption of Sade compensates for a masculinity whose realization is being violently withheld: withheld first by Dustan, and then by Dustan's death (which makes his refusal irreversible), as well as by Preciado's own deferral of definitive transition. But the "you" undercuts this compensatory mechanism: by addressing itself *to* Dustan, and thus insistently positioning him outside the text, *Testo Yonqui* emphasizes its own failure completely to absorb the masculinity associated with him. This is mourning, not melancholy, and the lost object remains outside the self. This means that while Preciado identifies with, and reperforms, the sadism Dustan had identified in him, this sadism also always has a referent *outside* what might otherwise seem to be the text's autonomous sexual dialectic of confessional bottom and theorizing top. Preciado's masochistic invocation of Dustan—"este placer as para ti"—thus places at the heart of autotheory a relation to a cruelty, an exteriority, that cannot be assimilated to the writing self.

So literal an address to the cruel and cruelly dead is of course not obligatory for autotheoretical writing, although I'll suggest below that something like this appears between the lines of Sedgwick's essay too. But Preciado's address to Dustan at the beginning of *Testo Yonqui* also functions to establish a broader logic of exterior reference that *does* seem characteristic of autotheory as a genre, a practice of writing about real-life persons, places, events, and texts, including of course the "real" author himself. (My sense of the importance of this referentiality is why I've resisted the option of treating Preciado the author and Preciado "the character" as two different figures here.[46]) As readers, we understand Preciado to be recounting things that really happened to him, and we take the book's characters to be real people, whether or not we had known of them before. The text thus seems to intend a process of reading that moves back and forth between the book and the world outside it, an intention flagged by its partial naming of the people it cathects. For instance, although I've identified the book's addressee as "the late writer Guillaume Dustan," in *Testo Yonqui* his name only appears in bibliographical footnotes, one of which follows a quotation and the phrase "decías tú."[47] In another generic context, I might understand this as a moment of found text collaged into the mouth of a fictional character, but knowing the kind of book this is means confidently following the footnote into the real. By the same token, a few seconds of googling make it clear that the "V. D." who becomes Preciado's romantic partner in the book is in fact the glamorous French writer and filmmaker Virginie Despentes. Obviously, this kind of lite research might attend any allusive text; but here the explicitly sexual relation to "you" and to "V. D." eroticizes the extratextual circuit, as if I'm looking outside the text to get a better view of its sex scenes.[48]

The more conventional scholarly references grounding *Testo Yonqui* as serious philosophy seem to have provided an infrastructure that is also being used to convey the reader to another kind of referent: a sexually electric scene of authors living in excess of their texts. What we find in photos and interviews are the traces of this excess, but click as we might, we won't access the source this way: not because Paul and Virginie aren't really out there somewhere but because they *are*. "Una ficción, es cierto."[49] And yet it's by marking itself as *non*fiction that autotheory prevents its masochistic submission *to* abstraction from ever being fully contained, mastered, managed through a sadistic identification *with* the theoretical. If theory is the "hardness" on which the confessional subject can shatter itself, then reality—a referent inaugurated by the text but not contained by it—is the negation of that negation, a field of materiality whose quantity, contingency, and temporality will always threaten to top the theorist and topple their textual self-mastery. To see this autotheoretical dynamic in action, we can turn to Sedgwick's essay, in which a theatrical display of intellectual domination serves to maximize the disruptive force of the real, precisely by seeming to manage it.

"With That Abstraction I Learned to Identify": Sedgwick's Trajectories

No one has staged the masochistic enticements of writing more beautifully than Eve Sedgwick. In her 1987 essay "A Poem Is Being Written" she says the following about her childhood desire to be a poet:

> the lyric poem was both the spanked body, my own body or another one like it for me to watch or punish, and at the same time the very spanking, the rhythmic hand whether hard or subtle of authority itself. What child wouldn't be ravenous for dominion in this place? Among the powers to be won was the power to brazen, to conceal, to savage, to adorn, or to abstract the body of one's own humiliation; or perhaps most wonderful,

to *identify with* it, creating with painful love and care, but in a temporality miraculously compressed by the elegancies of language, the distance across which this body in punishment could be endowed with an aura of meaning and attraction—across which, in short, the *compelled* body could be *chosen*.[50]

As the essay's title makes clear, Sedgwick's confessional description of her own early (and abiding) fantasy of writing-as-spanking is also, at the same time and less explicitly, a reading of Freud's "A Child Is Being Beaten." The description above is thus, we might say, classically overdetermined, shaped at once by personal memory—the memory of wanting and beginning to write poems, the memory of being spanked and of ruminating on being spanked—and by Freud's template, which corresponds too closely to what Sedgwick describes here not to be considered another of the passage's primal scenes.

To cite "A Child Is Being Beaten" is to invoke the enormous theoretical discourse on masochism and fantasy that has followed from Freud's article. And yet Sedgwick does not engage that discourse at all in her essay, merely acknowledging it on the first page by noting that her own essay's title "obviously means to associate the shifty passive voice of a famous title of Freud's, 'A Child Is Being Beaten,' with the general question of poetry."[51] The brevity of Sedgwick's reference to Freud and to the critical discourse that has made his title "famous" (and her reference "obvious") deserves note, particularly in light of the proximity to Freud avowed by her essay's title.[52] Taken together, these point to a certain ambivalence about masochism running throughout the essay, an ambivalence that manifests in an inconsistency between the way Sedgwick tends to characterize masochism in the essay, and the masochistic performance of the essay itself.

"A Poem Is Being Written" conducts an exquisitely thoughtful exploration of Sedgwick's own masochism in relation to her writing—an exploration that forms, I imagine obviously, something of an aspirational horizon for the book you're reading now. Yet amid her elucidation of masochism's complexities, Sedgwick repeatedly associates both the concept and the phenomenon of masochism with *simplification*, a move that sometimes seems tinged with condescension or even impatience. One way of explaining this impatience might be found in Sedgwick's attitude toward psychoanalytic criticism more broadly. Elsewhere in *Tendencies*, the 1993 collection in which "A Poem" is republished, she remarks that psychoanalysis's "transformational grammar for translating every organ, every behavior, every role and desire into a calculus of phallic presence or absence ... not only facilitates but virtually compels an irreducible theoretical elegance in its argumentative structure."[53] This "elegance"—which echoes in the "elegancies of language" Sedgwick associates with masochistic poetics in the long passage quoted above—is a distinctly backhanded compliment. As is well known, Sedgwick's own critical sensibility unceasingly favors complexity, asymmetry, and plurality, as in her famous proposal—also in *Tendencies*—that "queer" might refer to "the open mesh of possibilities, gaps, overlaps, dissonances and resonances, lapses and excesses of meaning when the constituent elements of anyone's gender, of anyone's sexuality aren't made (or *can't* be made) to signify monolithically."[54]

In "A Poem Is Being Written," this commitment to multiplicity informs Sedgwick's concern that a conceptual reliance on terms like "masochism" will tend to make things look too simple—and further, that masochistic sexuality itself *is* a reductive relation to the sexual field. Thus when Sedgwick introduces the narrative poem, written by her younger self, which will become the essay's main critical object, she writes: "Let me ... jump ahead here for a moment along the simplest of the trajectories to hand, the directly sadomasochistic one whose perversion lies in its exact, its *retardataire* simplicity."[55] At the end of this section ("Spanking and Poetry") she announces her intention to "retreat from that simplified trajectory," and at the start of the next section, "Fundamental Misrecognitions," she begins what she calls "the second part of my story, a more tortuously inclusive trajectory" which "cannot be read as directly as the first."[56] This second trajectory, marked off as counter to the initial, masochistic one, is where Sedgwick discovers anality, which she then presents as the destabilizing underside of the first section's masochistic spanking scenario: anality is the complexifying addendum that masochism and its analytic would both prefer to exclude.

I understand Sedgwick's use of the word "trajectory" here to mean both a thread within her personal development as a sexual subject, and an interpretive story she can tell about that development now as a theorist. If these two meanings seem to be collapsed in her references to the "simplified trajectory" of "sadomasochism," this may be because one effect of masochism's simplification—its ability "to abstract the body," as she writes in the long passage I quoted above—is that it performs *in* fantasy the very thing that theoretical interpretation is supposed to do *with* fantasy, rendering the latter task oddly redundant: masochism, already abstracting the body into a kind of distanced representation, may leave too little for theorization to do. The "sadomasochism" Sedgwick describes is always already theoretical, a process of self-objectification through which desire is able to see itself and thus remove itself from its own immediate instantiation, "creating ... the distance across which this body in punishment could be endowed with an aura of meaning." Writing the theory of this masochism, then, threatens to be a kind of gratuitous reiteration—as if in doing so, we might have gotten stuck just repeating the child's own fantasmatic move.

In order to push past masochistic "elegancies" toward true critical complexity, the essay has to discover a *different* sexual logic: thus we shift from the "simplified trajectory" of masochism to the "more tortuously inclusive" one of anality. This difference is scaffolded by two aesthetic polarities. The first is the generic opposition lyric/narrative: in adolescence, we learn, Sedgwick's writing underwent a shift from lyric to narrative poetry, a "generic leap from the tightly framed tableau of parental punishment to the social and institutional framing as narrative of exactly the same scene."[57] Sedgwick's identification of lyric with the "tableau" points to the second polarity, flatness/depth: where the scene of spanking is initially, in childhood and in the essay's first section, organized by the tableau's pseudoplanar frontality, that scene subsequently undergoes what might be described as a kind of thickening, a surge of three-dimensionality that disrupts the first section's planar framing. "Fundamental" is, of course, a joking reference to the ass, which will now become the essay's theoretical focus; but the word also emphasizes that this turn to corporeal specificity engages something *deeper* than masochism: something to write about that is not so evident on the discursive surface of things, and whose profundity is at once that of the full body, and that of systems—specifically the sex/gender system—that structure the subject at a deeper-than-phenomenal ("social and institutional") level. The elucidation of this something-deeper, we might well infer, will be the essay's profound contribution, a wresting-into-discourse of what masochism by itself would exclude: the fleshy obtrusion of the female ass, a dumb corporeal referent that, precisely unlike the always-already-figural child-body of masochism, actively disrupts the "aura of meaning" that masochistic fantasy, lyrically constrained and visually flat, would childishly reelaborate.

It is of course not lost on Sedgwick that the masochistic scene of spanking *is already* a mode of anal sex. If the signature move of masochistic fantasy is "creating ... the distance" across which "the *compelled* body could be *chosen,*" this imaginative self-distancing might also be glossed as the endeavor to get behind your own ass, to attain a perspective from which you could finally *determine* that ass's otherwise "terrifying involuntarity of meaning."[58] In this respect, it's not initially clear why "the sadomasochistic trajectory" should be conceived as eliding or evading the specificity of the ass, rather than as, say, magnetized by it. But even to speak of "the ass" as such, Sedgwick goes on to argue, is to abstract it away from predicates that make all the difference as to how an ass can function imaginatively, predicates that she glancingly acknowledges (more on this below) would include those of race but that in her analysis come down to a "*gen-*

der dimorphism of discourse [that] is almost un-thinkably extreme."⁵⁹ Whereas anal eroticism in men is "representationally central" to homosexuality and is therefore "not only an important and meaningful theme in Judaeo-Christian culture but arguably inextricable from modern Western *processes of meaning*" altogether, Sedgwick writes, "after classical times, *there has been no important and sustained Western discourse in which woman's anal eroticism means*. Means anything."⁶⁰ From the perspective of this awareness, the masochistic abstraction into form that initially produces the genderless phrase "A child" in Freud would thus be "*retardataire*" in that it seeks to imitate a pregenital phase of childhood, a point from which the fantasist or poet or essayist might avoid the discursive gap that is sexual difference.

It is, we might say, the abstraction *of* the ass *from* the body of a "gendered and sexed adult," and from the discursive norms to which the gendered body is subject, that produces the neuter figure *ein Kind* as the privileged body of masochistic fantasy here.⁶¹ Thus the "second" trajectory Sedgwick describes in "Fundamental Misrecognitions" is the one in which an initially gender-neutral ass has been refigured—its dimensional complexity restored—through a cultural system of sexual difference that turns out to have shoved the female ass down into obscurity while raising up the male. In Sedgwick's account, this process yields a female subject who finds recourse for her attachment to anal eroticism by identifying sexually as, while also knowing she is not, a gay man.

Now, Sedgwick is not saying that this complex erotic negotiation of (a) her own particular physical body and (b) the "social and institutional" systematicity of gender actually *replaces* masochism in some kind of progressive psychic development; on the contrary, her masochism is there to stay, as the grownup spanking scenes in her narrative poems amply demonstrate. "I should think that as the vastation of meaning surrounding women's anality propelled one leap of misrecognition, across gender, in a male homosexual identification," she writes, "it probably at the same time fortified something else, a stubborn *siege* of misrecognition, in a unshakeableness of the sadomasochistic identification with the punished child."⁶² What is more, she concedes that masochism itself might well be the driving force of the masochism/anality division that structures the essay: "I do see, however, as I know you do, that the move from the childish 'lyric' tableau of shame, exhibition, and misrecognized fury to the more adult 'narrative' pseudolinearity of differentiated gender and identity formation has represented not so much a subsumption as an acting out of those earlier dynamics."⁶³ In other words, conceiving the second, "adult" structure as distinct from the first, "childish" one has been, among other things, a way for her to place herself, critically as well as narratively, *apart* from the tableau of spanking; but this kind of self-distancing is precisely what the masochistic structure itself has always promoted. But if that's the case, then what exactly *is* childish about masochism? Why, that is, does Sedgwick persist in figuring masochism as a kind of infantilizing remnant, against which the grownup recognition of anality and/as gender supervenes?[64]

The answer, I think, is that the essay uses this conceptual separation to act out what I earlier called masochism's "erotic reliance upon a danger that comes from without," upon the threat of a site the writing subject has not mastered. This desire specifically invites the distressing invasion of its own fantasy, and thus *needs there to be something else* whose advent, though desired in anticipation, happens to the subject as if it had been unpredictable and alien. It seems to me that "A Poem Is Being Written" stages the upsetting corporeal and social *reality of the gendered ass* in just this way. In structuring her argument the way she does, Sedgwick obeys masochism's own structural imperative that there be something else in the offing, something masochistic desire itself could not contain: this exteriority is the position Sedgwick assigns to the female ass, which can thus embody the violent disruption that takes the masochistic subject unawares.

If, as Sedgwick herself intimates, masochism in this essay is not confined to the "earlier dynamics" of delimitation and abstraction but also prescribes or even scripts ("an acting out") the heaving into view of the gendered ass, then the very theatricality of this mise-en-scène might seem to imply that masochism is only ever pretending not to know what it's in for: that what looks like a radical disruption of masochistic fantasy has always been arranged by the fantasy itself. And yet the revelation of the essay's construction as a *kind of theater* does not boil down to a revelation that its surprises or interruptions are just pretend. I'll turn to Sedgwick's own explicit reference to theater in a moment, but first I want to pause on her account of the poetic device that figures masochism's relation to interruption in the essay: *enjambment*, which Sedgwick names as central to her early, masochistic passion for lyric.

"In terms of the beat(ing) of the poem, enjambment was, in this fantasy that shaped my poetic, the thrusting up out of the picture plane in protest by the poem's body of a syntactic thigh or shank that would intercept, would retard the numbered blow: would momentarily wedge apart with sense the hammering iteration of rhythm. Would say no."[65] This "no" figures initially as a "heroics" of "bravada resistance" to the regulating beat of punishment; but as Sedgwick goes on to observe, enjambment also "worked ... through whatever was most abstract and cognitively under control in the poem, through the forward-looking and distributive pressure of the syntactic. With that abstraction I learned to identify."[66] Enjambment produces what seems to say "no" to fantasy's composing force—here this resistance is embodied in the "shank," its indecorous meatiness, though its "no" might also recall the sadist's no—no, I won't hurt you like you want me to—in Deleuze's "stupid joke." And yet as a "no" to fantasmatic continuity, enjambment does not halt literary production but illuminates and eroticizes its diachrony. Its "no" reveals that the apparent "siege" of lyric stillness is in fact produced through an ongoing, dialectical process, which is to say that enjambment implies a *narrative of writing*. To "identify" with its procedure is to identify as a writer, where writing is a practice of cognitive "control" never finally synoptic, but "forward-looking," vigilant. The "cropped immobilized space of the lyric" or of masochism is thus never simply a space of aesthetic arrest.[67]

This suggests that the medium proper to masochism is not, in fact, the tableau but the tableau as repeatedly interrupted and reconstituted over time through fantasy's iterative and necessarily unfinished attempt to incorporate what it—fantasy—cannot abide. It's in this sense that we can recognize Sedgwick's masochism as theater. The masochist seeks out whatever will be too much for the "pasteboard landscape," as Gaitskill puts it, of her desire or pleasure; she is always on the hunt for a "second trajectory," one that will undercut her own fantasmatic equilibrium or stasis; and once she has incorporated this difference into her composition, she will begin looking out for the next. Sedgwick's remarkable description of the erotics of composition—that is, of writing—foregrounds writing's theatricality as, precisely, an art of spatial arrangement contending with change over time: "the presentation of a piece of writing as the now-under-control palimpsest of some earlier, plurivocal drama or struggle: among tones, among dictions, among genres. The visible marks of solicitous care and of self-repression, the scrupulously almost not legible map of exorbitance half erased by discipline, the very 'careful [one might add very pleasurable] orchestration of spontaneity and pageantry' (the same with which one's parents took one over their lap)."[68] Theater—an unmistakable referent of the phrases "plurivocal drama" and "orchestration of spontaneity and pageantry"—appears, here, as the essence of what spanking and writing can have in common; earlier, in fact, Sedgwick explicitly refers to spanking itself as "a small temporary visible and glamorizing *theater* around the immobilized and involuntarily displayed lower body of a child."[69] In this imagining, theater is not so much *a* form as it is form itself, the subjection of material multiplicity to determining aesthetic arrangement; as such it is also both a display of power (look what I can do with all this stuff) and the performative constitution of that power. But while it thus figures parental and authorial control—the "sado-" in Sedgwick's "sadomasochism"—I want to insist that the figure of theater also, and contrarily, serves Sedgwick's poetics by summoning an ongoing sense

that what is "*now*-under-control" will burgeon forth disruptively again, as
the outthrust ham of enjambment also suggests.

"I planned for each poem in a booklet I made at eight to be closely
framed by a golden proscenium hung with curtains": Sedgwick inserts this
parenthetical in a discussion of how the lyric-like "tableau" of childhood
masochism arrests and simplifies the body and abstracts experience from
the narratives that structure the social.[70] If we smile at her recollection,
this is perhaps because young Eve's approach takes so literally the promise of aesthetic form to define a space apart—safe—from the ugly welter
of reality, a reality that everywhere else subjects the poet to the relentless
cruelty of gender norms, or bullies her with the fat of her own ass. And yet
the theatrical frame Eve chooses for the inviolate space of the poem only
marks its susceptibility *to* violation: the proscenium is a frame that could
have no reference, no meaning, no function without the obtrusive presence of the very heterogeneity it tries and necessarily, constitutively *might
fail* to exclude.[71] Thus Lynda Hart, in her reading of this essay, pauses to
consider the proscenium frame as "an apt site for Sedgwick's masochistic
fantasy" because of the vulnerability of the frame's definitional and physical closure: "it is here that the 'real' and 'artifice' are most violently yoked
together, here that the visibility/invisibility divide is at once most powerfully enforced and most radically undone."[72] To put a proscenium frame
around the lyric poem, I'd add, is precisely to expose the breathlessness
with which the masochist lives every gesture of aesthetic autonomy; such
insistence on marking off text from context makes it impossible *not* to notice the reality that still accosts the art.[73]

The very gratuitousness of the frame around the poem—the poem
which, as Sedgwick helps us see, is itself already a vigorous act of
framing—suggests that what the masochistic child wants with the lyric is
not "simply" a purified space of artistic control but the promise of a confrontation with whatever would be alien to that space, even devastating to
it. This is why the poem needs to be imagined as adjacent to, indeed surrounded by, the space of theater, a cultural practice designed to expose
the (fantasmatically) autonomous textual object more or less mercilessly
to the vagaries of the "social and institutional" *and* the corporeal real. The
fundamental asymmetry of this confrontation, the insistence with which
reality will always reappear again beyond each attempt to aestheticize or
abstract it, must be recognized as belonging crucially to the masochistic
fantasy itself, which turns writing into a theatrical relation to the world.

A poem, then, is being written theatrically. And yet in spite of the essay's title and its focus on a series of Sedgwick's poems, I'm not sure poetry is really the kind of writing at the center of its account. In the passage
about the "palimpsest" quoted above, Sedgwick characterizes the latter

as a "trick of discursive authority" that, she writes, "became my utterance in prose as in poetry."[74] This phrasing, which gives "prose" an edge as the primary object of the description, and positions "poetry" as prose's simile, is worth pausing over: without marking it explicitly, Sedgwick seems to have shifted, if only in emphasis, from writing about writing poetry to writing about writing prose. This impression is underscored by the passage's quotation, with bracketed supplementation—"'careful [one might add very pleasurable] orchestration of spontaneity and pageantry'"—of a phrase that comes from the essay itself, three pages back. This recitation performs the "pleasurable" nature of *the autotheoretical essay's self-constituting return to itself*. In other words, this passage on the theatricality of writing, which comes in between Sedgwick's extended discussion of lyric enjambment and her account of her own "generic leap" from lyric to narrative poetry, is in fact focused less on either genre of poetry than on the genre of writing the essay itself is.[75] In the moment when Sedgwick most specifically describes the larger mechanism of what she calls her "sadomasochistic" poetics, the most immediate referent of this description is not one of the poems the essay reproduces but the autotheoretical (autobiographical, self-elaborating, self-theorizing) essay itself. In this sense, the title "A Poem Is Being Written" is a kind of caption for the essay itself, which *is* the definitive "Poem" in question.[76]

All this recursivity brings us back to the specter of autotheory as a kind of erotic self-mastery, or "sadomasochistic" self-sufficiency. Sedgwick seems to position herself, in this passage, as having mastered compositional technique and thus attained the "dominion" for which being spanked had made her "ravenous": seems to have graduated, as it were, from spanked to spanker, from child to parent, from masochist to sadist. And to the extent that autotheory here entails taking her own earlier writing as *corpus* or material, she does indeed seem to occupy both positions at once; she even demonstrates a potentially endless capacity to take what *was* her own earlier sadistic exercise of mastery *as the object* of this reflective dominion, perpetually topping herself. This is a version of the same feat we described in dramaturgical masochism, wherein the subject becomes, as we've said, a sadist in relation to the body and the pleasure from which she separates herself, which she constitutes as not hers, and which she also thereby subjects to form. So far, we might say, so sadomasochistic.

And yet as we've also said, there is in Sedgwick's masochism something that resists the "elegance" of this switch, an inclination to turn toward whatever would be unassimilable to the fantasmatic composition, and invite it to rush in and destroy the work, the form, the self. We can locate this gesture of invitation wherever something *sticks out* of the text like the jamb/ham begging to be punished, interrupting the diachronic flow.[77]

An example of such an excess—a slight mismatch between what the writer is invoking, and what she can compose—seems to me to occur when Sedgwick remarks that "rather than present the writer in this essay as an exemplary figure,... it's seemed more productive *to preserve and to invite in the reader* a distance from her that licensed freely the 'operations' of knowledge, even a certain examinative sadism, such as I would have found even harder with any other woman writer."[78] If the main thrust of this footnote is to acknowledge the potential risk, for a progressive and feminist project, of the ways Sedgwick is (as it were) being hard on herself, the reminder to the reader to be just as hard seems an almost awkward addition, without even commas to contain it. Indeed, the addition of "and to invite in the reader" almost threatens the referential stability of "with" in the last clause, such that we might well find ourselves puzzling over who is being hard with whom.

This may be where *you* come in again: now Sedgwick's "you," as in "I do see, however, as I know you do ..."[79] Unlike Preciado's "*tú*," Sedgwick's "you" is never explicitly named in the essay, so that it might really be you, might be anyone—"any other woman writer," for example; even me. Max Cavitch has pointed out that second-person address prevails across autotheoretical works, arguing both that this device tends to install in the reader a "fantasy of being recognized, singled out for attention" and that, as an author's *self*-address, the "you" conveys the "complex and fundamental self-experience of being non-self-identical that is endemic to autotheoretical works."[80] Kyle Frisina, however, offers a different account of the autotheoretical "you," which she derives from Claudia Rankine's *Citizen*: Frisina suggests autotheory's "you" addresses a *theatrical* audience, one whose irreducible and unpredictable difference from the speaker emphasizes the "limits of intersubjectivity," rather than overcoming those limits.[81] Sedgwick's "you" eroticizes just these theatrics of incommensurability, addressing an invisible audience that lurks in the darkness beyond the proscenium frame—or in any other corner of the shadows that flank the stage. The kind of theater Sedgwick invokes in framing her own text is a theater whose erotics center, for artists and anyone identified with them, on the wild fact that the audience response to one's authorial "pageantry"—that is, *your* response—could be *anything*; that in the darkened surround of the auditorium, it could come from anywhere, including, of course, from the wings, or from behind.[82]

The masochistic desire to suffer the violence of this unpredictable response would manifest not only in Sedgwick's direct appeals to "you" throughout the essay but also in the systematic expansiveness of the footnotes, which enact a heightened, almost frenzied awareness of how vulnerable the text might be to critical intervention. This desire also manifests, I think, in the elaborateness of Sedgwick's characteristic syntax, which Kathryn Bond Stockton has rightly likened to that of Henry James.[83] Sedgwick's writing, as Ramzi Fawaz observes, works to "stylistically model, and sometimes performatively bring into being or affectively invest, the reality of human multiplicity," even as it is "always inviting a counter-response, a particular, *other* claim."[84] Though Fawaz presents these two characterizations separately, their conjunction brings out the sense in which Sedgwick's textual striving to "orchestrate" or contain more and more differences even within a single sentence is not just, as she self-deprecatingly suggests, a performance of her own sado-mastery but is also a way of building into the text a kind of thrilled receptivity to all the vectors of challenge or complexification that might surge up to meet her argument—of which the charge of flaunting her mastery would surely be one. Despite the eagerness with which she anticipates this charge, her manner of allowing "plurivocal drama or struggle" to show up in her text manifests not only her ability to manage such vectors, but more fundamentally the pleasure she takes in *looking out for more* of them, as if to enact her appetite for the always-potentially-painful ungovernability of the corporeal and social arenas in which her discourse happens.[85] "One pays for the energy one's 'perversia' lend to her writing by certain moments of giving away with both hands, at the textual places where those energies break the surface, the poise or secret or charade of authorial control over the identifications of 'the' reader," Sedgwick writes in one such long footnote.[86] It seems to me that she could just as easily have redistributed these terms: one also pays *with* the charade of authorial control *for* the "moments of giving [it] away," which are themselves a source of enormous erotic "energy."

Writing passionately toward whatever might be powerful enough to interrupt its passion, masochism eroticizes the limit of desire itself. Sedgwick thus constructs "A Poem Is Being Written" in such a way that an initial "tableau of the small, bounded, and violence-inscribed torso" grounds an initial theory of the erotics of writing ("Spanking and Poetry"), which must then *yield* in the face of the "terrifying involuntarity" of the gendered ass: an initially "simplified" scenario is displaced by a "more tortuously inclusive trajectory" arising to overtake the essay as if from another angle—arising, that is, from precisely the direction Sedgwick describes herself as having "gazed raptly away from" in constituting the masochistic scene.[87] This staging of disruption, I've suggested, manifests a specifically theatrical mode of desire, constructed around the thrilled sense that something else—something that doesn't properly belong to the tableau of one's fantasy—always threatens/promises to knock one's careful orchestration off-course. The something-that-doesn't-properly-belong to the abstractive initial fantasy of "A Child"/"A Poem"—the ass and/as sexual difference—responds to an address that originates within the masochistic scene, and constitutes that scene's theatricality.

The theatricality of masochism cannot be reduced, then, to the way either Deleuze or, sometimes, Freud seems to understand it: it cannot be defined as either the bounded space of aesthetic suspension and idealization (like Deleuze's tableau) or the frivolously stagy pretending, the "acting out of fantasies in play," performed by Freud's so-called feminine masochist in "The Economic Problem of Masochism," both of which we considered in chapter 1. In chapter 2, we traced masochistic attachments to the inevitable gaps between writing and occurrence that theater's repetitions offer, in *Hedda Gabler* and "Nona Vincent," to eroticize. Echoing those late-Victorian texts, the theatricality Sedgwick evokes in her description of proscenium-framed writing-as-spanking is a determined invocation of the uncontainable, unmanageable alterity whose threatening proximity the frame implies. Here, theater is the excitingly doomed attempt to manage a contingency whose violence will inevitably break our hearts (or other parts of us) anyway. This means that in order for Sedgwick's essay—indeed, I want to say, for her whole theoretical edifice—to function erotically as masochistic theater, it both needs to show that it can incorporate or "take" the interruptions and disruptions that rise to threaten syntactic and fantasmatic unity at every turn—as it does with female anality—*and* it needs to construct a further external referent that is still too much for her mise-en-scène to incorporate, and whose threatening presence just outside the frame can keep charging up, provoking, guaranteeing that there will always be more need for this elaborate capaciousness.

Sedgwick's ass is the reality effect, the version of exteriority that *is* being mastered here, brought conceptually and compositionally under control: the spontaneity of its tableau-disrupting force has, of course, been orchestrated by the masochism of the essay itself. By enacting the erotics of this structure, however, the essay cues us to look out for whatever the next iteration of this disruption might be, one that the essay has *not* mastered, that might lurk just beyond the essay's frame. This might be one way to understand the relation of Sedgwick's essay to Lavery's critique. On the one hand, Sedgwick's work notably fails to anticipate the content of that critique, which is why Lavery's argument makes a powerful intervention in arguing that Sedgwick's work contributes to a "construction of queer universalism … predicated on the impossibilization of transition" that lends itself to being "deployed in trans-antagonistic contexts."[88] When Lavery remarks, with exasperation, "I am not trying to cancel Sedgwick," the disclaimer both denies and acknowledges a sense of how profound a threat this critique might indeed pose.[89] And yet the very move to characterize

Sedgwick's theory as "egg" responds, I think, to a fundamentally anticipatory stance *in Sedgwick's writing*, insofar as the "egg" is a structure negatively shaped by a shattering event—for Lavery, this would be the event of gender transition—that has yet to happen, and which the egg, qua egg, needs *not* to be able to see coming. One implication of Lavery's argument is that the refusal to recognize real trans possibility confers a certain unacknowledged fragility on the abstract systems queer theory labors to establish. What my reading would suggest is that the most thrilling aspect of erecting such a theoretical system might just *be* the sense of this fragility, the prospect of this shattering.[90]

As the word "fragility" itself may suggest, Sedgwick's text—or for that matter a reading like mine above, which no doubt follows that text too obediently to be the kind of reading its masochism actually demands—also lays itself open to another kind of critique, which would expose another structuring system that is symptomatically being left unexplored in the essay. Such a critique would point out that the field of meanings from which masochistic fantasy in her account must tenaciously "abstract the body" is of course not only the system of sexual difference but the even more "fundamental" modern differential system that is race. So while the essay brings anality bursting through the gender-neutral masochistic tableau of "a child," confronting both subject and reader with the violently binary difference between "men's" and "women's" anal eroticism—and hence between men and women—the essay enacts no corresponding reveal of the binary racial logic that always accompanies and structures the former divide. The essay's composition stages our discovery that the lyric moment of masochistic fantasy had been keeping sexed embodiment outside the frame, but it barely acknowledges that this fantasy also worked *and is still working* to screen out racialization, its elegant abstraction tendering an "escape" not only from embodiment as sexed but from embodiment as raced, as always inscribed within (not only patriarchal but) white supremacist domination. This is to say that even as the essay stages a reveal of masochism's imbrication with sexual politics, it never quite faces up to the whiteness that attaches both to the "childlike" scene of masochism *and* to the event of its disruption by Sedgwick's (white) ass.

Sedgwick's article does not—cannot—manage the advent of such a reading, but I think the article invites it, not only by omission but also in the few moments where Sedgwick does glancingly mention race. She characterizes her own family as "the quiet and agreeable space of the Biedermeier family culture of upwardly mobile assimilated American Jews in the 1950s," where "upwardly mobile" unmistakably refers not only to economic class but to the historical incorporation of Jews into the category of American whiteness during that period.[91] Describing the anthology of children's poetry that inspired her own early writing, she recalls the "illus-trations I'd so much admired and wanted, myself, to be like: white children in bonnets and smocks and pinafores, round-cheeked but slender, with no noses and no mouths."[92] (Reading this sends me into a kind of identificatory frenzy of my own, as I too was a plump, notably big-mouthed and increasingly big-nosed Jewish child, held painfully rapt by exactly that kind of alien Anglo image.) The abstraction of the body that Sedgwick associates with the childish masochism of lyric is thus, at its literary point of origin, not only an abstraction from sex and gender but also a disfiguring subtraction of racializing features, yielding a fantasmatic tableau that is not only gender neutral but also, by implication, impossibly white. The subsequent, enjoyably violent disruption of this tableau by the gendered but racially unmarked ass raises the question, therefore, of whether in spite of this disruption, the initial fantasy's whiteness has been left intact, and the suspicion that indeed it has. In staging the disruptive revelation of anal sexual difference, the essay keeps an even more troubling structure of meaning lurking in the wings. This means that the essay still defers a recognition that we—not the essay itself—will have to enact: the painful, double implication of Sedgwick's ass, both as not-quite-white and as undeniably white, in white supremacy.

The most notable moment in which Sedgwick's essay seems to be asking for this kind of intervention is, characteristically, halfway through a long footnote. Writing that for "the adult European female body" in a fat-obsessed culture, the ass is "the locus ... of an always potentially discrediting scandal, the scandal really of the very materiality and difference of female bodies," Sedgwick goes on to remark: "I understand that there are strong cultural differences in these perceptions: for instance that Afro-American eyes find it easier to see women's bodies ... as being strengthened, not discredited by their substance. (Still ... I am told, though I can't make a generalization of my own about this, that a high valuation in Afro-American culture of women's substance including the rear end coexists with an attitude toward anal eroticism that is as severe as the Euro-American ...)."[93] Sedgwick is correct to say that she "can't make a generalization of [her] own about this"—but, of course, says it after having just done so. The implication of both what she has been "told" and the fact that she has been told it, which she herself doesn't pursue, is that the ass itself is an inherently racialized site in the social imaginary, a signifier of racial difference that subtends and shapes the sexual difference the ass also embodies. If it is possible for Sedgwick to "understand that" Black people value large asses, Aliyyah Abdur-Rahman has argued that this commonsense trope—which circulates throughout "the collective cultural imagination"—is indissociable from racism: "black women's asses have been treated [by popular culture] for the past century as the main focus of (black) men's sexual interest, the supposed effect of cumulative and widespread racial and cultural retardation."[94] This racializing logic has been subjected to extensive critique; as Jennifer Nash points out, "Black feminist theory has long argued that the buttocks are *the* location of imagined black sexual difference," to such an extent that "the buttocks act as an analytic centerpiece of black feminist theorizing on sexuality, visual culture, and sexual politics."[95] What Sedgwick's footnote tries, rather halfheartedly, to place beyond the essay's frame is not just Black bodies and "eyes" per se but the system of racialization which constructs *all* asses, including Sedgwick's own, as "fundamentally" raced. This moment of theoretical faltering epitomizes the masochism of Sedgwickian rhetoric, which acts as if it were signaling confident self-possession (I already know what your objection will be!), while actually cueing us to a critique under which the text might buckle.

"In Deep Again": Sedgwick with Gary Fisher

"Pull down your pants": this phrase, Sedgwick confesses in *A Dialogue on Love* (1999), has been the most important verbal unit in her sexual fantasies.[96] This later book, which chronicles Sedgwick's experience in psychotherapy and the reflections her therapy occasions, would offer another rich field for exploring the masochism of autotheory. Instead, however, I want to use it as a jumping-off point for considering a different literary project that coincided with its writing, and that comes up in *A Dialogue on Love* a few times: Sedgwick's controversial editing and publication of the writings of the young gay Black author Gary Fisher after his death from AIDS, an undertaking that in some ways seems to literalize the masochistic textual structure I've been excavating here. In presenting Fisher's text to the public, we might say, Sedgwick arranges for her own whiteness— held largely at bay within "A Poem Is Being Written"—to come crashing with unprecedented force into the frame.

Sedgwick met Fisher in the 1980s when he took her class as a graduate student in English at UC Berkeley, and was impressed by what she calls in *A Dialogue on Love* his "ravishing stories"; after seeing him again years later, Sedgwick tells her therapist "I've fallen in deep again with Gary."[97] In a subsequent conversation with the therapist about Gary, Sedgwick reflects on her inability to "get anywhere" with the subject of racism, reflecting on "all the ways I feel like my upbringing twisted me into a small, tight, raw pretzel around this topic.... For me, this is a wrackingly depressive topic—I mean I don't get anywhere new with it, there's a load of habituated pain, there's a vindictively strong ethical line that never seems to *work*, I feel both wretchedly self-righteous and also a hundred percent in the wrong all the time."[98] Sedgwick's articulation of her own white fragility avant le lettre is the more striking because it arises through a profound emotional and erotic attachment to Fisher and his work. Being "in deep" with the socially and corporeally precarious Fisher makes Sedgwick vulnerable too, in more superficial but still powerful ways: in that their attraction must be asymmetrical; in that, loving Fisher, she must confront the "wrackingly depressive" problem of her own implication in white supremacy—a problem whose depressive force seizes her, she suggests, precisely in her capacity *as a theorist*; and most of all, in that she will lose Fisher to AIDS. This painful (but also pleasurable) attachment to Fisher drives her commitment to publish his work, which she does after he dies.

A Dialogue on Love suggests that the project of editing Gary's texts is rife with masochistic affordances.

> A few hours with some of Gary's papers, which I'll be editing for publication: two-hundred-proof taste of what the coming months hold as I plunge into the vat of his unmakings. Including, intensely: abyssal, glazed over boredom.
>
> Not because his writing fails to astonish.
>
> This kind of boredom doesn't mean no-cathexis: this kind, to me, means overstimulation, stimulation of wrong or dangerous kinds; hell; rape; dissolution. The kind of boredom that's a penetration.
>
> "Informed" by my studious father, unable to escape.[99]

The posthumous "penetration" that Fisher's texts enact on Sedgwick—which might remind us of the graphic way Preciado interpolates the dead Dustan—threatens a "dangerous" "overstimulation" not only because of how much there is that Fisher has written and Sedgwick must now read but also, presumably, because of what these pages contain, including Fisher's incessant return to erotic scenes of racialized sexual humiliation visited upon narrators (often Fisher himself, as he records in his diary) by white dominants. Fisher expresses his racialized masochistic fantasies overtly in violent, sexually explicit texts, which document his avid pursuit of white tops who will degrade him with racist slurs as well as physically. These scenarios could hardly be more different from the masochistic fantasies Sedgwick presents throughout "A Poem Is Being Written," fantasies that, I've suggested above, energetically exclude racial difference from the scene. For Sedgwick, we might hazard, Fisher's texts engender their "abyssal" affect at least in part because they open the abstractive tableau of her own masochistic fantasy to the depressive depths of an inevitable psychic implication in white supremacy.

Sedgwick's recasting of Fisher's corpus, in this passage, as the aggressor to whose "penetration" she submits—and whom she knowingly conflates (shades of Anna Freud!) with her own "studious father"—might well remind us of Fanon's classic analysis of white masochism.[100] In Sedgwick's case, however, I'd argue that what the fantasy of violation enables is less a justification for ongoing self-assertion than a determination to let Fisher's text bore through her own corpus and into the light of day. Masochistic desire here bears the grieving white fantasist through the otherwise-unbearable psychic "danger" of a posthumous collaboration with a particular Black subject whose painful words exceed Sedgwick's own powers of composition, in order that those words and the structures they expose might claim the attention of readers beyond herself, in the unpredictable world outside the proscenium frame of her own fantasy. In this sense, describing Sedgwick's work with Fisher as masochistic doesn't mean reducing it to a self-pleasuring exercise; indeed, I've been arguing that Sedgwick challenges her own characterization of masochism *as* a field of reduction. Sedgwick's "plunge into the vat" of Fisher's text is masochistic precisely in its opening toward uncertainty and heterogeneity, what José Esteban Muñoz, in an essay about their collaboration, calls a "queer politics of the incommensurable."[101] Opening toward the violent differences of Fisher's text, Sedgwick also beckons the various kinds of pain to which his text might subject her, including the trouble that might—and does—ensue when she presents it to the world, in what Muñoz, drawing on Jean-Luc Nancy, terms their "sharing out of the unshareable."[102] The sharing *out* of publication, not unlike that of theater, solicits a response from the world it pours itself into; and in this case, Sedgwick's editorial promotion, as a white woman, of Black work that flagrantly sexualized anti-Blackness drew some of "the harshest criticism" of Sedgwick's career.[103] Here again, we might say, she had arranged to be caught with her pants down.

Published in 1996, *Gary in Your Pocket* contains stories, poems, and entries from Fisher's diary, which begin in high school and end five months before his death at age thirty-two. Many of the entries are about his romantic and sexual relationships and his longing for intimacy. The passages that directly express Fisher's cross-racial masochism, and that thus occasion what Robert Reid-Pharr calls "the shock of Gary Fisher," have been the most intensively discussed, by Reid-Pharr and others; it doesn't seem necessary to reproduce them here.[104] Instead, I want to turn to one of the short stories in the collection, "Red Cream Soda." I've argued in this chapter that autotheory works masochistically in part through the insistence of its reference to what lies or lurks beyond its frame, and this text offers the chance to explore one such path of Sedgwick's reference more concretely, descending for a moment into what she calls the "vat" of Fisher's "unmakings."

If Fisher's writing has posed a kind of threat to writers who encounter it—as not only Sedgwick but also Reid-Pharr and Muñoz suggest—this may have something to do with the way Fisher works to disrupt any sense of writing (specifically confessional writing) as a reliable way of managing masochistic fantasy, or sustaining a self. Braiding together self-making and self-unmaking in their literary encounters with whiteness, Fisher's elaborations thus echo the scenes of writing in Kennedy's plays; Fisher's writing, like Kennedy's, purposely engages in what Avgi Saketopolou calls a "confrontation with his own negation."[105] Indeed, Fisher's journals literalize Kennedy's illumination, in *Ohio State Murders*, of *the university library* as a crucible of both desire and peril for a young Black writer. Fisher believed himself to have contracted HIV while having sex at the UNC Chapel Hill library as an undergraduate; the library was also the scene of his burgeoning sexual masochism. His journals, like Kennedy's play, thus construct the university library as the site of a deadly interracial intimacy, where the Black literary subject enters into an eros inseparable from harm. In Fisher's journals, however, this eros—a far cry from Kennedy's in both content and tone—becomes exuberantly sexual and explicitly masochistic. As Muñoz puts it: "The library is narrated in [Fisher's] journals as the space where his sexuality took a certain form, and the young, smallish, black man began to understand his own sexual desire as the impulse to be mastered by older, larger, dominant, white men."[106] Reid-Pharr also considers the significance of the library in Fisher's journals, reading a passage where Fisher playfully describes his own use of the buildings as a study site as well as a cruising venue. "In order to master fully the intricacies of Western modernity, one must expose oneself to degradation and disease," Reid-Pharr writes, "even though the likely consequence of such exposure is death … Fisher's mastery of his subjects was coterminous with the disease's mastery of his flesh" in a "piling-on of forms of mastery—literary, scientific, sexual—[that] is so very overdetermined as to seem obscene."[107] The interimplication of literary and sexual "mastery" in Fisher's work is never a matter of their simply running in parallel; instead, these registers have the capacity to intersect and disturb each other, as "Red Cream Soda" shows.

In this story, the narrator—who is sick with AIDS, though the disease isn't named in the story—has a roommate named Randy. Randy, presumably white (at one point we read of "his blue eyes gone gray, his hair tossled and full of lamplight"), reacts to the news of the narrator's disease by beginning to tell him graphic stories of Randy's own ongoing masochistic sexual adventures, experiences not unlike ones Fisher describes in diary entries elsewhere in the collection.[108] The narrator of "Red Cream Soda," whom it's obviously tempting to conflate with Fisher, is also a writer, and in the story, Randy's anecdotes obtrude on the narrator's writing time. "He could joke about the way writing sinister-little-stories absorbed me, but when he did get me to sit and listen to him he wouldn't tolerate my funning him," the narrator says.[109] Strangely, the narrator not only listens to Randy's stories but begins to write them down himself, in the first-person, after hearing them: "He didn't ask me to, but in the weeks that followed I kept a diary of his stories."[110] The ensuing texts-within-the-text read like some of Fisher's actual diary entries, but the "I" that appears in the former refers, at least initially, not to the narrator but to the roommate Randy.

The narrator emphasizes that Randy's storytelling is an imposition—the narrator is "forced to listen"—but he also frames this power dynamic as a kind of inversion: "I would sit so passively through the next installments, neatly bound and gagged by what could only have been disbelief; forced to listen because I couldn't stop his talking, like the unsuspecting psychoanalyst roped to his own couch while the lunatic roams and imposes his disease in much the same way the analyst, given the chance, would impose the cure."[111] The narrator feels "true discomfort" at the roommate's stories of sexual submission, which he seems to find outlandish; but the analogy of the "psychoanalyst roped to his own couch" suggests that the power to enact such a discursive onslaught—to force stories of violent sex on an unwilling audience—ought to have been, or even originally was, the narrator's own.[112] It's as if, in this story, the revelation of the narrator's AIDS has displaced him from his proper function as both (sadistic) narrator and masochistic subject. A compulsively narrative masochism that *should have been his own*—and that we inevitably recognize, from the real diary entries in the collection, as "really" Fisher's—now confronts the narrator in the alien person of Randy, "all but foam[ing] at the mouth"; but we can surmise that this sexuality, and the ability to narrate it, has been appropriated from the narrator himself.[113] This interpretation helps to account for the narrator's otherwise mysterious decision to write down Randy's exploits himself in the first-person, a scribal act whose motivation is left provocatively open. By capturing Randy's stories as his own diary entries, that is, the narrator *re*appropriates the sexual-and-authorial subjectivity that has been taken from him. As we find out, however, this restitution can't actually establish anything like psychic security.

What the story stages, it seems to me, is the unobvious complexity of masochism's relation to confessional writing, a complexity whose operation in autotheory this chapter has been trying to trace. In the figure of white roommate Randy, we find a masochistic desire that insists on expressing itself *in person*, in (so to speak) full-throated performance.[114]

The narrator seems at first to be the "passive" audience of Randy's confessional discourse—and indeed he is also that—but like James's Mrs. Alsager he turns out to be (to have been), more fundamentally, its author. "Red Cream Soda" makes this turn literal in the final diary entry. After being sexually brutalized by a group of men, the diary's protagonist (whom we have, until this point, understood to be Randy) decides to wreak "vengeance" on one of the men who has been fucking him: "a big fellow, skin so white in the relentless dark that I thought a light had been aimed at him to make him glow."[115] The vengeance, we read, will consist of turning top and infecting the big white man with HIV—the first sign that discursive as well as sexual positions are shifting, since it's the narrator, not Randy, who carries the virus. The protagonist begins fucking the big white man, and is just about to come when "as if he'd heard me, Randy looked around—I rushed into myself, like a mother racing after her little son racing after his ball into the path of oblivion."[116] Suddenly, that is, Randy appears as a character *inside* (and at the receiving end of) what has now become a sadistic fantasy *of the narrator's*.

Precisely by acceding, as we've seen in previous readings, to the sadistic position, the narrator (re)establishes himself as a subject of desire and as the author of masochistic narrative. And yet the same trajectory that pulls the narrator "into [him]self" thereby also pulls him into a feminizing "path of oblivion." What looks at first like mastery, and then like self-mastery, opens out onto the abyss. In the story's final image, the narrator manages to save Randy from infection by pushing him off his cock as they "tumbl[e] over and down a grassy hill into a cool stream": "Sometime during the fall I pushed him away laughing and we unravelled our white guts like ribbons along the slanted, rushing green."[117] The image is sweet but sinister; death has not been dealt, but the story ends mid-descent.

In "Red Cream Soda," then, authorship emerges as a metaleptic displacement of the self, powered by the alternating current of a starkly binary erotics: top/bottom, black/white, HIV negative/positive. The narrator recovers his own story, his own desire, only by way of the theatrics that stage it, elaborately, as the other's. But this dramaturgical self-discovery also entails a violent loss of security, as the space that had seemed to be safely outside the described scene of violence turns out to be permeable, susceptible to it, and vice-versa. The eponymous can of cream soda is an emblem of this logic. At first, the can gives the narrator something comfortingly familiar to focus on while Randy tells his disturbing tales, grounding him in the realist milieu of their shared living room: "I found myself anchored by that little red can of pop ... and fortunately so, because I might have gone back there with him. ... I pretended to go, but some part of me stayed, with the can in just the corner of my vision."[118] Soon, however, the can begins to exhibit a paradoxical temporality: as time passes, it seems to be both a new can and the same old can, a fact that distresses the narrator far more than Randy's anecdotes themselves, and seems to propel the story into the final episode described above.[119] Thus the meaningless detail that, in classic reality-effect fashion, is meant to secure an outside to fantasy actually reveals the impossibility of maintaining such a demarcation: it turns out the frame was made to be broken. The soda can underscores another rupture as well, between erotic relation and murderous violence: the queasy conjunction of colors implied in "red cream" anticipates the "white guts" that spill at the story's end, making murder and sex indistinguishable *even as* the narrative seems to reestablish the boundary between them ("I pushed him away laughing"). If cream can be red, then the hand that writes semen as "white guts" inscribes friendly mutual ejaculation with the red shadow of disembowelment, tinging it with the death (by infection) it was supposed to replace. Writing, this language suggests, can never be safe sex.

This chapter has found two distinct movements in autotheory's masochistic deployment of abstraction. In the first, the writer takes up a masochistic relation *to* abstraction, which itself offers to negate the writer's embodied particularity, more or less violently interrupting the consistency of the personal. In the second movement, the writer identifies *with* abstraction, and invites an unmanageable exterior reality to come crashing through the elegance of their textually wrought conceptual systems. I've suggested both that Lavery's critique of Sedgwick constitutes an instance of this crashing, and that the "impossibilized" event of gender transition itself might be something that the egg theorist masochistically defers— not in order to suffer longer but in order to guarantee that there is *something else coming*, an unbearable jouissance whose nature the subject will not have recognized in advance.[120] I've also suggested that Sedgwick's unresolved critical relation to race, and the affective intensity produced for her around this "wrackingly depressive topic," might be understood as another vector of masochistic possibility in her writing—as might her work with Gary Fisher, whose own writing erotically invests writing itself as a dangerously (and pleasurably) permeable endeavor. We've seen autotheoretical authorship respond to this kind of permeability by sexualizing the frame that marks off the text from the world that produced it, making the relevance of anything that was, is, or could have been going on around the work an erotically loaded question. And it is from within this charged relation to context that, for the past decade, reading Sedgwick has meant encountering, as the ultimate instance of what her texts couldn't handle, the unmanageable fact of Sedgwick's own death.

Is it absurd to suggest that the fact of Sedgwick's death itself belongs to the masochism of her writing too, precisely by being that which her writing cannot describe, manage, or contain? Of course, *A Dialogue on Love* and other later Sedgwick texts, written after her cancer diagnosis, do engage the possibility of her imminent death, and the ways her desire can and can't route itself around this prospect; one critic has even used *A Dialogue on Love* to theorize a subgenre he calls "auto-thanato-theory."[121] Reading backward, however, it's hard to shake the feeling that "A Poem," written before the diagnosis, in some ways sets up the reality to come of Sedgwick's fatal illness by sketching an especially precarious *fantasy* of death that the subsequent events will unpredictably realize and thus disrupt.[122] The only lyric poem of her own that Sedgwick reproduces in the "Spanking and Poetry" section, "Stillborn Child," images the infant body in and as romanticized death: "Crumpled face ... / Eyes that see / Nothing. Void / Of expression ..."[123] How could the "crumpled face" of the dead child in the poem not be the crumpled face of little Eve or a sibling mid-spanking, arrested in the image of a death that is, let's acknowledge, always also on the table when an adult is beating a child? So that while the entire text of "A Poem Is Being Written" theorizes, demonstrates, and invites us to the erotics of a *lifetime of writing*—a sexual "trajectory" as a literary career—it also installs at the heart of this career the figure of the writer's own corpse. And precisely by installing this death *as* a figure—as a wish, a fantasy—Sedgwick arranges for (orchestrates) the awful noncoincidence of that wish with the actual, inevitable event: a particular grownup woman lies dead where the abstract neutrality of A Child ought to be.

In *The Deaths of the Author: Writing and Reading in Time*, Jane Gallop argues that Sedgwick's writing illuminates a structural relationship between death and authorship as such: "the author's death shadows the writer writing, leaving its mark in the writer's engagement with temporality."[124] For Gallop, Sedgwick's brief discussion of her own "unexpected diagnosis" in the protomemorial essay "White Glasses" (first delivered while its object, Sedgwick's friend Michael Lynch, was still alive but published in *Tendencies* after Lynch's death) constitutes "a particularly dramatic example of a more general temporality of writing."[125] Gallop continues: "Instead of being, as most of us are, embarrassed by the queer temporality of the printed word, Sedgwick would embrace and celebrate it. While the writer may go about revising and updating, the printed word is the province not of the writer but of the author. The printed word, necessarily anachronistic, is where the writer confronts her status as a dead author."[126] The notion of writing as a confrontation with, and even a production of, one's own death is, as we noted in the introduction, a familiar poststructuralist theme, but

Gallop's work to claim this process as a specifically "queer" relation fore-grounds the erotic affordance of such anachrony.

And yet if an authorial eros of autonecrophilia can thus be valorized as queer, it also seems important to emphasize Gallop's conditional: "Sedg-wick *would* embrace and celebrate" this fucked-up temporality; likewise, we might say—based on Sedgwick's descriptions of her own eros—that she *would* welcome death; that she *would* make her own work a venue for Fisher's; or indeed that she *would* identify as a man. These are all versions of the same *would*, I'm suggesting, that inhabits the masochist's classic of-fer to suffer "anything." They are not structures of actual relation or com-munication so much as they are passionate invitations launched toward the unknown, in the knowledge or belief or lascivious hope that whatever is out there will respond to your desire with a ferocity impossible to em-brace. This is exactly the way Sedgwick's actual death belongs to the mas-ochistic composition of her essay: by virtue of the fact that it cannot be-long there. And yet it does belong in this chapter, the one I am writing now, the one you're reading; indeed it has been here all along. Sedgwick's death is part of *this* composition just as Sedgwick's ass is part of the composition of "A Poem": an unmanageable reality is being managed. In a structurally analogous way, the devastating fact of Sedgwick's death has become "fun-damental" to the sex act of elaborating upon her text.

Equally fundamental, however, is the way this writing (writing that loves and wants to imitate Sedgwick's) also reiterates the masochistic ges-ture of beckoning the unbearable yet again, by opening onto something really unbearable for *its* writer, something my writing cannot manage. In the case of my chapter, this further "something" would have to be far less assimilable to the present composition than the death of a writer whom I love but never knew. I'm aware, for instance, that this chapter is marked by a certain failure of composure around both the work and the death of Lau-ren Berlant, who was my friend, and whose body of work on Sedgwick, let alone on desire, I seem unable to bring myself fully to face. There is also, however, another kind of death-of-the-author that I have felt breaking in on my reading, whose shattering force I now want to acknowledge, though I may not be able to manage it: the iterative laying-waste to form that we commonly call motherhood.

I'm referring to my "own" motherhood, about which I'll (always) be trying to say more in the next chapter: motherhood, the event I seem to have invited to shatter whatever shells of self I might have incubated in my compositions and my fantasies, fucking up my writing and the sub-ject who had been known to undertake it. For Sedgwick too—though, of course, differently—parentality stands in a sadistic relation to the writing subject. At the end of the passage in which she theorizes writing-as-spanking as theater, Sedgwick writes: "these stigmata of 'decisiveness' in and authority over one's language are recognizable as such by their family resemblance to the power, rage, and assault that parents present to the child with a demand for compulsory misrecognition of them as discretion and love."[127] Whether "parents" here means all parents or just some of them, the "family resemblance" between writer and parent is precisely not identity: Eve Sedgwick, the writer and the subject of the essay, is not a parent, and if she implicates herself in the real practice of parental cruelty, it is only as the latter's sublimating representative. "For this reason," Sedgwick appends in another footnote, "I always find it hard to figure the polylogic, at least in my writing, as liberatory *as opposed to* disciplinary."[128] The "figure" of the "disciplinary" in the text—that is, of the disciplinary as a literary mode, as Sedgwick's own literary mode—presents itself as rooted in the ground of a real-life behavior which is *not* Sedgwick's own but that of "parents" in the world at large. (Sedgwick even phrases the note in a way that suggests that actual/parental discipline is a kind of limit on literary power, making things "hard to figure.") "Parents," in other words, arise to constitute something like an absolute outside to the literary structure of desire that the essay both theorizes and constructs, even if parents are that structure's personal origin and mimetic referent. Parents function this way precisely because their most pertinent action in the essay—spanking, punishing—is here revealed as the real violence that masochistic writing will ceaselessly *figure* and thus never actually be.

In the short confessional chapter that follows here and closes the book, I try to perform an account of motherhood that likewise presents both its proximity to and its incommensurability with masochism. In my highly partial account, unlike Sedgwick's, the parent is not the agent of violence; instead, the advent of motherhood is itself a violent devastation that the subject to whom it happens can never satisfactorily describe, a reiterative disruption that she cannot transmute into form and thereby master. Perhaps it is this persistent impossibility, the way motherhood exposes the writing subject to a kind of disruption she cannot redeploy as writing, that has occasioned my own insistent sense that masochism and its writing also need to be thought in relation to power dynamics that *won't* switch—not "sadomasochistic" writing but the masochism of writing an experience that really threatens to unmake both desire and writing itself; writing as the ongoing attempt to achieve the impossible form, regarding which the subject would be able to say, as she *needs* to say, without lying: I loved it.

In understanding autotheory's masochism as a drive to open the self toward what threatens it with unknowable destruction, we'd have a new way to account for the prevalence of "parent-child relationships," and especially motherhood, as favorite themes of the genre.[129] The text on motherhood that follows here is not presented as an exemplary instance of autotheoretical writing; indeed its engagement with theory is very limited. But by including the text here, I mean its presence to recast this whole book as a kind of stealth autotheory. I want to show you, that is, the kind of theater these readings have been.

Pure Love

I haven't been sleeping much this summer. It's not even the baby's fault. I wake up around four because my husband coughs or rolls over and then I can't fall back. I lie there trying to breathe, to count, to drop back into loose images, but thoughts from real life grab ahold of me and I let them drag me into the day. I'm tired all the time. Feelings I don't recognize swell up suddenly, then drain off. My wallet disappears from my purse; glass jars slip from my hands and crash to the floor. In a daze, thumbing through the magazines piled up on the kitchen counter, I come across an article in *O Magazine* on becoming a successful writer. "Your only motive for the pursuit must be pure love," the author says.[1] Elsewhere in the news, a gallery on East Seventy-Eighth Street is showing a series of paintings based on *The Story of O*, a famous erotic novel from the fifties. The painter, Natalie Frank, is the same age as me. She first read the book as a kid. So did I: I found it in my dad's bookcase, wedged between ratty murder mysteries. But I couldn't handle all the whipping and rough anal sex; I didn't understand why O would accept it, why she had to do everything her boyfriend wanted, regardless of how it felt to her. I never made it all the way through the novel. I did, however, use some lines from it in the first play I ever put on in college, a punk-rock *Taming of the Shrew*. I must have imagined, impurely, that you would be in the audience. You didn't turn up.

On the day the art show is closing, I go uptown to see it. I've always found the Upper East Side kind of soothing, but when I get out of the train I realize I'm right by the hospital where V. was born almost two years ago, where they didn't let me sleep for five days and my brain forgot how. After that I couldn't sleep at all without sedatives, so for months we took turns doing eight-hour shifts with her, which meant we were each alone all the time. As I pumped I'd imagine I had run away from the maternity ward in the middle of the night, hobbling toward some murderous assignation in Central Park. I never got there: the fantasy would end before I hit Fifth Avenue. When I got pregnant we had agreed: we can't kill ourselves now. We can't even want to anymore. Never. And then afterward, those months sunk so far down it wasn't even like wanting.

The gallery, which takes up the top two floors of a brownstone, feels like a house where no one has lived. In the first painting I look at, O is on her back, her arms tied up above her head. She is staring out at nothing, as if she's been lying there a long time, left alone while an orgy rages in another room. Eve Sedgwick says she imagines death as a voice that says, "That's enough; you can stop now."[2] O's not dead, but her expression is empty, peaceful. I remember that feeling of relief, as if it's only when someone has literally tied your hands to the bed that you can take a break, even if it's just while he changes his shirt. Is that a real memory? Anyway I find myself envying her now, that dull leisure. In the next picture O is on all fours getting fucked by a transparent man whose cartoony hand is pressing on her back while another man's fist holds her mouth ajar. Her face is stretched into someone else's toothy, dopey smile, a picture of a woman turning into a picture. Ugly as it is, I have a hard time looking away from the dumb grin, the Mickey Mouse hand, O evaporating into a grotesque mask. I walk around the gallery's rooms, checking out the rest of the pictures. The last one has animals in it—a baboon, a frog, a hippo—and a little girl, standing at O's shoulder, about to touch her. I know if my daughter saw this picture she would shout "baboon!" with pride and delight, so I feel happy too, imagining. Then someone else comes in, tattoos all over their arms. For a second I wonder if it's you. I don't look at their face. I walk back through the rooms again and take a couple of photos, then go home.[3]

I don't own *The Story of O* anymore, so I go to the Strand, where I find stacks of a recent edition on the banned books table. It's only seven dollars and less ugly than the bright pink copy I had in college, though I realize I'd been hoping to discover my dad's shabby pulp version again. I walk around the store for a while, looking for something else to buy with it so I won't be too embarrassed, but on four hours' sleep everything I pick up seems painfully difficult, even a rhyming picture book called *Feminist Baby*. So finally I bring *The Story of O* to the register, where the clerk rings it up unperturbed. I carry it around in my purse until it's the weekend again, then read it during naptime.

It turns out I was wrong. I thought the novel didn't care about O's pleasure; that's literally all it's about. What's confusing, what must have confused me before, is that it keeps saying it's about love: "I love you, I love you … I love you, do whatever you want with me, but don't leave me, for God's sake don't leave me."[4] But the men O seems to be talking to are ciphers, not characters; as the story goes on, it becomes clear that O isn't really experiencing all this sex in relation to anyone else at all. The word "love" is a kind of asterisk, a footnote directing you to everything else you've read or seen that has claimed to be about love—and it hints unnervingly that all that stuff, too, might be as insular, narcissistic, and lonely as this novel, trapped inside one middle-aged lady's burning brain:

> Would she ever dare tell him that no pleasure, no joy, no figment of her imagination could ever compete with the happiness she felt at the way he used her with such utter freedom, at the notion that he could do anything with her, that there was no limit, no restriction in the manner with which, on her body, he might search for pleasure? Her absolute certainty … that all he cared about was his own desire, so overwhelmed and gratified O that each time she saw a new proof of it, and often even when it merely occurred to her in thought, a cape of fire, a burning breastplate extending from the shoulders to the knees, descended upon her.[5]

Reading this passage, which comes close to the end, I mark it with my pen. I know right away it's the heart of the novel—or maybe its "belly" (in French, *ventre*), a word the writer resorts to a lot in her funny refusal to use dirty language—anyway I think I've found the reason why so many people see something they recognize here. Because of course the lover who can "do anything" with you, who only cares about his own desire, is a phantom, a desperate projection of your own selfishness, a fall guy onto whom you thrust the insistence of your own unbearably ugly hunger. What is especially brilliant and cruel about the passage is that O embarks on this train of thought right when her lover is jerking her off "so roughly she thought she would faint": at the very moment when she's totally lit up by the fantasy of being *used*, of her pleasure not mattering, he's making her come.[6] It's as if she can only bear pleasure by creating the most elaborate possible image of having transcended it. Freud: "the girl escapes."

What this book is about—and Natalie Frank, the painter, must have seen this too—is escaping from having a body by making it up, by turning it into pictures. The pictures I frame in fantasy are never pictures of my body, *this* body, and will never match any experience my body might have. The silly introduction to my 2013 edition of the book says the narrative is like "a naked light bulb in the room, casting an unforgiving glare on O's vulnerable flesh." (Apparently the book also "enthralls rather than titillates": pure love again.)[7] But actually we never see O, never really get to know what she looks like, and only from the fact that everyone who sees her wants to fuck her do we assume that she is, as it says on the back of the book, "beautiful." What we see instead is the machinery that helps everyone else see her: precise descriptions of how her costumes display her, her makeup routine, endless scenarios of her body being shown.

> "A little more light," said one of the men ...

> "Come over here so we can see you," her lover said ...

> They decided that she would be [whipped], irrespective of the pleasure they might derive from her screams and tears, as often as necessary so that some trace of the flogging could always be seen upon her ...[8]

All that marking and remarking never shows O to *us*, that is, to herself: instead it weaves a blanket of attention that covers up her body until she's just a pure point of experience. At the end of the book, O accompanies her owner to a party wearing nothing but an owl mask that conceals her head entirely; he makes a spectacle of her disappearance. This is what the whole book does, reaching again and again for whatever forms might accommodate my longing to disappear, to make you do all the fucking, to know that at last all the traces of my disgusting lust—including my "screams and tears"—are hidden under the blazon of your seeing, so that no one else (no one real) can see, so that I can't see myself.

And so of course O is—as we learn after the first round of flogging and fucking when she has to go back to work—a fashion photographer, someone whose task is making sex into images of other people. Since we mustn't see O, the book needs to come up with an actual beautiful body, one that doesn't belong to a subject, one that doesn't have desires. This is why it produces the model Jacqueline: "Her lips were slightly parted, and her eyes half-closed. Beneath the gleaming, liquid gloss of the photograph she looked like some blissful girl who had drowned, she was pale, so pale.... Her skin was actually darker than her hair, a grayish beige like fine-grained sand just after the tide has gone out. On the photograph, the red silk would be black."[9] The sinister language confesses: we're turning this girl into a dead thing so we can finally get a look at a body. And Jacqueline, who is a heartless bitch, is definitely asking for it: "completely egotistical," dumb but conniving, out for what she can get, even ethnically demonized by her "high Slavic cheekbones."[10] All Jacqueline has to do is lie there and show her pleasure: "To make sure that Sir Stephen could see Jacqueline in detail—and O thought to herself that if she were Jacqueline she would have guessed, or noticed, his invisible presence—O took pains to pull back her legs and keep them spread in the light of the bedside lamp which she had turned on."[11]

The narrator flaunts the powerlessness of this other cunt, not O's, not mine, which we can all examine with death-dealing precision. And isn't this murderous impulse against the vagina something most of us who have one feel? Cocks are so abstract, so linear, so easy to sublate into mere fact that it's almost like they're not there at all; but the mess of stuff we've got going on keeps us in the thick of the physical, swamps us with our own presence, fucks up the picture. Who wouldn't want to consign that morass to someone else, make them take it? Isn't that the first thing we'd have to do to be pure, to be free?

Meanwhile, as the summer winds on, I'm taking photographs almost constantly—probably way more than O, who seems pretty busy with other activities. My snapshots of Natalie Frank's paintings disappear into the welter of images on my phone, which are otherwise all, of course, of V., arrested over and over amid the wild storm of her two years' life. The earliest photos are unrecognizable now, as darkly enigmatic as the sonograms that preceded them. I scroll through them every once in a while; partly it's a way of hurting myself, but it also feels like there's something I'm trying to find, or hold on to. What do I want with these fierce, reproachful, lake-eyed shrimplings? But for that matter, what did I want at 7:31 this morning on the playground, when I whipped out my phone to catch her climbing up the monkey bars the same way she does every morning, her face exploding into the giant eyes and giant grin I now know better than I've ever known anything, the lion's mane of (stupidly there's no better way to say it) golden curls, all of which her dad and I have already captured hundreds and hundreds of times?

You could say we're objectifying her, wrestling her into these images as a reprieve from the chaos of loving her, the same way the text of O tries to submerge the unbearableness of its own desire in images of Jacqueline. A less brutal way to account for our photography might be through an almost-synonym that the philosopher Theodor Adorno uses in his *Aesthetic Theory*: objectivation. Adorno writes that objectivation—an artwork's taking fixed form—is essential to art. There has to be a thing there, like a text or an object or a picture, not just an event or happening. This is because through thing-ness, the artwork declares that it wants to outlast the world as we know it; this crazy aspiration—this fantasy—gets communicated to us as a kind of protest against the real world, the time and space in which we actually encounter the work; and that protest is what defines art as art.[12] In addition to whatever else it might be saying, then, the work of art is always also saying something like: "I have seen the truth, and it isn't this poisonous bullshit in which we are drowning. In fact I'm looking at it right now, even though I can't tell you what it is."

Maybe the problem, I find myself saying at lunch to my friend Shonni, another new mom, is that motherhood is all happening and no objectiva-

tion, no hint of transcendence. It's as if you've been smeared onto immediate physical space, the space you share with the baby. In the nearness of
that little body—a nearness that follows you wherever you go, even when
the baby doesn't—space becomes newly tyrannical; it's not just that you
can't leave the place where you are (though it is usually that too) but that
the very idea of leaving, of being elsewhere, has become somehow incoherent. You're grounded: flight could only be a kind of lethal unraveling,
your insides spilled out. And the same is true for time, to which you are now
fully subjected in a way that before was reserved to anomalous sites like
waiting rooms. As a parent, you're obsessed with time at all scales, and the
scales themselves feel cruelly continuous. Minutes on the breast: too few
means the baby is probably starving; too many means the baby is not feed-
ing efficiently so is probably starving. Minutes, hours of crying, counted to
reckon the chances there might really be "something wrong" with her besides the incalculable terror of suddenly existing. Hours of sleep: in a day
or at a stretch, in the bouncer versus the stroller versus the crib, and what
it all says about your chances of ever getting "back to normal," ever sharing a bed with your husband again. Then later, and presumably almost forever: hours of childcare, paid and unpaid, owed and begrudged; virtuous
hours of romping on the playground; sinful hours of television; hours until
the next mealtime, counted to determine whether you should appease her
demands, then yowls, for more strawberries; hours until bedtime; and finally, but not at all finally, hours before she'll be up again, which you must
somehow parcel out between the warring intimacies of conversation, sex,
violence, eating, TV, and sleep, a calculus roughly mooted by the insomnia
that ends up hogging most of these hours anyway.

But beyond all this, and much more terribly, the existence of this child
finally makes real what before you knew only in theory: you're getting old,
and you're going to die. That is: someday she'll be grown, and when that
happens, you'll lift your head and look about you as the tide of all this goes
out, and what you'll see is simply the damp sand of your old, neglected,
wrinkled, irreparably injured body, which no one will ever want to touch
again, if indeed—by now it's hard to remember—they ever really did. ("It
just gets worse," says your mother on your thirty-seventh birthday, when
you tell her you can't believe how old you look now, how ugly.) And the
person for whom, or with whom, or in whom you are undergoing all of
this—the child, despotic ruler of your whole heart—will never once have
stopped running, jumping, clamoring, transforming, will never once have
just stood there, stood still and returned your gaze, pausing the world in
its chaos so that you can actually see what it is that you have given your
life over to doing. That's why you take pictures: because in staring at that
still image you can imagine catching your breath, stepping back from this

relentless flux, as if there were someplace else to step back into. You can't really do it, but you can imagine it. Her objectivation in the photograph is something you perform upon yourself, and in it, like the work of art, you say absurdly: I am—there is—something other than this.

Suddenly I realize the pronouns have shifted around: the "you" has become a general you, that is, has collapsed into me. Throughout this piece of writing I had been trying to save it for someone else: *you*, the stranger, the other, the one who will see. But when the going got tough, like O I ended up using you to cover my ass, afraid of copping to my own passion. Embarrassed by the pitch of my confession, I wanted to disappear into that you, but instead it was you who vanished, and with it the hope that I might be delivered. In my life before, when I was feeling bad, I would sometimes do this exercise: lie on your back, close your eyes, remember that you are a creature like any other, and so in that most basic sense you are already perfect, already enough. It doesn't work anymore because it isn't true. Now the most essential part of me is something that careens beyond the grasp of any comfort. If I lie on my back and close my eyes, she might fall out the window. You will never be enough again.

The truth O's author heroically ignores is that most people, even men, don't really want to hurt us—not in the ways we want to be hurt. Long ago, I found someone who did. "Being ordinary and being married are both antiutopian wishes, desires that automatically rein themselves in," José Esteban Muñoz writes.[13] But for us, those reins *were* utopia, impossible negation of everything we'd been taught to value, everything human. We weren't building a good life together; we were walling up the garden of our wickedness, and the world of common sense could fuck off. Standard-issue apolitical bourgeois fantasy? Reactionary isolationist domesticity? Unwitting, belated echo of O's own midcentury values? Of course. But I'm trying to describe how fierce it was in us, how strong, this sudden access to something we could both recognize—could *feel* with our whole bodies—as truth, as something that, like art, seemed to be the opposite of everything else we knew.

Does everything else always have to win? "Anyone who brings a baby into this world has a lot of courage," a childless male friend observed sagely after V. was born. Whatever our courage had been, it crumpled in the face of the new terror wailing in our arms. The nothing you had promised to make me, that I'd begged to become, was itself nothing in the face of the baby's need, which left no room for desire because it left no room anywhere at all. We struggled to find the energy we'd always used for courting death, to channel it instead toward survival—hers, ours; it fizzled like a safety match, and we were thrown back on our own resources, the old, stupid, human ones, the ones we'd brought with us separately and stuffed away scornfully on entering the fortress of our love: patience, humility, brainless perseverance. Ideals I used to hate with all my heart.

The thing that might rescue us is language. V. has spent the last year learning to talk. She learned animals first, then colors, objects. She loves announcing the moon, sometimes in bright daylight; we're skeptical, but it turns out to be up there more often than we'd have thought. She says more and more sentences, says what she wants, what things are, what happened today, or on another day she remembers; she starts to invent, to tell tales. We don't always understand. The week she turns two she shocks me: I'm wiping cream cheese off her face when, writhing as usual, she yells: "Jesus Chwist!" and adds, a couple days later: "Fuck!" I immediately worry that she will offend the kind Christian woman who runs her daycare. "Don't say that," I plead, "you'll make people sad," though at the same time it's all I can do not to burst out laughing, and secretly I'm proud that she's already learned to enjoy the danger of speech. But amid all this, the thing she still can't get straight is pronouns. "I wanna carry you," she says when she wants me to pick her up for a while. "My g'asses," she explains at a quarter to six a.m., grabbing my glasses off the bedside table and thrusting them at me to put on so I can get started on her oatmeal. And "I wanna picsha you an' mama" when she wants me to hand her the photograph that sits on our bookshelf, out of her reach. It's a selfie I took when she was three months old; it shows the two of us just after nursing. Because of the camera angle, her sleeping face as it rests on my chest is enormous, much larger than mine. I am looking out at the camera vacantly, my hair uncombed, shadows under my eyes. The "you" in her "you an' mama" means "me," that is, her. The "mama" refers to that other one, the messy ghost.

A ghost: this is how, never having finished reading *The Story of O*, I had always assumed O would end up. A friend had mentioned that that the book got "pretty disturbing," and I figured that must mean O's last lover would end up killing her. But I was wrong about that too. As it turns out, there's almost no death in this novel; the pain in its world never gets anywhere near lethal, and even Jacqueline presumably comes away just fine. In fact, the last thing that happens is that Sir Stephen and his friend take off O's owl mask and fuck her on top of a table. At this point—spoiler, I guess— the narrative retreats to its artsiest level, and the last lines of the book are these: "There exists a second ending to the story of O, according to which O, seeing that Sir Stephen was about to leave her, said she would prefer to die. Sir Stephen gave her his consent."[14] That's it. As you can imagine, when I close the book I'm disappointed. By this point they've branded her, inserted pieces of iron through her labia, made her wear corsets that deform her permanently, whipped her until she bleeds, and all with a level of ritualistic formality that implied, I thought, some kind of final sacrifice as the culmination. But this sounds more like a marital spat: "Guess I'll just slit my wrists then!" "Yeah sure, go ahead."

I suppose there are two ways to understand what's disappointing about this "second ending." The first is that it's a failure of nerve, a result of the same squeamishness that makes the narrator transpose all anatomy into euphemism while remarking coyly on "the coarseness of the terms the men were using," which we're never allowed to hear.[15] Susan Sontag, who had a stronger sense of the book's "literary merit" than I do, notes that its "prose style is rather formal, the level of language dignified and almost chaste."[16] For me, it's hard not to read in this chastity the author's fear of getting us all in trouble. To show O getting slaughtered might break the fantasy that contains this story—her fantasy—and we'd suddenly find ourselves tumbled outside of it, outside of desire, realizing too late what we didn't want. Booted from the Eden of O's subjectivity, we'd be vulnerable to the shitty insistence of what Freud calls the reality principle, that know-it-all mechanism that constantly reminds us of what's actually the case: for instance, that in real life men are killing women literally all the time, and there's nothing sexy about it. O's death has to remain hypothetical, abstract, so that the novel can avoid this cold shower—and the prosaic, undignified questions that might follow.

And yet the more I think about it, the more I start to feel that there is also something perfect about O maybe dying of her lover's mere indifference. It's the logical end point of that "cape of fire," the fantasy that my own desire can be erased, made irrelevant, by the other's. What I want is to be nothing but a character in your dream. And how can I know I have achieved this—how can I be sure—unless at some point, at the limit, your dream ends? It's morning: you sit up in bed refreshed, no trace left of what we did together. I sink from the world like a stone. You look down fondly at the person asleep beside you, the early daylight gleaming off their cheek. They are lovely, nothing like me; even in their sleep they are sweet, strong, full of thought. Following their passion! Even though neither of you is real—even though the truth is that *you're* just characters in *my* dream—I can't think about this, here in the dark, without crying. I take it back, says O, going under. It's not what I want.

But then it is. After I've stopped sniffling I close my eyes and let myself imagine that descent, the incredible relief of the dark becoming total, the permission at last to quit fighting, as if I hadn't even realized I'd spent the past two years with both hands clenched into fists. In one, the precious fragments of whatever I used to think I was, what I'd be, what I'd write, how I'd show it to you. And in my other hand, the tiny captive hand of my daughter, which I try not to squeeze but to hold gently, lightly, even as she bucks and wriggles and plumps down yelling in the middle of the street we always seem to be crossing and I have to lift her up and my longing to be gentle flickers in the wind of the danger that assails her at all times and from all sides, including, since the very beginning of her life, from inside her little body itself, the intestinal turmoils that kept her screaming, the dreams that now make her cry out in the night, whatever pain it is that makes her clutch wildly at the blue bucket when another child reaches for it in the sandbox: "No! Mine!" The exhaustion, finally, of never letting *her* let go, never letting her fall out of the world, even though I know the thing inside her that wants to, that will always want to.

"You've got guts," says a hell demon in an episode of my favorite TV show, "I think I'd like to slice you open and play with them." The lines I mouthed along with my favorite rock album at fourteen: "I'm happy and bleeding for you." The stocky older girl I followed around at camp all summer who would wipe her nose on me, shove me against a wall covered with spiders. The blond boy from my health ed class who sat down beside me on the crosstown bus and started scraping skin off the back of my hand with his thumbnail: "Does that hurt? I know it does. Want me to stop?" Once at a talkback I said my plays were always worlds I wanted to live in. "That's a very violent world," said a man in the audience. A graduate student who is writing an essay on those plays says: "I guess I want to understand that desire." I want him to understand, want everyone to understand, want you to. But don't you? The middle-aged white girls who elected a monster for president do. My lonely, angry dad did, and all the other losers who secreted away their copies of The Story of O, or who have since devoured Fifty Shades in all its media, or blissed out to Lana Del Rey's empty angel voice singing, "Tell me you own me," "Fuck yeah, give it to me," "Gimme all of that ultraviolence."[17]

And most and worst of all, the mothers. When the time comes to decide, let's not lie to ourselves: a baby means more pain, more death, and the savage pleasure that leaps like a flame from both of these. But where O's cape of fire sublimes her body into the ecstasy of the perfect zero, motherhood is nothing like that nothing. Again and again, it shoves us back among the crusts and crumbs, the spills and slops and organs and bones, the remnants, the beginnings. This is not self-sacrifice, but the mutation of the self into something utterly ungovernable, a formless roiling, a wild incessant howl that the world has taught us to attribute to the baby, and that indeed has nothing to do with the grownup person the world used to know, even if it already knew how to ignore her—her plans, ambitions, dreams; the forms she fought to take, dark eyes shining. We will never find our form now, never come to rest. And as we wander among the forms of others, the hunger in us will only grow. We walk around in a daze, fluids spattered on our clothes, hair sticky, bitten, bruised. The things we used to care about, when we can still attend to them, reach us distorted and muted, like echoes. You can't hold us. But if pure is what makes it through the blaze, then we must be on the right track. We are burning.

2018

Curtains

I know, I know, swerving into personal writing at the end of a book like this is not an original move. Lynda Hart does it with an experimental epilogue in *Between the Body and the Flesh: Performing Sadomasochism*; Kaja Silverman does it more briefly in the afterword to *Male Subjectivity at the Margins*, in which she wonders: "What is my own connection to these 'deviant' masculinities?"[1] Takeo Rivera ends *Model Minority Masochism* with a coda about the first theater he made in college; it's like we can't resist.[2] Chris Kraus's "Emotional Technologies," an autotheoretical essay on S&M, includes personal narrative throughout, but in the version of the essay published in the recent *Kink* anthology, Kraus also includes her own afterword, which situates the essay within the trajectory of her life as an artist and reflects on her S&M practice as "an exorcism of grief."[3] The fact that Kraus's piece is the last in *Kink* means that this turn to personal revelation is the closing gesture not only of "Emotional Technologies," but of the anthology as a whole, which is otherwise made up mostly of erotic narrative fiction. And in fact, erotic fiction has its own classic version of this maneuver: Georges Bataille's afterword to *Story of the Eye*, in which the author confesses to sources of the novel's sexual obsessions in his own childhood.[4] All of which is to say that what I just did, in ending this book with my own little confessional, is yet another instance of repetition.

Why this compulsion to end with a (return to) genre departure? As our discussion of autotheory showed, masochistic authorship may operate as a relay between different genres or discursive levels—not in order to deconstruct that difference but, on the contrary, to insist on it, eroticizing the difference as negation. The perverse theater we've been excavating throughout these chapters activates a heightened awareness of the incommensurabilities that structure writing, making gaps and hollows that are sites of both threat and retreat. This way of feeling writing corresponds,

I've suggested, to Freud's masochistic (and "sadistic") girl, who elaborates fantasies in order to disappear from them: authorship as a practice of removing yourself from the scene. What's key is that the move is iterable: by writing about this writing, the masochist can repeat the self-removal again and again—attaining to a position of critical exteriority, only to sacrifice it by implicating herself in further reflection, so that yet another disappearance will have to take place. It strikes me now that the confessional turn taken by all these final chapters operates as something like a tour of that structure. By showing you *where else I was* when I was writing the other chapters of this book, I reassure myself that there will always be another elsewhere for me, a recess beyond the frame that guides your attention at any given moment—a place like Mrs. Alsager's box, say.

Years after composing the above piece, and shortly after Leo Bersani's death, I reread *Intimacies*, the book Bersani had coauthored with Adam Phillips in 2008. Reading through Bersani's theorization of barebacking gangbang porn, I was slightly startled to find an extended discourse on the phrase I had chosen as the title for my essay on motherhood. Bersani argues that the practice of intentionally contracting HIV through unprotected group anal sex on film "perpetuates ... an ethic of sacrificial love startlingly similar to the officially condemned form of Catholic mysticism articulated toward the end of the seventeenth century by Quietism and the proponents of what was known as '*pure love*.'"[5] Citing the religious historian Jacques Le Brun, he notes that for Quietists, "Self-annihilation is the precondition for union with God; only those who have given their eternity to God can be the perfect receptacles for all that God, in His unfathomable arbitrariness, may will to give them."[6] Both barebacking and Quietism "can be thought of as disciplines in which the subject allows himself to be penetrated, even replaced, by an unknowable otherness"; both renounce "what we usually think of as the humanizing attributes of intimacy within a couple, where the personhood of each partner is presumed to be expanded and enriched by knowledge of the other"; instead, "their individualities are overwhelmed by the massive anonymous presence to which they have surrendered themselves."[7] Pure love is impersonal the way a virus is, the way God is. How close, I wondered, was Bersani's notion of "pure love" to mine—or to O's, or O's?

Bersani allows that both Quietism and barebacking may seem like "appalling examples of prideful masochism," but counters that "it is difficult to locate in either case the pleasure inherent in masochism or, more radically, the subject to whom pride might be imputed."[8] This dismissal of masochism's relevance surprises me, given Bersani's own famous account of masochism as a momentary shattering of the ego, which he rehearses in the next chapter of *Intimacies*; presumably, it would always be "difficult to locate" the subject in jouissance, that is, the sexual subject.[9] Our readings throughout this book have also emphasized a further sense in which masochistic enjoyment may be inherently "difficult to locate," where the masochist imagines pleasure in and as the obviation of her pleasure, and refuses to ground enjoyment in her particular body. The Quietist determined to suffer not this or that particular trial but *anything* God wants would seem to be this kind of masochist, a commitment that links him not only to the barebacking bottom as Bersani suggests, but also to Gaitskill's Beth, or, of course, to O.

Bersani published his own reading of *The Story of O* in the 1980s; like Sontag before him, he considers the novel's preponderant religiosity, observing that Réage "insists, in a rather heavy-handed way, on the analogies between O's willing enslavement to her lovers and a nun's surrender to God"; ultimately, he decides that "with a perversity familiar to theologians and saints, O finds in the very loss of self an occasion for self-glorification."[10] Bersani's reading of bug-chasing gangbangs in *Intimacies* reverses this emphasis. He admits that "the bottom's hypermasculinized ego" is a prominent feature of barebacking porn, but "self-glorification" doesn't seem to win out this time: the bug-chaser, it turns out, actually "perpetuates something quite different," a neo-Quietist movement toward impersonality.[11] Bersani's earlier reading of *The Story of O*, while sustained and thoughtful, never finds in it anything like the counterintuitive or transgressive possibilities he later discerns in this genre of all-male porn. Instead, *O*'s scenes "merely repeat, with increasing intensity, the single project of an already fixed identity."[12] Where I see the main action of *The Story of O* as something like an ongoing attempt to *give* form to a terrifyingly formless experience—an attempt I relate to the impasse of motherhood as I've come to know it—Bersani renders the novel as a bold but ultimately conservative reiteration of already-familiar fantasmatic structures.

Bersani's reading of this fixity seems to be rooted in his willingness to take seriously the subjectivity of O's male lovers, which I can't bring myself to do; he even suggests that they are the novel's true psychic point of origin. While it is O "whose experience we share," he writes, "to be in O's consciousness is, necessarily, to be fascinated by a *far more important subjectivity*, one which comes to us, as it comes to her, only through the scenarios she agrees to perform."[13] The novel is, he suggests, most revelatory "as a kind of fantasy-blueprint of pure heterosexual desire, a mad dream of the 'ideal' resolution (especially by men) of Oedipal conflicts."[14] By reassigning the novel's founding desire to straight men—by turning away, I almost want to say, from the generative subjectivity of its female lead—Bersani seems to cut off the potential for finding the kinds of productive incoherence he is almost always so adept at discovering. As we might well expect, then, the "pure heterosexual desire" structuring *The Story of O* has little in common with the "pure love" of the barebacking orgy and its heretical precedent, and perhaps even less in common with the all-male world Bersani weaves into his argument in the next chapter of *Intimacies*: Plato's academy.

What role could a body like mine have to play in such scenes of pure love? None, and that's one of the reasons why I love them. In these chapters of *Intimacies* I find my own desire—as, in their own ways, in their respective masochistic scenes, Sedgwick and Silverman also do—expressed in a scene that pointedly excludes me, the scene of men fucking, thinking. "There's no part for *me*!"[15] It's a familiar comfort.

But in the final chapter of *Intimacies*, something different happens. Bersani's coauthor Adam Phillips offers to supplement Bersani's account of impersonal love by proposing another protagonist for it, alongside the barebacker and the Platonic lover. What about, Phillips says, *the mother*? After all, "mothering could be described, however counterintuitively, as a profoundly impersonal intimacy."[16] Reading this, the thrill of gratitude I feel is anything but impersonal. That's right, it's me! With my cesarean scar and my syrup-smeared jeans, *I'm* the most fucked-up pervert around, the most uncompromising philosopher!

But wait: does this thrill of self-revelation mean I'm not the girl after all, but the boy? Not Mrs. Alsager but Wayworth, dying for my chance to stumble out in front of the footlights, desperate to be seen? Has it always just been me in full view?

Well, yes. But whatever it is I've been trying to show you all this time, let's both remember: there's even more you'll never see. And isn't that the point of all these masochistic afterwords? "After this," Hedda announces, "I will be quiet."[17] The book is ending now, and you're not here.

Acknowledgments

A lot has happened since I started writing this book and I'm grateful to everyone who kept me here anyway. Shonni Enelow, you are the best evil twin a fellow could have. Thank you for giving this project so much of your time, rigor, and glamour, and thank you always for your comradeship—it means, actually, the world. Wendy Anne Lee, thank you, sister, for your ferocity and insight and all that good holding. Martin Harries, thank you for your exquisite guidance and kindness this whole time. Thank you to Tim Reid, to Zach Samalin for psyching me up and talking me down, and to Jonathan Flatley for being such a good person to think with. Thank you, Lauren Berlant.

I started this writing as an assistant professor in the English department at New York University, surrounded and supported by colleagues as remarkable as Una Chaudhuri, Sonya Posmentier, Richard Halpern, Brandon Woolf, and Elaine Freedgood: thank you, and I miss you. Deep gratitude also to my remarkable colleagues at Brown University, Rebecca Schneider, Patti Ybarra, Thalia Field, Kym Moore, Sophia Skiles, Leon Hilton, and especially the passionate artists who have taken care of the MFA playwriting program so I could sneak away and write: Melissa Kievman, Lisa D'Amour, Stacey Karen Robinson, B Reo, thank you. Extra special thanks to the Brown MFA playwrights '20–present, who are badass and brave and who have kept lighting up my brain through dark times, and to the PhD students in my spring '21 grad seminar in performance studies, who got on zoom once a week to talk about a lot of the texts in this book. Thank you, Kate Bothe and Eamon Brown, for being our Providence family. Darcie Dennigan, thank you for writing with me.

Back before any of this, I was a grad student in the Department of Rhetoric at the University of California, Berkeley, alongside Simon Porzak, K-Sue Park, and Damon Young, brilliant people who introduced me to psychoanalysis and queer theory. Thank you, Simon, for deciding we should start a Working Group on Violence, Pleasure, and Writing, and thanks to Daniel Boyarin and the Center for the Study of Sexual Culture for funding it—really, this project started there. Gratitude always to the late Felipe Gutterriez for his inspired mentorship, and to Shannon Jackson for hers—and for teaching me how to write a book even when it seems impossible.

I'm grateful to the English Institute for inviting me to give a paper in their session on Abstraction in the fall of 2019, and to everyone there who talked to me about it afterward; it's because of that weekend that I started figuring out what this book would really be. Thanks to Nan Da for her help and encouragement, and to Alan Thomas, Anahid Nersessian, and the press's anonymous readers, whose feedback has been truly thoughtful and helpful. Other people whose generous engagement with this work in progress I want to acknowledge include Elin Diamond, Josh Kotin, Andy Parker, David Kurnick, Sasha Weiss, and Nick Ridout. This has been going on for almost a decade so I know there are many more of you, too, which is a fact I should think about more often, because it's incredibly cheering. Thanks.

To the artists who have made Minor Theater with me in these years, you already know I know how lucky I am, but I'll say it again. Jennifer Seastone, Ben Williams, my heart sharks. Kedian Keohan, Sebas Alarcón, Kim Gainer, Haruna Lee, Linda Mancini, Pete Simpson, Jordan Baum, Ann Marie Dorr, and lots more, I'm so grateful. Ásta Bennie Hostetter, you are Björk *and* PJ and I can't imagine being a person without you.

Thank you to my mom, Fredrica Jarcho, and my brother, Nick Jarcho, for being so good to me when I need it, which is too often. Thank you, Cody Carvel, for so, so much. Thank you, Jane Velko, for being better than anything.

Notes

Introduction

1. Sigmund Freud, "The Economic Problem of Masochism," in *The Standard Edition of the Complete Psychological Works of Sigmund Freud*, ed. James Strachey, vol. 19, *The Ego and the Id and Other Works* (London: Hogarth Press, 1961), 162, PEP Web.

2. Scott Mendelson, "Box Office: 'Fifty Shades Freed' Pushes The Trilogy Past $1 Billion Worldwide," *Forbes*, February 10, 2018, https://www.forbes.com/sites /scottmendelson/2018/02/10/box-office-fifty-shades-freed-dakota-johnson-jamie -dornan-universal-el-james/?sh=42b3c6d015c5; Liz Bury, "50 Shades Makes EL James World's Highest-Earning Author," *Guardian*, August 13, 2013, https://www.theguardian .com/books/2013/aug/13/50-shades-el-james-highest-earning-author.

3. Jillian Keenan, "Finding the Courage to Reveal a Fetish," *New York Times*, November 9, 2012, https://www.nytimes.com/2012/11/11/fashion/modern-love-a-spanking -fetish-is-not-revealed-easily.html.

4. Gayle Rubin, "Thinking Sex: Notes for a Radical Theory of the Politics of Sexuality," in *Culture, Society, and Sexuality*, ed. Peter Aggleton and Richard Parker (London: Routledge, 2006), 151, 153.

5. For a particularly incisive account (and critique) of the controversy around S&M in late twentieth-century feminism, see Lynda Hart, *Between the Body and the Flesh* (New York: Columbia University Press, 1998), 36–82.

6. R. O. Kwon and Garth Greenwell, "Introduction," in *Kink*, ed. Kwon and Greenwell (New York: Simon & Schuster, 2021), xii.

7. Gilles Deleuze, "Coldness and Cruelty," in *Masochism*, trans. Jean McNeil (New York: Zone Books, 1991), 40. Chapter 1 will return to this passage from Deleuze's essay.

8. Molly Haskell, letter to the editor, *New York Times*, March 5, 2021, https://www .nytimes.com/2021/03/05/books/review/kink-frankenstein-and-other-letters-to-the -editor.html.

9. R. O. Kwon, "Safeword," in *Kink*, 58.

10. Peter Mountford, "Impact Play," in *Kink*, 102–24.

11. Amber Jamilla Musser, "The Literary Symptom: Krafft-Ebing and the Invention of Masochism," in *Mediated Deviance and Social Otherness: Interrogating Influential Representations*, ed. Kylo Hart (Cambridge: Cambridge Scholars Press, 2007), 287; Musser, "Reading, Writing, and the Whip," *Literature and Medicine* 27, no. 2 (Fall 2008): 205, http://dx.doi.org/10.1353/lm.0.0034.

12. David S. Marriott, *Lacan Noir: Lacan and Afro-Pessimism* (Cham, Switzerland: Palgrave Macmillan, 2021), 13.

13. For two classic accounts of the complexities of identification (including cross-racial identification), see José Esteban Muñoz, *Disidentifications* (Minneapolis: University of Minnesota Press, 1999), and Diana Fuss, *Identification Papers* (New York: Routledge, 1995). On the complexities of identification in modern drama and, specifically, in Adrienne Kennedy's work, see Elin Diamond, *Unmaking Mimesis: Essays on Feminism and Theater* (London: Routledge, 1997), especially 106-41.

14. Sigmund Freud, "A Child Is Being Beaten," in *The Standard Edition of the Complete Psychological Works of Sigmund Freud*, ed. James Strachey, vol. 17, *An Infantile Neurosis and Other Works* (London: Hogarth Press, 1955), 180, PEP Web.

15. Amber Jamilla Musser, *Sensational Flesh: Race, Power, and Masochism* (New York: NYU Press, 2014), 18-19.

16. In discussing the predominant whiteness of my masochism canon, I have not quite known what to do with the fact that this canon is also (like me) largely Jewish. Just as I would not claim that being Jewish has excluded me from the privileges or exempted me from the culpabilities of whiteness, I would not want to invoke Freud's Jewishness—or Sedgwick's, Silverman's, Bersani's, Edelman's—in some attempt to qualify the whiteness of this literary and theoretical archive. Of course, Freud was not really white in his own time; the complex ramifications for psychoanalysis of Freud's Jewish identity—which was traumatically racialized, not only by the Nazi regime that ultimately forced him into exile but throughout a life lived in an openly anti-Semitic society—has been the object of much fruitful critical discussion. But Freud's work did address itself to a white culture within whose canon it has now been long enshrined, and we encounter his work today in a societal context whose racial logic has as it were whitened him for us. This is obviously not the last word on the matter; as Eliza Slavet writes: "The scholarship on Freud's Jewish identity is immense." Slavet, *Racial Fever: Freud and the Jewish Question* (New York: Fordham University Press, 2009), 199 n. 40. Slavet offers a helpful summary of this discourse in her introduction, 1-30. Some important contributors to it include Cathy Caruth, *Unclaimed Experience: Trauma, Narrative, and History* (Baltimore: Johns Hopkins University Press, 1996); Sander Gilman, *Freud, Race, and Gender* (New York: Verso Books, 2007); Jay Geller, *On Freud's Jewish Body: Mitigating Circumcisions* (New York: Fordham University Press, 2007); and Ann Pellegrini, who argues that "Freud's theories of sexuality and sexual difference may represent Freud's attempts to work his own way out of the damning alignment of male Jewishness, the feminine, and sexual 'deviance.'" Pellegrini, *Performance Anxieties: Staging Psychoanalysis, Staging Race* (New York: Routledge, 1997), 4.

17. Of course this theory is partial; it could only ever supplement the objective analysis of how canons serve the interests of social and economic domination. But I believe it is valuable to examine the imaginative and erotic experiences such formations offer to those who identify with them. For examples of work in cultural studies that shares this conviction, see Sharon Holland's *The Erotic Life of Racism* (Durham: Duke University Press, 2012), which considers white subjects' libidinal investments in anti-Blackness; Grace Lavery's analysis of how masochistic desire operates among cis men in Trumpism (see her 2019 article "The King's Two Anuses: Trans Feminism and Free Speech," *differences* 30, no. 3 [2019]: 118-51, https://doi.org/10.1215/10407391-7974030); or perhaps most famously, Lauren Berlant's *Cruel Optimism* (Durham: Duke University Press, 2011).

18. One recent exception is Olivia Noble Gunn's *Empty Nurseries, Queer Occupants: Reproduction and the Future in Ibsen's Late Plays* (New York: Routledge, 2020). Citing Ibsen's predisposition to absent children and replace them with other, queerer "futures," Gunn enlists him as "a kind of antisocial ally" for theorists in the tradition of Bersani and especially Edelman (33). She notes that "approaches to gender and sex in Ibsen studies" have been dominated by "the story of the Father and the question of the freedom of the individual" (40). A notable recent example of psychoanalytic work (informed by queer theory and queer of color critique) that attends extensively to one particular piece of contemporary realist drama is Avgi Saketopoulou's writing on Jeremy O. Harris's *Slave Play*; see Avgi Saketopoulou, *Sexuality Beyond Consent: Risk, Race, Traumatophilia* (New York: NYU Press, 2023).

19. Hart, *Between*, 64.

20. My curiosity about how masochism operates in unsafe situations, as opposed to normative ones, aligns these readings to some extent with Saketopoulou's theorization of "limit consent" as a sexual practice that courts a state she calls "overwhelm": "unlike self-shattering, which presumes a quick, and better, reconstitution of the subject, as in Bersani's work (1986), overwhelm opens up to actual risk," Saketopoulou writes. Saketopoulou, *Sexuality*, 58, see also 100. Like masochism in many of my readings, "limit consent is about inviting surprise that opens up space for fresh experience. This invitation is risky through and through; one steps into the space at the risk of being injured or assuming the risk of injuring the other" (91). While Saketopoulou repeats this warning throughout the book, her argument consistently emphasizes the possibility for positive psychic change ("expanded psychic freedoms," 92) issuing from these experiences. This emphasis isn't one that *Throw Yourself Away* shares.

21. Michel Foucault, *The History of Sexuality*, vol. 1, *An Introduction*, trans. Robert Hurley (New York: Vintage Books, 1990), 32.

22. Foucault, *History*, 34.

23. For an example of excellent work in the latter vein, see Ariane Cruz's *The Color of Kink* (New York: NYU Press, 2016).

24. Claire Jarvis, *Exquisite Masochism: Marriage, Sex, and the Novel Form* (Baltimore: Johns Hopkins University Press, 2016), 12.

25. Jarvis, *Exquisite Masochism*, 161.

26. My suggestion that form can be the content of masochistic fantasy seems to me to resonate with Eugenie Brinkema's recent work on form and/as violence: see Brinkema, "The Violence of a Fascination with* a Visible Form (on Martyrs, Cruelty, Horror, Ethics) [*on and vs. with vs. as]," *Postmodern Culture* 30, no. 2 (January 2020), https://www.pomoculture.org/2021/01/07/the-violence-of-a-fascination-with -a-visible-form-on-martyrs-cruelty-horror-ethics-on-and-vs-with-vs-as/.

27. Jarvis retains Deleuze's emphasis on "the frozen, suspended qualities of [masochistic] sexuality" and echoes his insistence on masochism's separateness from sadism, as well as his treatment of dominant women as masochistic characters, though she differs from Deleuze in emphasizing a "masochistic dyad … constructed by two active participants, not one"; see Jarvis, 10–15.

28. Deleuze, "Coldness," 14.

29. For the centrality (and primacy) of masochism in Freud's thought, see Jean Laplanche, *Life and Death in Psychoanalysis*, trans. Jeffrey Mehlman (Baltimore: Johns Hopkins University Press, 1976).

30. Freud, "Economic Problem," 161; Freud, "Das ökonomische Problem des Mas-ochismus," *Gesammelte Werke*, vol. 13 (Frankfurt: S. Fischer, 1972), 374, PEP Web.

31. Freud, "Economic Problem," 159.

32. Musser, *Sensational Flesh*, 8. In this respect, masochism seems to partake of the paradoxical structure Eve Kosofsky Sedgwick famously ascribes to the modern concept of homosexuality, a concept she argues is both "minoritizing" and "universalizing" and hence "is organized around a radical and irreducible incoherence." Sedgwick, *Epistemology of the Closet* (Berkeley: University of California Press, 1990), 85.

33. Freud, "Economic Problem," 162.

34. Leo Bersani, *The Freudian Body* (New York: Columbia University Press, 1986), 39.

35. Bersani, *Freudian Body*, 43. This sentence and the following come from my article "Anything," published in *ELH* 88, no. 2 (Summer 2021): 353–54, https://doi.org/10.1353/elh.2021.0016.

36. Bersani, *Freudian Body*, 41.

37. Timothy Murray, ed., *Mimesis, Masochism, and Mime: The Politics of Theatricality in Contemporary French Thought* (Ann Arbor: University of Michigan Press, 1997), 18.

38. This is the poststructuralist discourse on "theatricality" as a subversion of representational, identitarian logic and/or phallogocentric power, a discourse in relation to which Timothy Murray points out that post-Freudian accounts of the split, fragmented, or "fading" subject "can be said to align theatricality with the intensity and pleasure of masochism," while "masochism is understood to theatricalize the constitution of the symbolic order in *différance* and to provide a representational means for forging this order differently by and for its Others." Murray, ed., *Mimesis*, 18–20. Murray's anthology is conceived around this alignment, although it seems to me that the essays collected in the volume rarely explore masochism in a sustained way, treating it instead mainly as a conceptual switchpoint for questions of representation, subjectivity, and power.

39. Derrida develops the logic of the supplement, which is at once writing and sexual fantasy, throughout his reading of Rousseau's work in *Of Grammatology*. Jacques Derrida, *Of Grammatology*, trans. Gayatri Chakravorty Spivak (Baltimore: Johns Hopkins University Press, 1997). Masochism as we'll encounter it in the following chapters will sometimes echo—or, we might say, will try to stage—Derrida's account of the supplement, which always "dislocates the subject that it constructs" and "torments its language" (141), ensuring that "pleasure is the menace of death" (154). In language—which as always, for Derrida, means writing—"spoken plenitude begins to become what it is through losing itself, hollowing itself out, breaking itself, articulating itself" (270). By the same token: "Writing *represents* (in every sense of the word) enjoyment. It plays enjoyment, renders it present and absent. It is play" (312)—this even though, and because, "writing carries death" (290).

40. Michel Foucault, "What Is an Author?" trans. Josué V. Harari, in *Aesthetics, Method, and Epistemology*, ed. James D. Faubion (New York: The New Press, 1998), 206–7.

41. See Jean Laplanche and J.-B. Pontalis, "Fantasy and the Origins of Sexuality," *The International Journal of Psycho-analysis* 49, no. 1 (1968): 1–18, ProQuest.

42. Leo Bersani, *A Future for Astyanax: Character and Desire in Literature* (New York: Columbia University Press, 1984), 10–11.

43. Berlant, *Cruel Optimism*, 138.

44. Darieck Scott, *Extravagant Abjection: Blackness, Power, and Sexuality in the African American Literary Imagination* (New York: NYU Press, 2010), 255, my emphasis.

45. Scott, *Extravagant Abjection*, 155, 166–69.

46. Musser, *Sensational Flesh*, 170.

47. Musser, *Sensational Flesh*, 170.

48. Musser, *Sensational Flesh*, 46–47. See Frantz Fanon, *Black Skin, White Masks*, trans. Charles Lam Markmann (London: Pluto Press, 2008), 109–62.

49. Musser, *Sensational Flesh*, 52. While Musser offers her own rereading of Fanon that does locate masochism in the Black male subject he describes, she remarks that Fanon himself never "describe[s] sexual desire on the part of the Negro" at all; see 49–52, 93.

50. Freud, "Economic Problem," 169.

51. Sigmund Freud, "A Child," 180. On this moment in Freud, see also Scott, *Extravagant Abjection*, 107. Fanon also references (French translations of) *Uncle Tom's Cabin* in his discussion of white masochism; see Fanon, *Black Skin*, 133.

52. David Savran, *Taking It Like a Man: White Masculinity, Masochism, and Contemporary American Culture* (Princeton: Princeton University Press, 1998), 33. For perhaps the most influential critique of white subjects' pleasurable identification with spectacles of Black suffering, see Saidiya Hartman, *Scenes of Subjection: Terror, Slavery, and Self-Making in Nineteenth-Century America* (New York: Oxford University Press, 1997).

53. Aliyyah I. Abdur-Rahman, *Against the Closet: Black Political Longing and the Erotics of Race* (Durham: Duke University Press, 2012), 26–27.

54. Abdur-Rahman, *Against the Closet*, 32.

55. Saidiya Hartman's reading of white abolitionist writers also characterizes their explicit identification with the enslaved as "masochistic fantasy," which she describes as another form of violence: if "black suffering … can become palpable and indignation can be fully aroused only through the masochistic fantasy, then it becomes clear that empathy is double-edged, for in making the other's suffering one's own, this suffering is occluded by the other's obliteration." Hartman, *Scenes*, 19.

56. Abdur-Rahman, *Against the Closet*, 42.

57. Abdur-Rahman, *Against the Closet*, 42, original emphasis.

58. Musser, *Sensational Flesh*, 175–76. Musser bases her account of this violence in a reading of Hortense Spillers's classic 1987 essay "Mama's Baby, Papa's Maybe: An American Grammar Book," which Scott also cites in the remarks quoted here. See Spillers, "Mama's Baby, Papa's Maybe: An American Grammar Book," *Diacritics* 17, no. 2 (Summer 1987): 67, JSTOR. In describing Black women as the "limit of theory" Musser draws on Sharon Holland's *The Erotic Life of Racism*; see Musser, *Sensational Flesh*, 156–58. Saketopoulou also discusses the "antiracist racism" of refusing to recognize possibilities of perverse desire in Black subjects; see *Sexuality*, 124–28.

59. Scott, *Extravagant Abjection*, 156.

60. Scott, *Extravagant Abjection*, 163–64.

61. Cruz, *Color of Kink*, 10, 25.

62. Takeo Rivera, *Model Minority Masochism: Performing the Cultural Politics of Asian American Masculinity* (New York: Oxford University Press, 2022), 45.

63. Hortense Spillers "'All the Things You Could Be by Now, If Sigmund Freud's Wife Was Your Mother': Psychoanalysis and Race," in Spillers, *Black, White, and in Color:*

Essays on American Literature and Culture (Chicago: University of Chicago Press, 2003), 376. This 1996 essay is republished in the 1997 collection *Female Subjects in Black and White: Race, Psychoanalysis, Feminism,* ed. Elizabeth Abel, Barbara Christian, and Helene Moglen (Berkeley: University of California Press, 1997), which contains many more examples of work that pursue a critical rapprochement between critical race theory and psychoanalysis. In addition, see—from the same year—Christopher Lane, ed., "The Psychoanalysis of Race," special issue, *Discourse* 19, no. 2 (Winter 1997), JSTOR.

64. Spillers, "All the Things," 384–85. In *Black Skin, White Masks* Fanon opens the chapter "The Negro and Psychopathology" by noting similarly: "one should investigate the extent to which the conclusions of Freud or of Adler can be applied to the effort to understand the man of color's view of the world." Fanon, *Black Skin,* 109. Spillers engages and critiques Fanon's argument in the essay discussed here.

65. Fanon, *Black Skin,* 73.

66. Fanon, *Black Skin,* 77–78.

67. For a useful one-paragraph distillation of Fanon's relation to psychoanalysis, see Christopher Lane, "The Psychoanalysis of Race: an Introduction," in Lane, ed., "Psychoanalysis of Race," 9.

68. Elizabeth Freeman observed in 2010 "sadomasochism's absence from the historical turn in queer theory" and noted that "it has been easy for critics who would condemn queer theory in the name of a more properly historicist analysis to fasten on sadomasochism as a sociosexual and critical fad, whose fading from academic interest ought to be viewed with relief." Freeman, *Time Binds: Queer Temporalities, Queer Histories* (Durham: Duke University Press, 2010), 140–41. Freeman's own beautiful argument that sadomasochism can itself be a way of engaging history—and specifically, the ongoing history of Black enslavement—is very suggestive for my own reading of Kennedy in chapter 3. Its application there is limited by the fact that her argument is directed towards an account of embodied sadomasochistic practice that "conjures up the possibility of a future beyond ... writing." Freeman, *Time Binds,* 151. I'll suggest that in Kennedy's play *He Brought Her Heart Back in a Box,* it's precisely *through writing* that the encounter with history becomes live, or that history can become an encounter.

69. José Esteban Muñoz, *Cruising Utopia: The Then and There of Queer Futurity* (New York: NYU Press, 2009), 11. Muñoz is here referring to the "antisocial" strand of queer theory pursued most famously by Bersani and Edelman. Michael Hames-García traces the disciplinary "shift from queer theory to queer ethnic and indigenous studies," or queer of color critique, in "What's After Queer Theory? Queer Ethnic and Indigenous Studies," *Feminist Studies* 39, no. 2 (2013): 388, JSTOR. Prominent examples of this shift include work by Muñoz, Roderick A. Ferguson, Anne Anling Cheng, and later also Holland, Juana María Rodríguez, Scott, and Musser (to name a very few). In *Sensational Flesh,* Amber Jamilla Musser adapts the familiar critique of universalism in white queer theory to her own focus on masochism, calling for "another type of reading practice" for masochism "which would center difference, flesh, and multiplicity" (19); in her subsequent book, *Sensual Excess: Queer Femininity and Brown Jouissance* (New York: NYU Press, 2018) she develops an interpretive practice that "works around" psychoanalytic discourse (11, see also 72). Although here she occasionally draws on Lacan and other psychoanalytic writers, she argues for a critical shift away from "sexuality's emphasis on desire, subjectivity, and agency" towards a focus on sensuality, alterity, and embodiment (21).

70. Spillers, "All the Things," 426.

71. Scott's analysis focuses purposely on Black male subjects; he worries that a "focus on the abject in relation to black women too easily might appear to be a confirmation of the defeat with which abjection works rather than a complication of it," since the analysis of Black female figures *as* abject would lack the "more counterintuitive" force of reading abjection in Black masculinity. Scott, *Extravagant Abjection*, 265. Scott's suggestion that there might be something dangerously *obvious* in figuring Black female subjugation—and especially in relating that figure to desire—will echo below in my reading of Kennedy's *Funnyhouse of a Negro*, which I'll describe as a consciously evoked "nightmare of tautology."

72. Scott, *Extravagant Abjection*, 2; see also 13.

73. Christina Sharpe, *Monstrous Intimacies: Making Post-Slavery Subjects* (Durham: Duke University Press, 2010), 3.

74. Sharpe, *Monstrous Intimacies*, 121, 185, 173. For a related argument see Nahum D. Chandler, "Of Exorbitance: The Problem of the Negro as a Problem for Thought," *Criticism* 50, no. 3 (Summer 2008): 345–410, JSTOR.

75. Sharpe, *Monstrous Intimacies*, 187.

76. Gérard Genette, *Narrative Discourse*, trans. Jane E. Lewin (Ithaca: Cornell University Press, 1980), 235 n. 51.

77. See Paul de Man, "Autobiography As De-Facement," in *The Rhetoric of Romanticism* (New York: Columbia University Press, 1984), 67–81.

78. Henrik Ibsen, *Hedda Gabler*, trans. Edmund Gosse and William Archer (New York: Dover, 1990), 37.

79. Kaja Silverman, *Male Subjectivity at the Margins* (New York: Routledge, 1992), 189.

80. See Robyn Wiegman, "Heteronormativity and the Desire for Gender," *Feminist Theory* 7, no. 1 (2006): 89–103, https://doi.org/10.1177/1464700106061460; Andrea Long Chu, *Females* (New York: Verso Books, 2019), 35.

81. Jessica Benjamin's 1988 work *The Bonds of Love* is one of the most sophisticated and useful accounts treating masochism as a psychic result of patriarchy, distinctive both in its commitment to psychoanalytic complexity and its genuine curiosity about masochism: unlike many contemporaneous critiques, *Bonds of Love* proceeds as if masochism might teach us something about power that we *don't* already know. See Benjamin, *The Bonds of Love* (New York: Pantheon, 1988). In *Taking It Like a Man* (1998) Savran also argues for masochism's continuity and complicity with oppressive social structures (specifically capitalism), although he makes this argument about male rather than female masochism, arguing that the former is in fact utterly normative.

82. Cruz, *Color of Kink*, 32–34. Writing in 1994, Sedgwick describes both of these positions:

> Both mainstream and feminist anti-S/M propaganda have refused to perceive any complexity at all in what they see as the completely continuous relation between S/M violence and violence *tout court*. This has resulted, reactively, in a public self-presentation of S/M that emphasizes the *dis*linkages between the social realities of power and violence, on the one hand, and the sexualized representation of power and violence, on the other; that emphasizes, too, the crisp way in which S/M play can explicitate and therefore manage issues of power, consent, and safety that often remain dangerously obscured in more conventional sexual relations.… What

remains underarticulated outside of fiction, though, is the richness of experimental and experiential meaning in these scenes when they are understood as neither simply continuous with, not simply dislinked from the relations and histories that surround and embed them.

Eve Kosofsky Sedgwick, afterword to *Gary in Your Pocket*, by Gary Fisher (Durham: Duke University Press, 1996), 282–83.

83. See Cruz, *Color of Kink*, 56.

84. Musser, *Sensational Flesh*, 2.

85. For an exemplary nonrelational account of masochism, see Bersani's "Is the Rectum a Grave?": Bersani reiterates his account of sexuality as grounded in masochistic ego-shattering and writes: "Desire, by its very nature, turns us away from its objects." Bersani, "Is the Rectum a Grave?" in *October* 43 (1987): 221, JSTOR. For an account that emphasizes relation in sadomasochism, see Hart: considering the preponderant dynamics of lesbian S&M fantasies ("both the fictive ones and most testimonials"), Hart suggests that masochistic "suspense … could be understood as a desire to extend the relationship as long as possible" and claims: "One point on which all sadomasochists agree is that the surrender is mutual or it is not s/m." Hart, *Between*, 78–79. See also Saketopoulou, *Sexuality*, 68–69 and 77–78.

86. Garth Greenwell, "Gospodar," in *Kink*, 145.

87. Greenwell, "Gospodar," 147–48.

88. Greenwell, "Gospodar," 155.

89. Greenwell, "Gospodar," 164.

90. Greenwell, "Gospodar," 165.

91. Greenwell, "Gospodar," 145–46.

92. Greenwell, "Gospodar," 159.

93. Greenwell, "Gospodar," 159–60.

94. Greenwell, "Gospodar," 164.

95. Bersani, "Is the Rectum a Grave?" 212.

96. Juana María Rodríguez observes that "the spaces of sexual exploration and expression so common in the narratives of urban gay male sexuality … are places that can prove deadly to female-bodied people, female-presenting people, and others perceived as physically vulnerable…. We are not only threatened physically, we are often punished personally and politically for even stating a desire to participate in these alternative sexual formations that exist outside monogamy and domesticity." Juana María Rodríguez, *Sexual Futures, Queer Gestures, and Other Latina Longings* (NYU Press, 2014), 14.

Chapter 1

This chapter began as a talk at the English Institute in October of 2019. The talk, much of which is included here, was subsequently published as "Anything," alongside the other talks, in *ELH* 88, no. 2 (Summer 2021): 343–59.

1. Deleuze, "Coldness," 14.

2. Elfriede Jelinek, *The Piano Teacher*, trans. Joachim Neugroschel (New York: Grove, 2009); Mary Gaitskill, *Two Girls, Fat and Thin* (New York: Simon & Schuster, 1991); Mary Gaitskill, *Bad Behavior* (New York: Simon & Schuster, 2009).

3. Sontag includes *The Story of O* in the "authentic" category. Susan Sontag, "The Pornographic Imagination," in *A Susan Sontag Reader* (New York: Farrar, Straus and Giroux, 1982), 206. Daphne Merkin rehearses Sontag's classifying gesture when she opens her 1996 confessional New Yorker piece by describing the section of her bookshelf "given over to … sadomasochism"; Merkin briskly divides her collection into books that (presumably) have a claim to literary or theoretical seriousness and "the cheesier stuff, … books that get straight down to business without indulging in any niceties." Merkin, "Unlikely Obsession," *New Yorker*, "Special Women's Issue," February 26 and March 4, 1996, 98. As Lynda Hart observes in her critique of Merkin's piece, the "authors are unremarked in the latter category"; Hart suggests that this dismissive gesture corresponds to Merkin's anxious reassertion of her own "upper-class status" throughout the essay. Hart, *Between*, 32.

4. Roland Barthes, *A Lover's Discourse: Fragments*, trans. Richard Howard (New York: Penguin, 1990), 3–5.

5. Leopold von Sacher-Masoch, *Venus in Furs*, in *Masochism*, trans. Jean McNeil (New York: Zone Books, 1991), 202.

6. Pauline Réage, *The Story of O*, trans. Sabine d'Estrée (New York: Ballantine, 2013), 115, 185.

7. Mary Gaitskill, "A Romantic Weekend," in *Bad Behavior*, 43, 36, 42.

8. Deleuze, "Coldness," 125.

9. As Roxane Gay wryly puts it, "The trilogy tries valiantly to make the reader believe female pleasure is the most important part of a sexual experience." Gay, *Bad Feminist* (New York: Harper, 2014), 196.

10. E. L. James, *Fifty Shades Trilogy* (New York: Vintage, 2012), 504.

11. Sacher-Masoch, *Venus*, 200; E. L. James, *Fifty*, 506.

12. Réage, *Story of O*, 76.

13. Gaitskill, "Romantic," 40.

14. Gaitskill, "Romantic," 40.

15. W. H. Auden, *September 1, 1939*, quoted in Gaitskill, *Bad Behavior*, front matter.

16. Gaitskill considers the way in which "a contemporary idea of complexity" operates as a norm of American realism in her 2011 review "Form Over Feeling: a Review of *Out* by Natsuo Kirino," in *Somebody with a Little Hammer* (New York: Vintage, 2017), 210–14.

17. See Roland Barthes, "The Reality Effect," in *The Rustle of Language*, trans. Richard Howard, ed. François Wahl (Berkeley: University of California Press, 1989), 141–48.

18. Barthes, "Reality," 142.

19. Barthes, "Reality," 147.

20. Barthes, "Reality," 145–46.

21. Gaitskill, "Romantic," 27.

22. Gaitskill, "Romantic," 36–37.

23. Gaitskill, "Romantic," 45. The claim that bad sex in Gaitskill—and specifically, the badness of sex with an actual sadist—functions in conversation with Flaubert's barometer and sundry furnishings seems to me to find support in Beth's impression that her lover's grandmother's apartment is "brutally ridiculous, almost sadistic in its absurdity"—the story's only use of the s-word. Gaitskill, "Romantic," 35.

24. Gaitskill, "Romantic," 27.

25. Gaitskill, "Romantic," 28.

26. Gaitskill, "Romantic," 27.

27. Gatskill, "Romantic," 46.

28. The term "variable focalization" comes from Genette, *Narrative Discourse*, 189.

29. Gaitskill, "Romantic," 38.

30. Maggie Nelson, *The Art of Cruelty* (New York: Norton, 2011), 221–22.

31. Deleuze, "Coldness," 45.

32. Gaitskill, "Romantic," 48.

33. Gaitskill, "Romantic," 48.

34. Berlant, *Cruel Optimism*, 148. Berlant makes this comment in a chapter on Gaitskill's 1991 novel *Two Girls, Fat and Thin*. Another of the stories in *Bad Behavior*, "Secretary"—also a sustained exploration of masochism—was made into an actual romantic comedy in 2002. Gaitskill has been critical of the film, calling it "the *Pretty Woman* version of my story" and noting: "In the movie, the heroine awakens to her masochistic sexuality and lives happily ever after. In the story, the heroine awakens to her masochistic sexuality and learns a hard truth: that she is a small, fallible container for a primary force beyond her understanding." I would suggest, though, that Gaitskill's fiction is remarkable at least partly because it invents and occupies new and disturbing modes of proximity to romantic comedy. Gaitskill, "Victims and Losers: A Love Story," in *Somebody with a Little Hammer* (New York: Vintage, 2017), 76, 83.

35. As in Avgi Saketopoulou's account of "exigent sadism," the sadist here appears as someone whose erotic significance for their partner lies in the sadist's drive to "intervene against the other's effort to master their unconscious through binding." *Sexuality*, 88. Both Saketopoulou and Gaitskill, that is, imagine the sadist as enjoying defeating their partner's efforts at self-mastery (which would include the self-mastery of a coherently held desire). For Saketopoulou, however, the exigent sadist is engaged in a deeply ethical and self-aware "form of care" (12)—definitely not what Beth's lover is up to.

36. Gaitskill, "Romantic," 30.

37. Gaitskill, "Romantic," 28–29.

38. Gaitskill, "Romantic," 30.

39. Gaitskill, "Romantic," 45.

40. Gaitskill, "Romantic," 48.

41. Gaitskill, "Romantic," 28.

42. Gaitskill, "Romantic," 43, 46.

43. Gaitskill, "Romantic," 46.

44. Gaitskill, "Romantic," 41.

45. Gaitskill, "Romantic," 27, 30, 48, 31.

46. Gaitskill, "Romantic," 29, 48. Among other signifying functions, the glancing references to Asian images or subjects that pepper this story underscore the whiteness of both main characters, leaving unchecked the common assumption that masochism is, to cite Ariane Cruz again, "a kind of Anglo phenomenon." Cruz, *Color of Kink*, 10. Larissa Pham's short story "Trust," published in the 2021 *Kink* anthology, seems to me to intervene in this scenario by riffing on "A Romantic Weekend" in several ways but establishing its own protagonist as Asian-American. Also about a masochistic woman and her cruel male lover who go away for a weekend together, "Trust" similarly employs variable focalization to explore the incommensurabilities between their desires. Indeed, Pham's narrative is more explicit in this thematic focus than Gaitskill's:

Do what you want with me, she says.... Though nothing he could do would ever be enough. What she wants is for him to understand her, to anticipate her every need. She wants to submit to him so thoroughly that he possesses even her desires, recognizing her so thoroughly that she never has to ask for a thing.... Suddenly, he wants to hurt her. Not in the way she wants him to.... She wants him to do what he wants, but she wants those wants to be her wants.

Larissa Pham, "Trust," in *Kink*, 35–36.

47. Gaitskill, "Romantic," 43.

48. Gaitskill, "Romantic," 43.

49. Gaitskill, "Romantic," 30.

50. Gaitskill, "Romantic,"42.

51. Silverman, *Male Subjectivity*, 265.

52. Sigmund Freud, "A Child," 195; see also 190. Sometimes Freud does not use the qualifier, and refers to the fantasies as simply "sadistic," both before and after the revelation of their masochism: see "A Child," 186, 199.

53. Freud, "A Child," 186.

54. Freud, "A Child," 191, 190, 180; Freud, "Ein Kind wird geschlagen," in *Gesammelte Werke: chronologisch geordnet*, vol. 12 (Frankfurt: S. Fischer, 1968-78), 211, 210, 198, PEP Web.

55. Sacher-Masoch, *Venus*, 150, 271.

56. Musser argues that Jean Paulhan's introduction to the anonymously published novel effectively "claims O as male fantasy," and observes that Aury's later confession positions her own writing as an emulation of the Marquis de Sade; see Musser, *Sensational Flesh*, 59.

57. Sigmund Freud, "Psychopathic Characters on the Stage," in *The Standard Edition of the Complete Psychological Works of Sigmund Freud*, ed. James Strachey, vol. 7, *A Case of Hysteria, Three Essays on Sexuality and Other Works* (London: Hogarth Press, 1953), 305, PEP Web, original emphasis. The Standard Edition dates this article to 1905 or 1906.

58. Freud, "Psychopathic Characters," 305-6.

59. Freud, "Psychopathic Characters," 306.

60. "das Drama [soll] aber tiefer in die Affektmöglichkeiten herabsteigen, die Unglückserwartungen noch zum Genuß gestalten, und zeigt daher den Helden im Kampf vielmehr *mit einer masochistischen Befriedigung* im Unterliegen." Freud, "Psychopathische Personen auf der Bühne," in *Gesammelte Werke: Texte aus den Jahren 1885 bis 1938*, Nachtragsband (Frankfurt: S. Fischer, 1987), 657, PEP Web, my emphasis.

61. Aristotle, *Poetics*, trans. Malcolm Heath (New York: Penguin, 1996), 11-13 (1450a-b) and 46 (1461b-1462a).

62. Freud, *"Psychopathische Personen,"* 657, my translation.

63. Aristotle, *Poetics*, 28 (1455b).

64. Gaitskill, "Romantic," 48.

65. Gaitskill, "Romantic," 48, ellipsis in original, emphasis mine.

66. Jarvis, for example, insists that the formal masochism she theorizes "is entirely separate from sadism" (*Exquisite*, 11). Similarly, Ruth McPhee finds that by "resolutely dissociating masochism from sadism Deleuze does much to start dismantling the reductive binary logic that has conceptually bound this perversion," a move which clears

the way for understanding "the radical potential of masochistic desire and pleasure." See McPhee, *Female Masochism in Film: Sexuality, Ethics and Aesthetics* (Surrey: Ashgate, 2014), 24.

67. Deleuze, "Coldness," 13–14, 38–40.

68. Deleuze, "Coldness," 42.

69. Deleuze, "Coldness," 40–41.

70. Deleuze, "Coldness," 23, my emphasis.

71. Deleuze, "Coldness," 67.

72. Deleuze, "Coldness," 26–35.

73. Deleuze, "Coldness," 31–33. See Sigmund Freud, "Fetishism" (1927), in *The Standard Edition of the Complete Psychological Works of Sigmund Freud*, ed. James Strachey, vol. 21, *The Future of an Illusion, Civilization and its Discontents, and Other Works* (London: Hogarth Press, 1961), 147–58, PEP Web.

74. Deleuze glosses Freud's concept of fetishistic disavowal this way: "the knowledge of the situation as it is persists, but in a suspended, neutralized form." "Coldness," 32.

75. Deleuze, "Coldness," 40.

76. See Deleuze, "Coldness," 43–46 and 132–34.

77. Deleuze, "Coldness," 133.

78. Deleuze, "Coldness," 66.

79. Deleuze, "Coldness," 57, 59.

80. Freud, "Economic Problem," 161–62. In German: "das Material ist sehr gleichartig, jedem Beobachter, auch dem Nichtanalytiker, zugänglich." Freud, "Das ökonomische Problem," 374.

81. Freud, "Economic Problem," 162; "Das ökonomische Problem," 374. As David Savran glosses Freud's description: "Like a theatrical performance based on a written script, the actors are only standing in for imagined subjects whose presence is perpetually deferred, who are neither 'in' the script nor 'on' the stage." Savran, *Taking It*, 28. While Savran's reading offers a metaphysical grounding for the "only"-ness or slightness Freud imparts to masochism here, I am most interested in the sleight as itself an erotic performance.

82. See in this connection Freud's remark in *Beyond the Pleasure Principle* that "a theatrical production never creates so great an impression the second time as the first." Freud, *Beyond the Pleasure Principle*, in *The Standard Edition of the Complete Psychological Works of Sigmund Freud*, ed. James Strachey, vol. 18, *Beyond the Pleasure Principle, Group Psychology and Other Works* (London: Hogarth Press, 1955), 35, PEP Web.

83. Freud, "Economic Problem," 162.

84. Freud, "Economic Problem," 162; "Das ökonomische Problem," 374.

85. Max Nordau, *Degeneration*, 2nd ed., anonymous trans. (London: William Heinemann, 1898), 412–14, Project Gutenberg. Richard von Krafft-Ebing, whose *Psychopathia Sexualis* formulated and popularized the concept of masochism, established its "feminine" nature (in men) and maintained it throughout subsequent editions; as Musser notes, "the theory that masochism was the product of an overly active feminine sexual drive remained consistent; only the case studies changed." See Musser, "Reading," 204–22, 207.

86. Freud, "Economic Problem," 169.

87. Freud, "Economic Problem," 169–70.

88. See Freud, "Economic Problem," 166–70; Freud, *The Ego and the Id*, in *The*

Standard Edition of the Complete Psychological Works of Sigmund Freud, ed. James Strachey, vol. 19, *The Ego and the Id and Other Works* (London: Hogarth Press, 1961), 12–66, PEP Web.

89. Leo Bersani, *The Culture of Redemption* (Harvard University Press, 1990), 37. For Bersani, the pleasure produced in sublimation is fundamentally masochistic, as sexuality itself is; in *The Freudian Body*, he locates sexuality in an experience of self-shattering "without any specific content" (40). For Joan Copjec's Lacanian critique of Bersani's account of sublimation—and in particular, of his claim that it constitutes an independence from particular objects—see Copjec, *Imagine There's No Woman: Ethics and Sublimation* (Cambridge, MA: MIT Press, 2002), 48–80.

90. Freud, "Economic Problem," 165.

91. Deleuze, "Coldness," 28.

92. For Hart, "The [feminist] promise of the Deleuzean model falls away rather rapidly as we discover that the idealism of the masochist places the woman on top *as the fantasy construct of the masochist.... * In this theory it is still women who must 'save the world' by saving men from themselves." Hart, *Between*, 72.

93. Freud, "A Child," 199, translation modified; Freud, "Ein Kind," 220–21, my emphasis. We'll return to this passage in chapter 2.

94. Deleuze, "Coldness," 42, my emphasis.

95. See note 96 in the introduction above.

96. Deleuze, "Coldness," 65.

97. Deleuze, "Coldness," 66, my emphases.

98. Deleuze, "Coldness," 67.

99. Deleuze, "Coldness," 14.

100. Deleuze, "Coldness," 69.

101. In an illuminating analysis of Anna Freud's 1922 paper "Beating Fantasies and Daydreams," which revisits and complicates one of the cases referred to in "A Child Is Being Beaten"—to wit, the case of Anna Freud herself—Rachel Blass foregrounds Anna Freud's conflicted desire for creative expression and authorship, and the psychic struggle with her father that this entails. Attending to the context of Anna Freud's paper, which was written as a requirement of her acceptance into the Vienna Society, Blass offers the intriguing formulation: "The masochistic fantasy here described is ... in part one of having one's inner creative experience (wish, fantasy, dream, story) beaten out." Rachel Blass, "Insights into the Struggle of Creativity: A Rereading of Anna Freud's 'Beating Fantasies and Daydreams,'" *The Psychoanalytic Study of the Child* 48 (1993): 87, PEP Web. I will return briefly to the topic of Anna Freud's paper in chapter 2.

Chapter 2

Portions of this chapter are adapted from two previously published articles. The first of these articles is "Cold Theory, Cruel Theater: Staging the Death Drive with Lee Edelman and Hedda Gabler," published in *Critical Inquiry* 44, no. 1 (Autumn 2017): 1–16. Copyright 2017 by The University of Chicago, 00093-1896/17/4401-0005. https://doi.org/10.1086/694127. The second is "Being Acted: Dramaturgical Masochism in Henry James's 'Nona Vincent,'" published in *Textual Practice* 35, no. 1 (2021): 153–70, copyright Taylor & Francis, available online: https://www.tandfonline.com/doi/10.1080/0950236X.2020.1811754.

1. Freud, "Das ökonomische Problem," 374.

2. Laplanche and Pontalis, "Fantasy," 17.

3. Lauren Berlant, *Desire/Love* (Brooklyn, NY: Punctum, 2012), 75.

4. Berlant, *Desire/Love*, 73.

5. Sigmund Freud, "A Child," 186.

6. Hart, *Between*, 63–64.

7. Silverman, *Male Subjectivity*, 166.

8. For biographer Leon Edel's classic account of this engagement, see Edel, "Henry James: The Dramatic Years," in *Henry James: Guy Domville with Comments by Bernard Shaw, H.G. Wells and Arnold Bennet*, ed. Leon Edel (Philadelphia: J. B. Lippincott, 1960), 11–121. See also David Kurnick's *Empty Houses: Theatrical Failure and the Novel* (Princeton: Princeton University Press, 2012), 105–52.

9. Diamond, *Unmaking Mimesis*, 31. In her reading, Diamond cites both Freud's "Psychopathic Characters" and James's review of the London premiere of *Hedda Gabler* (alongside other contemporary responses), moves I have borrowed from her here.

10. Diamond, *Unmaking Mimesis*, 31.

11. Lee Edelman, *No Future* (Durham: Duke University Press, 2004), 9.

12. Sigmund Freud, *Civilization and Its Discontents*, trans. James Strachey (New York: Norton, 2005), 117.

13. See Freud, *Beyond the Pleasure Principle*, 53–55.

14. For some key instances of this tradition in theater and performance studies, see Herbert Blau, *Take up the Bodies: Theater at the Vanishing Point* (Urbana: University of Illinois Press, 1982); Peggy Phelan, *Unmarked* (New York: Routledge, 1993) and *Mourning Sex: Performing Public Memories* (London: Routledge, 1997); Marvin Carlson, *The Haunted Stage: The Theatre as Memory Machine* (Ann Arbor: University of Michigan Press, 2003); and Rebecca Schneider, *Performing Remains: Art and War in Times of Theatrical Reenactment* (London: Routledge, 2011).

15. Edelman, *No Future*, 3.

16. Edelman, *No Future*, 27.

17. Edelman, *No Future*, 22.

18. Edelman, *No Future*, 17–18.

19. Jennifer Doyle, "Blind Spots and Failed Performance: Abortion, Feminism, and Queer Theory," *Qui Parle* 18, no. 1 (2009): 35, JSTOR. Doyle argues persuasively that the book enacts a "citational erasure" of its own feminist precedents: Doyle, "Blind Spots," 34. For related critiques of Edelman, see John Brenkman, "Queer Post-Politics," *Narrative* 10, no. 2 (2002): 174–80, Project MUSE; responses by Robert Caserio, J. Halberstam, José Esteban Muñoz, and Tim Dean in Caserio, Edelman, Halberstam, Muñoz, and Dean, "The Antisocial Thesis in Queer Theory," *PMLA* 121, no. 3 (May 2006): 819–28, JSTOR; and Muñoz, *Cruising Utopia*. Since its publication, *No Future* has often been invoked as a privileged synecdoche for the limitations of white queer theory; see note 68 in the introduction above for more on this critique, as well as Calvin Warren, "Onticide: Afropessimism, Queer Theory, and Ethics," *Ill Will*, November 18, 2014, https://illwill.com/print/ontocide. For a critique of *No Future* oriented by Black feminism, which finds fault with previous critiques and argues that *No Future* unwittingly ("symptomatically") describes queerness as what is in fact a Black position, see James Bliss, "Hope Against Hope: Queer Negativity, Black Feminist Theorizing, and Reproduction without Futurity," *Mosaic* 48, no. 1 (March 2015): 83–98. Edelman himself responds to

some of these critiques in his most recent book, *Bad Education* (Durham: Duke University Press, 2022); see especially ix–xix and 1–43.

20. See Edelman, *No Future*, 30, 102–7, and 165–66 n. 10. Although Edelman's discussion of Antigone is several pages long, his concern is with Judith Butler's reading of Lacan's account of the character, not with Antigone "herself."

21. Halberstam, in Caserio et al., "The Antisocial Thesis," 824.

22. Halberstam, in Caserio et al., "The Antisocial Thesis," 824. For an account and critique of the Ludlam production, see Alisa Solomon, *Re-Dressing the Canon: Essays on Theater and Gender* (London: Routledge, 1997), 144–54.

23. See Solomon, *Re-Dressing*, 46–49.

24. Ibsen, *Hedda Gabler*, 35. I have replaced the translators' ö with the original ø in character names throughout. Diamond notes that Ibsen apparently considered specifying that Løvborg's book is about "progress *resulting from the comradeship between man and woman*," though he decided against it: quoted in Diamond, *Unmaking Mimesis*, 25–26.

25. Ibsen, *Hedda Gabler*, 6, 34, 57–59.

26. See Ibsen, *Hedda Gabler*, 9, 63.

27. Ibsen, *Hedda Gabler*, 7.

28. Edelman, *No Future*, 43–44.

29. Ibsen, *Hedda Gabler*, 32.

30. For more on the distinction between desire and the drive in Lacan, see Slavoj Žižek, "From Desire to Drive: Why Lacan Is Not Lacaniano," *Atlántica de las artes* 14 (Aug. 1996), zizek.livejournal.com/2266.html.

31. See for example Bertolt Brecht, *Brecht on Theatre: The Development of an Aesthetic*, trans. Jack Davis et al., ed. Marc Silberman, Steve Giles, and Tom Kuhn (New York: Hill and Wang, 2015), 237.

32. Shonni Enelow, *Method Acting and Its Discontents: On American Psycho-Drama* (Evanston: Northwestern University Press, 2015), 18. See also Fuss, *Identification Papers*, and Diamond, *Unmaking Mimesis*.

33. Elizabeth Robins, *Ibsen and the Actress* (New York: Haskell House, 1973), 18.

34. See Diamond, *Unmaking Mimesis*, 31–32, and Susan Torrey Barstow, "'Hedda Is All of Us': Late-Victorian Women at the Matinee," *Victorian Studies* 43, no. 3 (2001): 389, https://doi.org/10.1353/vic.2001.0044. Solomon analyzes the feminist importance of Ibsen's dramaturgy in *Re-Dressing*, 46–69.

35. Toril Moi, "Hedda's Silences: Beauty and Despair in *Hedda Gabler*," *Modern Drama* 56, no. 4 (Winter 2013): 436, Project MUSE.

36. Moi, "Hedda's Silences," 436.

37. Ibsen, *Hedda Gabler*, 59.

38. Freud, *The Interpretation of Dreams*, trans. and ed. James Strachey (New York: Bard, 1998), 547–48. See Jacques Lacan, *The Four Fundamental Concepts of Psychoanalysis*, trans. Alan Sheridan, ed. Jacques-Alain Miller, vol. 11 of *The Seminar of Jacques Lacan* (New York: Norton, 1998), 57–60.

39. The elimination of soliloquies and asides is frequently cited as a signal realist achievement; see for example Oscar G. Brockett, *History of the Theatre*, 7th ed. (Boston: Allyn & Bacon, 1995), 430. See also Barstow, "Hedda," 399.

40. Ibsen, *Hedda Gabler*, 30.

41. Moi, "Hedda's Silences," 447.

42. Moi, "Hedda's Silences," 447.

43. Ibsen, *Hedda Gabler*, 70.

44. Ibsen, *Hedda Gabler*, 25.

45. Ibsen, *Hedda Gabler*, 59; Edelman, *No Future*, 59. As Moi shows in *Henrik Ibsen and the Birth of Modernism*, Hedda's aestheticism is also part of Ibsen's ongoing (and sometimes immanent) critique of idealism; see Moi, *Henrik Ibsen and the Birth of Modernism* (Oxford: Oxford University Press, 2006), 316–20.

46. See Diamond, *Unmaking Mimesis*, 28.

47. Ibsen, *Hedda Gabler*, 48.

48. Charles Dickens, "A Christmas Carol," *Charles Dickens: Christmas Books*, ed. Ruth Glancy (Oxford: Oxford University Press, 1988), 8.

49. Solomon, *Re-Dressing*, 17–18.

50. *A Doll's House*, by Henrik Ibsen, English version by Simon Stephens, directed by Carrie Cracknell, produced by the Young Vic, BAM Harvey Theater, Brooklyn Academy of Music, Brooklyn, NY, March 20, 2014.

51. See Solomon, *Re-Dressing*, 66.

52. Henrik Ibsen, *A Doll's House*, in *Six Plays by Ibsen*, trans. Eva Le Gallienne (New York: Modern Library, 1957), 76.

53. Ibsen, *Hedda Gabler*, 71.

54. Ibsen, *Hedda Gabler*, 72; *Hedda Gabler*, by Henrik Ibsen, directed by Thomas Ostermeier, BAM Harvey Theater, Brooklyn Academy of Music, Brooklyn, NY, Nov. 21, 2006, DVD, New York Public Library Performing Arts Research Collections. I'm grateful to Shane Boyle for suggesting I watch Ostermeier's production when I was developing this reading of the play.

55. Ibsen, *Hedda Gabler*, 37.

56. Ibsen, *Hedda Gabler*, v, translation modified.

57. Ibsen, *Hedda Gabler*, 37, translation modified.

58. Bert O. States, *Great Reckonings in Little Rooms* (Berkeley: University of California Press, 1985), 127.

59. Edelman, *No Future*, 59.

60. Ibsen, *Hedda Gabler*, 9.

61. Moi, *Henrik Ibsen*, 316.

62. Ibsen, *Hedda Gabler*, 15.

63. Ibsen, *Hedda Gabler*, 59, 68, translation modified. Moi observes that Løvborg has been shot "*i underlivet*"—in the genitals, and not just "in the bowels" or as otherwise euphemistically translated; see Moi, "Hedda's Silences," 453 n. 4, and Moi, *Henrik Ibsen*, 365 n. 2.

64. Moi, "Hedda's Silences," 437; see also Moi, *Henrik Ibsen*, 316, and Solomon, *Re-Dressing*, 66. Hedda's self-diagnosis may also return to theater by another route; in Freud's early writings, Fuss notes, identification itself "is fundamentally a question of *lowness*," naming the bourgeoise hysteric's imaginary relationship to the "fallen woman" (Fuss, *Identification Papers*, 24). If identification always entails the threat of debasement, then Hedda's theatrical power to compel our identification is precisely the power to bring "all of us" down.

65. Antonin Artaud, *The Theater and Its Double*, trans. Mary Caroline Richards (New York: Grove, 1958), 79.

66. Artaud, *Theater*, 75.

67. Jacques Derrida, *Writing and Difference*, trans. Alan Bass (Chicago: University of Chicago Press, 1978), 239. Lynda Hart's theorization of lesbian sadomasochism and theater turns to Artaud's theater (and Derrida's reading of it) as an analogy in a somewhat similar vein: "I think that lesbian sadomasochism is a performance that yearns for an experience that is beyond the closure of representation, and it seeks that beyond through the apparently paradoxical method of discipline, regulation, and prescription." Hart, *Between*, 159. Whereas Hart's "beyond" would be the longed-for transcendence of what has been prescribed, however—and in that sense seems to me not unlike normative accounts of the magic of theater—here I'm more interested in the desire for cruelty as a disastrous irruption of contingency that sends us crashing back to earth. This may be closer to what Hart elsewhere describes as "the anticipation that the limits will be pushed to the breaking point, that the 'scene' will cross over into the 'real'" (Hart, *Between*, 91).

68. Interestingly for us, Freud observes that "if a child has been told a nice story, he will insist on hearing it over and over again rather than a new one; and he will remorselessly stipulate that the repetition shall be an identical one and will correct any alterations of which the narrator may be guilty." Freud, *Beyond the Pleasure Principle*, 35.

69. Artaud repeatedly invokes humor as a destructive force, praising "laughter's power of physical and anarchic dissociation." Artaud, *Theater*, 42; see also 90–92, 125, 142.

70. Judith Butler, *Antigone's Claim: Kinship between Life and Death* (New York: Columbia University Press, 2002), 82; quoted in Edelman, *No Future*, 103.

71. Edelman, *No Future*, 106.

72. On this and other structures of desire in James see Kevin Ohi's remarkable *Henry James and the Queerness of Style* (Minneapolis: University of Minnesota Press, 2011).

73. See Ohi, *Henry James*, 25–26 and 149–51.

74. Silverman, *Male Subjectivity*, 176; Leo Bersani and Adam Phillips, *Intimacies* (Chicago: University of Chicago Press, 2008), 11–24.

75. In addition to Silverman's reading of *The Awkward Age* in *Male Subjectivity at the Margins*, see Kathryn Bond Stockton, "Eve's Queer Child," in *Regarding Sedgwick: Essays on Queer Culture and Critical Theory*, ed. Stephen M. Barber and David L. Clark (New York: Routledge, 2002), 181–99.

76. This latter tendency to minimize the *pain* (for both characters and readers) of giving up the impossible communion is probably the only respect in which a celebratory queer reading like Ohi's may need supplementation through a theory of masochism. On *The Ambassadors*, for example, Ohi writes: "the dominant affect as the novel draws to its close and Strether declines to get anything for himself is not disillusion or disappointment, not resignation or renunciation, not sadness but joy." Ohi, *Henry James*, 165. It seems to me that the negative affects Ohi lists are actually indispensable to such passages, which nevertheless engage the enjoyment *of* painful feelings—hence the need to think their queerness as, also, perverse.

77. Freud, "A Child," 186, my emphasis.

78. Freud, "A Child," 185–87.

79. Freud, "A Child," 186.

80. Freud, "A Child," 191.

81. My formulation here owes a great deal to Silverman, who draws on Freud's essay to theorize masochism as a willing subjection of the self to alterity: "This peculiar form

of identification, which might be said to 'ex-corporate' rather than to in-corporate, enables the psyche to take up residence within a different bodily terrain.... The self ... is precisely what is sacrificed through this 'ex-corporation.'" Silverman, *Male Subjectivity*, 259. See also Ohi's reading of "apposition" in *The Wings of the Dove*, where a character "seems to 'feel' outside of herself—that is ... to experience feeling in an externalized mode." Ohi, *Henry James*, 66.

82. Henry James, "Nona Vincent," in *Henry James: Complete Stories 1892-1898* (New York: Library of America, 1996), 4. Except where otherwise noted, all references are to the revised edition of "Nona Vincent" that James published in 1893 in *The Real Thing and Other Tales*. The story first appeared in serial form in 1892 in *The English Illustrated Magazine*.

83. James, "Nona Vincent," 1.

84. James, "Nona Vincent," 24-26.

85. James, "Nona Vincent," 30.

86. James, "Nona Vincent," 31.

87. Henry James, "Nona Vincent" (serialized edition), *The English Illustrated Magazine, 1891-1892* (London: Macmillan, 1892), 502.

88. James, "Nona Vincent," 31.

89. Bersani, *Freudian Body*, 70.

90. James, "Nona Vincent," 31.

91. James, "Nona Vincent," 6.

92. Freud, "A Child," 196-98.

93. Freud, "A Child," 198.

94. James, "Nona Vincent," 23. See Peter Collister's reading of this passage as a "climactic, scenic version" of theater's challenge to authorial autonomy, "which mixes desire and fear." Collister, "Henry James, the 'Scenic Idea,' and 'Nona Vincent,'" *Philological Quarterly* 94, no. 3 (Summer 2015): 277-79, ProQuest.

95. Deleuze, "Coldness," 125; see 123-34.

96. Deleuze, "Coldness," 125.

97. James, "Nona Vincent," 5-6.

98. On "going behind" in James see Silverman, *Male Subjectivity*, 157-81; on Jamesian anal erotics see also Eve Kosofsky Sedgwick, *Touching Feeling* (Durham: Duke University Press, 2003), 47-61.

99. James, "Nona Vincent," 17-18.

100. Berlant, *Desire/Love*, 77.

101. Freud, "A Child," 190, 191, 180, translation modified.

102. Anna Freud, "The Relation of Beating-Phantasies to a Day-Dream," *International Journal of Psychoanalysis* 4 (1923): 100, PEP Web.

103. Anna Freud, "Relation," 102.

104. See Hart, *Between*, 29-30. Hart also cites Teresa De Lauretis, who seems to identify the girl's turn to writing with Anna Freud's grownup career as "writer, training analyst, and heir to the Freudian institution," and thus with a complicitous relation to psychoanalysis's "dismissive attitude towards lesbianism" (quoted in Hart, *Between*, 30). See De Lauretis, *The Practice of Love* (Bloomington: Indiana University Press, 1994), 37-38.

105. James, "Nona Vincent," 2-3.

106. James, "Nona Vincent," 3.

107. James, "Nona Vincent," 5–6.

108. James, "Nona Vincent," 6.

109. I'm indebted to Julie Rivkin's excellent reading of this passage (and of the story as a whole), which argues that Mrs. Alsager, "who speaks here as the advocate of 'performance,'" articulates the story's proto-Derridean concern with showing the way "the artistic ideal itself is an effect of representation, constituted by the very act of performance that might also be seen as betraying it." Julie Rivkin, *False Positions: The Representational Logics of Henry James's Fiction* (Stanford: Stanford University Press, 1996), 17–18; see also 16–26.

110. Freud, "A Child," 199, translation modified; "Ein Kind," 220–21.

111. Freud, "A Child," 186.

112. Freud, "A Child," 190; "Ein Kind," 210.

113. James, "Nona Vincent," 30.

114. James, "Nona Vincent," 8.

115. James, "Nona Vincent," 3.

116. Sitting still in a chair, the way Mrs. Alsager presumably does at Violet's house, is in fact, a classic exercise of Constantin Stanislavki's method acting, which—like "Nona Vincent," as we'll discuss below—developed in a close relationship with turn-of-the-century dramatic realism. See Stanislavski's *An Actor Prepares*, trans. Elizabeth Reynolds Hapgood (New York: Theatre Arts, 1936), 31–35. Stanislavski's insistence that someone apparently doing nothing can constitute a meaningful event resonates powerfully with James's poetics; see, for example, Henry James, "The Art of Fiction," in James, *Partial Portraits* (London: Macmillan, 1888), 392–93, ProQuest.

117. James, "Nona Vincent," 30.

118. James, "Nona Vincent," 29.

119. James, "Nona Vincent," 27–28.

120. James, "Nona Vincent," 27.

121. Joanne Gates, *Elizabeth Robins, 1862–1952: Actress, Novelist, Feminist* (Tuscaloosa: University of Alabama Press, 1994), 46.

122. Robins, *Ibsen*, 16.

123. Henry James, "On the Occasion of *Hedda Gabler*," in *Henry James: The Scenic Art*, ed. Allan Wade (New Brunswick: Rutgers, 1948), 250–51.

124. James, "Occasion," 250, 254.

125. Robins, *Ibsen*, 55.

126. Solomon, *Re-Dressing*, 51.

127. Robins, *Ibsen*, 18.

128. As Susan Torrey Barstow has argued, Ibsen's plays—and their popularity with the mostly female audiences of London's late-Victorian matinees—played a critical role in galvanizing "a new feminist self-consciousness … that would later realize itself in the theatricalized struggles of the Edwardian suffragette movement." Barstow, "Hedda," 387–88.

129. Robins, *Ibsen*, 53.

130. Robins, *Ibsen*, 47, my emphasis.

131. Barstow, "Hedda," 392.

132. Quoted in Barstow, "Hedda," 392–93. Diamond discusses this dangerous female metabolizing of Ibsen in terms of the prominent medical and theatrical discourse of hysteria. She also examines an actual "woman's play"—*Alan's Wife*, written and

staged by Robins and Florence Bell in 1893—in terms that resonate with this theme of cannibalization: "In *Alan's Wife*, Robins and Bell have produced a limit-text of Ibsenite realism: mimesis gone wild. A body imitating hysteria generates other hysterias, and the solid geometry of representation, the theater of knowledge, is radically disturbed." Diamond, *Unmaking Mimesis*, 37.

133. Nordau, *Degeneration*, 412–14.

134. James, "Occasion," 256, ed. note.

135. James, "Occasion," 249.

136. See, for example, Ezra Pound's "Henry James," in *Literary Essays of Ezra Pound*, ed. T. S. Eliot (New York: New Directions, 1968), 308.

137. Robins, *Ibsen*, 44–45.

138. James, "Nona Vincent," 15.

139. In "Nona Vincent" there are a few other men around—the unnamed male actors, the manager Loder—but they are effectively nonentities; and like Wayworth himself, they are powerless to make the play a success. Meanwhile, Wayworth's family consists of a "mother and sisters": James, "Nona Vincent," 10.

140. James, "Nona Vincent," 31.

Chapter 3

1. To elucidate the problems that attend any reading of a Black woman's desire as masochism, Musser revisits Hortense Spillers's 1987 essay "Mama's Baby, Papa's Maybe: An American Grammar Book," focusing on Spillers's famous argument that slavery reduced human beings to the status of "flesh," a "zero degree of social conceptualization" that rendered Black bodies entirely available to their captors' discursive and sexual, as well as economic, use. Spillers, "Mama's Baby," 67. Enfleshment—which, Spillers suggests, continues to inform Black women's subjectivity today—implies "the very real possibility that 'sexuality,' as a term of implied relationship and desire, is dubiously appropriate" for describing the relations (and nonrelations) that this structure of oppression produces; terms like "pleasure" and "desire" are thus "thrown into unrelieved crisis" (76). Interestingly, Musser suggests that when feminists such as Audre Lorde and Alice Walker condemned Black women's sadomasochistic practice in the 1980s, they were in a certain way reiterating the process of enfleshment, by refusing to recognize sexual agency and desire in Black female submissives themselves: "In their refusal to allow for individual agency … [these writers] enact Spillers's argument that black women are discursively outside of sexuality and individuality." Musser, *Sensational Flesh*, 172.

2. As Musser puts it, "race disrupts attempts to think sexuality as the primary frame of difference." Musser, *Sensual Excess*, 178. Musser cites David L. Eng, Roderick Ferguson, Jasbir Puar, and Chandan Reddy as exemplifying "scholars working within queer of color critique" who "have been making [this argument] for years." Musser, *Sensual Excess*, 203 n. 42. For other key texts in this critical tradition, see for example Sylvia Wynter, "Unsettling the Coloniality of Being/Power/Truth/Freedom: Towards the Human, After Man, Its Overrepresentation—An Argument," *CR: The New Centennial Review* 3, no. 3 (Fall 2003): 257–337, https://doi.org/10.1353/ncr.2004.0015; and Frank B. Wilderson III, *Afropessimism* (New York: Norton, 2020).

3. I will, however, suggest that a specific (white, male) character in one of Kennedy's

plays *is* a typical Freudian male masochist; see below. For an extended argument that masochism can be a useful theoretical lens for analyzing works of Black literature, including works in which masochism is never made explicit, see Biman Basu, *The Commerce of Peoples: Sadomasochism and African American Literature* (Lanham: Lexington Books, 2012). For Basu, sadomasochism/masochism is a structure overdetermined by modern political economy, history and historiography, phenomenology, and utopian desire; the elements of masochism he finds in Black texts tend to reflect nonpsychological aspects he has theorized as fundamental this structure, such as the Foucauldian claim that "masochism enacts the [historical] mutation of power from punishment to discipline" or the Deleuzo-Guattarian investment in masochism as a form of transgressive "becoming." Basu, *Commerce*, 87, 134–35.

4. Adrienne Kennedy, *Funnyhouse of a Negro*, in *Adrienne Kennedy Reader* (Minneapolis: University of Minnesota Press, 2001), 14.

5. Basu's observation, in reading Nella Larsen's novel *Passing*, that "the political economy of passing cannot be separated from its economy of desire"—in other words, that the practical benefits of becoming what Sarah calls "an even more pallid Negro" are fundamental to the subject's desire for that condition but cannot be parsed out such that the latter would be only a symptom of the former—is relevant here. Basu, *Commerce*, 86.

6. Kennedy, *Funnyhouse*, 11–12.

7. Kennedy, *Funnyhouse*, 25.

8. See Adrienne Kennedy, *People Who Led to My Plays* (New York: Theatre Communications Group, 1987), 96, 118.

9. Kennedy, *Funnyhouse*, 25.

10. Raymond is marked not only as white but also as Jewish: "I would like to lie and say I love Raymond. But I do not. He is a poet and is Jewish. He is very interested in Negroes." Kennedy, *Funnyhouse*, 15. On Jews in Kennedy's plays see Diamond, *Unmaking Mimesis*, 124, and Claudia Barnett, "'An Evasion of Ontology': Being Adrienne Kennedy," *TDR* 49, no. 3 (Autumn 2005): 179–80, https://doi.org/10.1162/1054204054742417.

11. Kennedy, *Funnyhouse*, 25–26.

12. Abdul JanMohamed, "Negating the Negation as a Form of Affirmation in Minority Discourse: The Construction of Richard Wright as Subject," *Cultural Critique* 7 (Autumn 1987): 245–66, https://doi.org/10.2307/1354157. JanMohamed describes the negation of negation as a fundamental principle of Wright's work, reading *Black Boy* as "a remarkable document of Wright's total absorption of the racist attempt to negate him and his own total negation of that attempt," 260. What JanMohamed calls Wright's "absorption" of white supremacy corresponds to some degree with what I (following Sharpe) am calling Kennedy's "intimacy" with it. As the title of JanMohamed's article suggests, however, his concept of double negation in Wright is more decisively affirmative and less ambiguous than the one I am trying to describe in Kennedy.

13. bell hooks, "Critical Reflections: Adrienne Kennedy, the Writer, the Work," in *Intersecting Boundaries: The Theatre of Adrienne Kennedy*, ed. Paul K. Bryant-Jackson and Lois More Overbeck (Minneapolis: University of Minnesota Press, 1992), 180–81.

14. hooks, "Critical Reflections," 181.

15. hooks, "Critical Reflections," 181.

16. hooks, "Critical Reflections," 183–84.

17. hooks, "Critical Reflections," 182, original emphasis.

18. See hooks, "Critical Reflections," 183–84.

19. hooks, "Critical Reflections," 184.

20. Diamond suggests that the political power of Kennedy's work involves its resistance to fixed identity: "Kennedy's is a theater not of identity but of identification, and as such it interrogates the fixities of racism precisely by avoiding positivities of form or ideation." Diamond, *Unmaking Mimesis*, 117.

21. Scott, *Extravagant Abjection*, 30. Scott's focus is on the literature of Black masculine abjection.

22. These include the four *Alexander Plays* as well as the prose piece "Letter to My Students on My Sixty-First Birthday by Suzanne Alexander," in *The Adrienne Kennedy Reader* (Minneapolis: University of Minnesota Press, 2001), 137–227.

23. Kennedy, *Ohio State Murders*, in *The Adrienne Kennedy Reader*, 152.

24. Kennedy, *Ohio State Murders*, 154.

25. Kennedy discusses her love of the mystery genre in the preface to her novella *Deadly Triplets*, which is itself a murder mystery. Kennedy, *Deadly Triplets: A Theatre Mystery and Journal* (Minneapolis: University of Minnesota Press, 1990), vii–ix.

26. Kennedy, *Ohio State Murders*, 156–57.

27. I hope readers of Hardy will forgive my rather hasty take on the novel's moral logic. For an argument that helpfully clarifies the question of Tess's rape from a legal and narrative standpoint (and briefly summarizes the history of critical attention to this question), see William A. Davis Jr., "The Rape of Tess: Hardy, English Law, and the Case for Sexual Assault," *Nineteenth-Century Literature* 52, no. 2 (September 1997): 221–31, JSTOR. For a more theoretically ambitious account of Hardy's struggle with Tess, see Penny Boumelha, *Thomas Hardy and Women: Sexual Ideology and Narrative Form* (Brighton: Harvester, 1982), 117–34.

28. This excess manifests sharply in the sensuality of the first passage Hampshire reads from Hardy's *Tess*: "In spite of the unpleasant initiation of the day before, Tess inclined to the freedom and novelty of her new position in the morning when the sun shone.... She sat herself down on a coop, and seriously screwed up her mouth for the long-neglected practice. She found her former ability to have degenerated to the production of a hollow rush of wind through the lips and no clear note at all." Quoted in Kennedy, *Ohio State Murders*, 153–54.

29. Kennedy, *Ohio State Murders*, 153.

30. Kennedy, *Ohio State Murders*, 153.

31. Kennedy, *Ohio State Murders*, 169.

32. Kennedy, *Ohio State Murders*, 169.

33. Kennedy, *Adrienne Kennedy Reader*, 196.

34. Quoted in Kennedy, *Ohio State Murders*, 157.

35. See Diamond, *Unmaking Mimesis*, 130–38.

36. Kennedy, *Ohio State Murders*, 173.

37. Kennedy, *Ohio State Murders*, 173. In the scene description at the beginning of the play, Kennedy stipulates "*hundreds of books on an 'O' level beneath the library at Ohio State.... Sections of the stacks become places on campus during the play*" (152). In this sense, Elinor Fuchs's description of an earlier Kennedy play as "a text composed of writings" is true of this play too, though here the writings (as "literature") exhibit and exert a

specifically institutional force. See Fuchs, "Presence and the Revenge of Writing: Re-Thinking Theatre after Derrida," *Performing Arts Journal* 9, no. 2/3 (1985): 168, JSTOR. I return to this passage from Fuchs below.

38. Sharpe, *Monstrous Intimacies*, 5.

39. Sharpe, *Monstrous Intimacies*, 24.

40. Sharpe, *Monstrous Intimacies*, 4; see also 33–34.

41. Sharpe, *Monstrous Intimacies*, 122.

42. Sharpe, *Monstrous Intimacies*, 147.

43. In *Extravagant Abjection*, Scott considers this possibility at length in relation to literary representations of Black men being sexually violated; see 153–71.

44. Diamond, *Unmaking Mimesis*, 141.

45. hooks, "Critical Reflections," 184.

46. In *Ohio State Murders*, Suzanne refers to "maps I had made likening my stay [at Ohio State] to that of Tess's life at the Vale of Blackmoor" (161); the play returns repeatedly to this theme of racial violence as geography.

47. Adrienne Kennedy, *He Brought Her Heart Back in a Box*, in *He Brought Her Heart Back in a Box and Other Plays* (New York: Theatre Communciations Group, 2020), 7, 17.

48. Kennedy, *He Brought Her Heart*, 4–5.

49. Kennedy, *He Brought Her Heart*, 28.

50. Adrienne Kennedy, "Unraveling the Landscape," interview by Branden Jacobs-Jenkins, December 2017, in *He Brought Her Heart Back in a Box and Other Plays* (New York: Theatre Communications Group, 2020), 30.

51. Kennedy, *People*, 98.

52. Sharpe, *Monstrous Intimacies*, 29.

53. Quoted in Sharpe, *Monstrous Intimacies*, 27–28.

54. Sharpe, *Monstrous Intimacies*, 29.

55. Kennedy, *He Brought Her Heart*, 5.

56. For an argument that "the racial border" is not only permeable to but constituted through and by sexual violence, see JanMohamed's article "Sexuality on/of the Racial Border: Foucault, Wright, and the Articulation of 'Racialized Sexuality,'" in *Discourses of Sexuality: From Aristotle to AIDS* (Ann Arbor: University of Michigan Press, 1992), 94–116. Asking why "the sexual violation of the socio-political borders [does] not call into question the validity and the enforcement of the entire racial border," JanMohamed argues that "rape … subsumes the totality of force relations on the racial border, which is in fact always a sexual border" (99, 109).

57. Kennedy, *He Brought Her Heart*, 5.

58. Kennedy, *He Brought Her Heart*, 14.

59. Kennedy, *Adrienne Kennedy Reader*, 47.

60. Kennedy, *He Brought Her Heart*, 19. The play's premiere production at Theatre for a New Audience handled this doubling by using a bone-white mannequin in a suit to represent Harrison Aherne; Tom Pecinka, the actor playing Chris, manipulated the mannequin while he spoke Harrison's lines at the end of the play. I should confess that while watching this production, I didn't understand that these lines (which are mostly quotations from Marlowe) were Harrison's rather than Chris's—which is to say that Kennedy's conflation of son and father remained effective in spite of the prop. *He Brought Her Heart Back in a Box*, by Adrienne Kennedy, directed by Evan Yionoulis, Theatre for a New Audience, Brooklyn, NY, January 18, 2018.

61. Kennedy, *He Brought Her Heart*, 28.

62. Kennedy, *He Brought Her Heart*, 17.

63. Kennedy, "Unraveling," 29.

64. Kennedy, *He Brought Her Heart*, 10.

65. Hartman, *Scenes*, 89, quoted in Sharpe, *Monstrous Intimacies*, 33.

66. Kennedy, *He Brought Her Heart*, 10.

67. Kennedy, *He Brought Her Heart*, 15-16.

68. See Sharpe, *Monstrous Intimacies*, 187.

69. In the same passage of the interview I cited earlier, Kennedy emphasizes her awareness of her own writing as a reiterative process: "What amazes me is that I tend to think about the same things I've thought about all my life, and I always try to unravel those things. I just had another go at trying to unravel that town … and that's really what it is." Kennedy, "Unraveling," 30.

70. Theater is also central to the plots of some other Kennedy plays: *An Evening with Dead Essex*, *Motherhood 2000*, and *Mom, How Did You Meet the Beatles?* But I'd argue that none of these pieces is as thoroughly structured by and as theater as *He Brought Her Heart Back in a Box*. See *Adrienne Kennedy Reader*, 117-35 and 228-33, and Adrienne Kennedy and Adam P. Kennedy, *Mom, How Did You Meet the Beatles?*, in *He Brought Her Heart Back in a Box and Other Plays*, 73-115.

71. Kennedy, *He Brought Her Heart*, 7-8.

72. Kennedy, *He Brought Her Heart*, 11-12.

73. Kennedy, *He Brought Her Heart*, 8, 27-28. Although these are the last words spoken live in the play, the last words we hear are in fact from "*a radio, December 7, 1941:* 'Today is the day that will live in infamy.'" There would of course be many things to say about this ending, one of which is that it emphasizes the play's desire to engage with the echoic structure of American history as such—with Roosevelt's lines serving as a ready synecdoche for that history. Kennedy, *He Brought Her Heart*, 28.

74. Kennedy, *He Brought Her Heart*, 19.

75. W. S. Van Dyke, dir., *Bitter Sweet* (Warner Bros., 1940).

76. Kennedy, *He Brought Her Heart*, 28.

77. Kennedy, *He Brought Her Heart*, 28.

78. "I haven't been to the theater in years. And I don't consider myself a playwright, because I haven't had very many pleasant experiences when I've had my plays put on.… I don't really like the theater that much, from my experiences when I've had my plays put on." Kennedy, "Unraveling," 32.

79. See Peter Szondi, *Theory of the Modern Drama*, ed. and trans. Michael Hays (Minneapolis: University of Minnesota Press, 1987), 7-10. For a rich essay on Kennedy's work through the early 1990s that takes pains to articulate the work's divergences from dramatic convention, see Marc Robinson, *The Other American Drama* (Cambridge: Cambridge University Press, 1994), 115-49.

80. In this sense, the opening description in *Mom, How Did You Meet the Beatles?*, which features characters named after Adrienne and her son (and coauthor) Adam Kennedy, feels emblematic: "*Throughout the play, Adrienne looks at the audience. There are only a few moments when she glances back at the actor behind her.*" See Adrienne Kennedy and Adam P. Kennedy, *Mom*, 77.

81. Fuchs, "Presence," 168.

82. On the widespread tendency, among postdramatic playwrights, to make characters speak monologically in various forms of nondramatic "discourse" rather than interpersonally in "dialogue," see Andrzej Wirth, "Vom Dialog zum Diskurs: Versuch einer Synthese der nachbrechsten Theaterkonzepte," *Theater Heute* 1 (1980): 16-19.

83. See Sharpe, *Monstrous Intimacies*, 162-87. Sharpe engages with Copjec's analysis of the role of jouissance in Walker's work (183), and also argues that Copjec's reading of Kara Walker problematically "erases whites from the scenes and symptoms of (post) slavery" (185-86). I realize that, as another white critic taking up the work of a Black artist in the course of my own psychoanalytically informed project, my return to and indeed reliance on Copjec here might itself seem like a kind of symptomatic repetition, and can only say that the resonance I experience between Copjec's account and Kennedy's play has felt too powerful to ignore.

84. Copjec, *Imagine*, 96.

85. Copjec, *Imagine*, 102.

86. Copjec, *Imagine*, 102. In this passage, Copjec refers to female subjects specifically.

87. Kennedy, *He Brought Her Heart*, 21.

88. Kennedy, *He Brought Her Heart*, 25.

89. Kennedy, *He Brought Her Heart*, 15, 28.

90. Spillers, "Mama's Baby," 74; see 73-77.

91. Kennedy, *He Brought Her Heart*, 26.

92. Other versions of this white figure in Kennedy's plays would include Rosemary in *A Rat's Mass* and Dr. Freudenberger in *The Film Club* and *Dramatic Circle*; see Kennedy, *Adrienne Kennedy Reader*, 47-54 and 174-96. On the psychoanalytic implications of "Freudenberger," see Diamond, *Unmaking Mimesis*, 130-38.

93. Spillers, "Mama's Baby," 79. Spillers is citing this law as rendered in abolitionist William Goodell's 1853 book *The American Slave Code*, which she quotes here.

94. Spillers, "Mama's Baby," 80. Here Spillers is writing specifically about Black men, whom she distinguishes as "the *only* American community of males which has had specific occasion to learn *who* the female is within itself," 80. Her article is partly a response to the infamous Moynihan Report, which had faulted a supposedly disproportionate influence of Black mothers (and absence of Black fathers) on their sons for racial socioeconomic inequality in the US, so she is specifically concerned to respond to that view of Black men; but it seems to me her reading of Goodell might extend, albeit with different stakes, to Black daughters as well as sons.

95. Alongside his ruminations on his father's obsession with the cemetery, Chris also becomes increasingly aware that Harrison evidently collaborated with Nazis before the war, helping them design their own version of a systematically white supremacist society. Having pieced this secret together, Chris asks questions whose answers have become obvious: "what was he doing in Berlin? Why were we walking on Unter den Linden under the Brandenburg gate?... Why were we in that house on the Wannsee Lake?" See Kennedy, *He Brought Her Heart*, 16-17, 18-21.

96. Kennedy, *He Brought Her Heart*, 5.

97. In the first scene, Kay quotes a letter from Maggie, a family friend, who had identified Mary's body: "Kay, she had been stabbed to death. She was a sweet child and, Kay, I want you to know your mother loved you so much and as soon as she got well she was going to have Robert go and get you." Later, Kay seems to contradict her own quo-

tation by saying: "It was Maggie who told me my mother shot herself"; after that, in the passage reproduced above, Kay has her great-aunt contradict *that*: "She was killed and Maggie knows it." See Kennedy, *He Brought Her Heart*, 14, 20, 21.

98. Kennedy, *People*, 86.

99. Kennedy, *People*, 20–21.

100. Kennedy, *People*, 24. The book's first reference to *Snow White* occurs a few pages earlier: "I thought after seeing this movie that somehow in some way we were all sleeping and had to be awakened before we could really live" (18).

101. Kennedy, *He Brought Her Heart*, 17.

102. Kennedy, *He Brought Her Heart*, 3.

103. In this connection, I'm struck by Kennedy's comment that Hitchcock's *Vertigo* "was perhaps the most influential movie of its time, in the impact it had on my imagination." Although Kennedy refers this influence to "Hitchcock's use of the change of identities," *Vertigo* is also about a kind of uncanny reanimation, a lost love who troublingly comes back. Kennedy, *People*, 109.

104. Kennedy, *People*, 61.

105. Kennedy, *People*, 81.

106. For more on this iterative logic, see Schneider, *Performing Remains*.

107. Kennedy, *Adrienne Kennedy Reader*, 47, 297–98, and Kennedy, *Etta and Ella on the Upper West Side*, in *He Brought Her Heart Back in a Box and Other Plays*, 65–69. On the psychoanalytic and deconstructive dimensions of writing-as-repetition in Kennedy's work see Randi Koppen, who observes that "what starts out as a process of anamnesis gradually comes to manifest itself as the interminable repetitions and revisions of scriptural activity." Koppen, "Psychoanalytic Enactments: Adrienne Kennedy's Stagings of Memory," *Hungarian Journal of English and American Studies* 4, no. 1/2 (1998): 128, JSTOR.

108. As Diamond, writing on *Movie Star*, puts it: "Kennedy co-opts the cinematic image.... Colonized by these glamorous images, [protagonist] Clara/Kennedy in turn remakes and represents them in a context that bears the materiality of her consciousness (her language), if not her color—which is precisely the point." Diamond, *Unmaking Mimesis*, 127–28.

109. See Spillers, "Mama's Baby," and n. 1 above.

110. Kennedy, *He Brought Her Heart*, 11.

111. Sharpe, *Monstrous Intimacies*, 121. Sharpe locates the subjectivity that emerges from this behavior as ranging from "the mid-nineteenth century in Europe and America" through the present day—a range that would cover Freud's milieu and James's, Chris and Kay's, Kennedy's and our own.

112. Kennedy, *He Brought Her Heart*, 15.

113. Kennedy, *He Brought Her Heart*, 11, 13.

114. I suspect this abruptness is why Hilton Als's otherwise appreciative review essay calls the play "too short and thin to thrive on its own." See Als, "Adrienne Kennedy's Startling Body of Work," *New Yorker*, February 5, 2018, https://www.newyorker.com/magazine/2018/02/12/adrienne-kennedys-startling-body-of-work.

115. Sharpe, *Monstrous Intimacies*, 113.

116. Sharpe, *Monstrous Intimacies*, 128.

117. Freeman, also writing about *The Attendant*, argues similarly that Julien uses sadomasochism to approach "the possibility of encountering specific historical moments

viscerally, thereby refusing these moments the closure of pastness." Freeman, *Time Binds*, 145. See also Saketopoulou, who suggests that Gary Fisher's erotic engagement with "the trauma of slavery" in his writing "may be trying *to find a way to be with that history*." *Sexuality*, 114. I'll return to Fisher in the next chapter.

118. Freud, "Economic Problem," 162.

Chapter 4

1. Tim Dean, "Sex and the Aesthetics of Existence," *PMLA* 125, no. 2 (March 2010): 388, JSTOR.

2. For a different argument that also contests the apparent "solipsism" of autotheory, see Max Cavitch, for whom "autotheory addresses the need for relational, rather than merely reflexive, self-narration—including the need to attend to the intersubjectivity of writing and reading." "Everybody's Autotheory," *Modern Language Quarterly* 83, no. 1 (March 2022): 84, https://doi.org/10.1215/00267929-9475043. See also Kyle Frisina's account of autotheory's theatricality: Frisina, "From Performativity to Performance: Claudia Rankine's *Citizen* and Autotheory," in "Autotheory Theory," ed. Robyn Wiegman, special issue, *Arizona Quarterly* 76, no. 1 (Spring 2020): 141–66, Project MUSE.

3. Berlant, *Cruel Optimism*, 146. The ego-threatening nature of sex is also a central theme of *Sex, Or The Unbearable*, a textual dialogue between Berlant and Lee Edelman (Duke University Press, 2013).

4. Bersani, *Freudian Body*, 39, 41. It's important to note, however, that Berlant also distances her position from Bersani's famously nonrelational account of sex when she locates this "loss of sovereignty" specifically "in relation."

5. Michael Warner, "The Mass Public and the Mass Subject," in *Habermas and the Public Sphere*, ed. Craig Calhoun (Cambridge: MIT Press, 1992), 377, 382.

6. Warner, "Mass Public," 384–92.

7. Warner argues that our longing for the impossible reconciliation between "positivity and self-abstraction" produces what he calls figures of "metapopularity"—figures whose function is to disavow the alienation of public subjectivity, like Ronald Reagan—as well as an insatiable hunger for scenes of mass disaster, in which the public audience "finds its body with a revenge." Warner, "Mass Public," 396–97.

8. Lauren Fournier, *Autotheory as Feminist Practice in Art, Writing and Criticism* (Cambridge: MIT Press, 2021), 13.

9. Maggie Nelson, *The Argonauts* (Minneapolis: Graywolf, 2015), 3.

10. See the first chapter of Fournier's *Autotheory*, especially 32–37 and 41–45; Stacey Young, *Changing the Wor(l)d: Discourse, Politics, and the Feminist Movement* (New York: Routledge, 1991), 61–98; Carolyn Laubender, "Speak for Your Self: Psychoanalysis, Autotheory, and The Plural Self," in Wiegman, "Autotheory Theory," 39–64. For more on autotheory's (and *Testo Yonqui*'s) roots in French feminist theory, see Émile Lévesque-Jalbert, "'This Is Not an Autofiction': Autoteoría, French Feminism, and Living in Theory," in Wiegman, "Autotheory Theory," 65–84.

11. See, among others, Young, *Changing*, 61–98, and Nancy K. Miller, *Getting Personal: Feminist Occasions and Other Autobiographical Acts* (New York: Routledge, 1991). In *The Anti-Racist Writing Workshop*, Felicia Rose Chavez recalls the formative experience of reading the 1981 anthology *This Bridge Called My Back: Writings by Radical*

Women of Color: "Gloria Anzaldúa, Cherríe Moraga, and Toni Cade Bambara proved to be my real mentors, modeling how to be a woman of color who commands her own voice." Chavez, *The Anti-Racist Writing Workshop* (Chicago: Haymarket, 2021), 71.

12. Saidiya Hartman, *Lose Your Mother* (New York: Farrar, Straus and Giroux, 2008).

13. Eve Kosofsky Sedgwick, *Tendencies* (Durham: Duke University Press, 1993), 3.

14. Sedgwick, *Tendencies*, 11.

15. Sedgwick, *Tendencies*, 18.

16. Berlant, *Cruel Optimism*, 123–24, my emphasis.

17. *Oxford English Dictionary*, s.v. "demonstrative (adj. & n.)," accessed March 2022, https://www.oed.com/view/Entry/49846?redirectedFrom=demonstrative.

18. "Beatriz Preciado es filósofa." Because Preciado now uses he/him pronouns and goes by the name Paul B. Preciado, I am following his usage here.

19. Paul Preciado [named in this edition Beatriz Preciado], *Testo Yonqui* (Barcelona: Espasa, 2013), 15; Paul Preciado, *Testo Junkie: Sex, Drugs, and Biopolitics in the Pharmo-pornographic Era*, trans. Bruce Benderson (New York: Feminist Press at the City University of New York, 2013), 11.

20. Gilles Deleuze, *Présentation de Sacher-Masoch: le froid et le cruel* (Paris: Éditions de Minuit, 1967), 18.

21. Deleuze, "Coldness," 20.

22. Deleuze, "Coldness," 20, 18–19.

23. Roland Barthes suggests that Sade's "philosophy" is fundamentally to be located in the literary dimension of his relationship to language, rather than in his access to truth. See Barthes, *Sade/Fourier/Loyola*, trans. Richard Miller (Baltimore: Johns Hopkins University Press, 1997), 27.

24. Preciado, *Testo Yonqui*, 15; Maggie Nelson, "Riding the Blinds," interview by Micah McCrary, *Los Angeles Review of Books*, April 26, 2015, https://lareviewofbooks.org/article/riding-the-blinds/.

25. Preciado, *Testo Yonqui*, 302; *Testo Junkie*, 416.

26. Preciado, *Testo Yonqui*, 22; *Testo Junkie*, 19.

27. Preciado, *Testo Yonqui*, 23; *Testo Junkie*, 20.

28. Lévesque-Jalbert also understands Dustan's role in *Testo Yonqui* as formative for the book's elaboration of autotheory as a genre; for Lévesque-Jalbert, however, this is because Dustan represents the earlier genre of autofiction, a genre from which Preciado's coining of *autoteoría* explicitly takes its distance, even as (Lévesque-Jalbert argues) autofiction continues to "influence" Preciado. See "'This is not,'" 76–82. In this connection it may be worth noting Leo Bersani's observation that in Dustan's 1996 book *Dans ma chambre*, "there are no scenes … that would qualify as bona fide S/M. 'I am not a sadist,' Guillaume candidly writes." See Bersani and Phillips, *Intimacies*, 37. Bersani reads Dustan's text as working towards what Bersani will theorize as "impersonal intimacy," a notion that is suggestive for the particular collocation of intimacy and impersonality I'm ascribing to autotheory here—although in work like Preciado's, I'm suggesting, intimacy and impersonality function erotically by promising to negate each other, rather than (as in Bersani's account here) converging into a continuous relational system. Bersani and Phillips, *Intimacies*, 42.

29. Preciado, *Testo Yonqui*, 245; *Testo Junkie*, 347.

30. Preciado, *Testo Yonqui*, 46; see especially 25–46, 111–58, 179–220.

31. Preciado, *Testo Yonqui*, 285; *Testo Junkie*, 398.

32. Preciado, *Testo Yonqui*, 15; *Testo Junkie*, 11.

33. For example: "el cuerpo individual funciona como una extensión de las tecnologías globales de communicación" (the individual body functions like an extension of global technologies of communication); "el trabajo sexual como proceso de subjectivación [abre] la posibilidad de hacer del sujeto una reserva interminable de corrida planetaria transformable en capital, en abstracción, en dígito" (sexual work as a process of subjectivization [opens] the possibility of making the subject an inexhaustible supply of planetary ejaculation that can be transformed into abstraction and digital data—into capital); "en biotecnología y en pornocomunicación … se trata de *inventar* un sujeto y producirlo a escala global" (In the fields of biotechnology and pornocommunication … it's a matter of *inventing* a subject and producing it on a global scale). Preciado, *Testo Yonqui*, 39, 40, 45; *Testo Junkie*, 44, 46, 54.

34. Preciado, *Testo Yonqui*, 284; *Testo Junkie*, 397.

35. Grace Lavery, "Egg Theory's Early Style," *TSQ: Transgender Studies Quarterly* 7, no. 3 (August 2020): 384–85, https://doi.org/10.1215/23289252-8553034.

36. Lavery, "Egg Theory's Early Style," 389.

37. Preciado writes: "Yo no quiero cambiar de sexo, no quiero declararme disfórico de nada" (I don't want to change my sex, and I don't want to declare myself dysphoric about whatever it may be). *Testo Yonqui*, 168 (see also 173–74); *Testo Junkie*, 250.

38. Grace Lavery, "Trans Realism, Psychoanalytic Practice, and the Rhetoric of Technique," *Critical Inquiry* 46, no. 4 (Summer 2020): 722, https://doi.org/10.1086/709221.

39. Warner, "Mass Public," 382.

40. Berlant's description of the sexual role played by intellection (or what I am calling abstraction) in the lives of the main characters in Gaitskill's *Two Girls, Fat and Thin* seems especially relevant here, as it is to my book as a whole. Noting that "the relation between impersonal formalism and the project of unique self-cultivation is all tied up in the novel," Berlant observes that for its two main characters—whom she associates, throughout the essay, with Sedgwick and herself—"a new idea … interrupts the present and organizes the opportunity to identify with *pursuit*, with the raw energy of desire." Abstraction, that is, provides a means of sustaining oneself by negating the self's (and indeed others') particular content. Later in the reading, Berlant describes S&M as "a formalist mode of sex." *Cruel Optimism*, 132, 139, 151.

41. "It might indeed be said that the sadism which has been forced out of the ego has pointed the way for the libidinal components of the sexual instinct, and that these follow after it to the object." Freud, *Beyond the Pleasure Principle*, 54. Kaja Silverman—citing a related passage from Freud's *Three Essays on the Theory of Sexuality*—characterizes sadism as "the [perversion] which is most compatible with conventional heterosexuality" (*Male Subjectivity*, 187). But Freud also writes (in "The Economic Problem of Masochism") of the particularly "serious impression" made by "the cruelties of sadism, whether imagined or performed" (162). On whom this impression is made Freud does not say, but the implication is that most subjects would find sadists' fantasies highly disturbing, at least at the conscious level. This is a fact that Sade's work both trades upon and often frantically disavows.

42. Marquis de Sade, *Philosophy in the Boudoir*, trans. Joachim Neugroschel (New York: Penguin, 2006), 66.

43. Warner argues that "the perverse acknowledgement of [this kind of] pleasure …

allows Waters a counter-public embodied knowledge in the mode of camp." Warner, "Mass Public," 394. This instance of "perverse acknowledgement" might return us to the theme of masochism's stagey "insistence" on fundamental structures of sexuality and textuality (and we could now add, publicity), which I discussed in the introduction.

44. As Laubender writes, autotheory "is always in danger of enacting a self-expansion at the very moment it would be most committed to a dispossession." "Speak for Your Self," 59.

45. Preciado, *Testo Yonqui*, 164; *Testo Junkie*, 244.

46. For an example of a reading that makes this distinction, see Kim Coates, "'Both Sides at Once': Addiction and Autotheory in Paul B. Preciado's *Testo Junkie*," *TSQ*Now*, May 10, 2021, https://www.tsqnow.online/post/both-sides-at-once-addiction-and-autotheory-in-paul-b-preciado-s-testo-junkie. Kyle Frisina also argues for this distinction's importance in autotheory; see Frisina, "From Performativity," 146.

47. Preciado, *Testo Yonqui*, 19. "*The strongest is his voice, I think*, you were saying." *Testo Junkie*, 15. As Preciado's footnote records, the line is from a poem in Guillaume Dustan's *Nicolas Pages* (Éditions Balland, Paris, 1999), 17.

48. For more on the role of citation in autotheory, see Fournier, who relates it to what she calls "intertextual intimacy." Fournier, *Autotheory*, 133–74.

49. Preciado, 15. "Fiction, actually." *Testo Junkie*, 11.

50. Eve Kosofsky Sedgwick, "A Poem Is Being Written," *Representations* 17 (Winter, 1987): 115, JSTOR.

51. Sedgwick, "A Poem," 110.

52. Sedgwick refers to Freud, just as glancingly, twice more in the article: once in the passage where she describes the way the framed tableau of spanking becomes "a free switchpoint for the identities of subject, object, onlooker, desirer, looker-away" ("this is in Freud, too" she notes between em-dashes); and once when, in a discussion of anal excitation, a parenthesis directs us to "*vide* Freud, among others." Sedgwick, "A Poem," 115, 129.

53. Sedgwick, *Tendencies*, 95.

54. Sedgwick, *Tendencies*, 8.

55. Sedgwick, "A Poem," 118. In the previous paragraph, Sedgwick characterizes sexuality "as, necessarily, retardation; as, necessarily, perversion"—a context that makes clear that her attribution of "*retardataire* simplicity" to masochism is not meant to be taken as disapprobative. In a certain way, however, it seems to me that this characterization of sexuality as such makes masochism seem even *more* "simple," as if the latter were only a kind of line drawing or degree-zero of something (retardation, perversion) that gets more differentially developed in other sexual modes.

56. Sedgwick, "A Poem," 124.

57. Sedgwick, "A Poem," 118.

58. Sedgewick, "A Poem," 126.

59. Sedgwick, "A Poem," 140–41 n. 15, 129, my emphasis.

60. Sedgwick, "A Poem," 129.

61. Sedgwick, "A Poem," 124.

62. Sedgwick, "A Poem," 134.

63. Sedgwick, "A Poem," 134.

64. Here it's tempting to recall another moment in *Tendencies*, where Sedgwick questions discourses of innocence and ignorance that "make an appeal to, and thus re-

quire the expulsion of, *a time before*, a moment of developmental time, and why not call it for convenience's sake *a time before gender—factitious though that time may be.*" Sedgwick, *Tendencies*, 47. First emphasis in original; second mine. It seems to me that Sedgwick's construction of masochism in "A Poem Is Being Written" avails itself—however self-consciously—of precisely this factitious, expulsive appeal.

65. Sedgwick, "A Poem" 117.

66. Sedgwick, "A Poem." 117.

67. Sedgwick, "A Poem," 115. Here I'd want to contest Kathryn Bond Stockton's importation of Deleuze's account of masochism into her reading of "A Poem Is Being Written": I'm arguing that Sedgwick's essay ultimately unmakes the Deleuzian claim that masochism is a synchronic aesthetics of arrest. See Stockton, "Eve's Queer Child."

68. Sedgwick, "A Poem," 117.

69. Sedgwick, "A Poem," 114, my emphasis.

70. Sedgwick, "A Poem," 115.

71. Sedgwick touches on the theatrical proscenium's vulnerability in *Touching Feeling*, when, having argued that marriage is not only performative (as in the exemplary performative utterance "I do") but theatrically structured "for the eyes of others," she observes that in many Victorian novels, the "sexual plot climaxes, not in the moment of adultery, but in the moment when the proscenium arch of the marriage is, however excruciatingly, displaced." Sedgwick, *Touching Feeling*, 72–73.

72. Hart, *Between*, 109.

73. I have argued elsewhere that for some modern playwrights, theater's potential to convey a heightened sense of its own and its audience's immersion in a shared historical present—which is also to say, the relative weakness of theater's claim to aesthetic autonomy—seems to provoke, in turn, a heightened aspiration to aesthetic negativity, or resistance to the present. Here, I'm considering the erotic affordances of a related intuition about theater: that theatrical work is always made and experienced in a condition of palpable vulnerability to disruption, interruption, and mischance. See Jarcho, *Writing and the Modern Stage: Theater Beyond Drama* (Cambridge: Cambridge University Press, 2017).

74. Sedgwick, "A Poem," 117.

75. Sedgwick, "A Poem," 118.

76. We might consider the possibility that Freud's title works the same way: that his essay doesn't just analyze a fantasy in which a child is being beaten but itself enacts a version of the beating. This would be in keeping with my suggestion in chapter 1 that Freud's writing about masochism sometimes adopts precisely the sadistic posture invited by the fantasies he is describing.

77. "I knew about parts of the body, *la jambe*, and foods, *le jambon*—and … I knew enjambment, not just for a technical word in the introduction to my rhyming dictionary, but for a physical gesture of the limbs, of the flanks, the ham." Sedgwick, "A Poem," 116.

78. Sedgwick, "A Poem," 139 n. 8, my emphasis.

79. Heather Love discusses another example of Sedgwick's address to the reader in "Truth and Consequences: On Paranoid Reading and Reparative Reading," in "Honoring Eve," ed. Erin Murphy and J. Keith Vincent, special issue, *Criticism* 52, no. 2 (Spring 2010): 235–41, JSTOR.

80. Cavitch, "Everybody's Autotheory," 91–92.

81. Frisina, "From Performativity," 147.

82. For a short story that literalizes this theatrical logic in a fantasy of actually getting fucked by the audience, see Kim Fu, "Scissors," in *Kink*, 166–76.

83. Stockton, "Eve's Queer Child," 182.

84. Ramzi Fawaz, "'An Open Mesh of Possibilities': The Necessity of Eve Sedgwick in Dark Times," in *Reading Sedgwick*, ed. Lauren Berlant (Durham: Duke University Press, 2019), 6–33.

85. This is also, perhaps, to characterize Sedgwick's writing (and reading) as pleasurably *paranoid*, even though "paranoid reading" is an object of critique in one of her most famous essays: see Sedgwick, "Paranoid Reading and Reparative Reading, or, You're So Paranoid, You Probably Think This Essay Is About You," in *Touching Feeling*, 123–52. In the wake of that essay's enormous influence, some of Sedgwick's readers have been moved to argue that Sedgwick is far from jettisoning critical paranoia or embracing a wholly "reparative" practice, especially where the latter is assumed to exclude paranoia or negativity more broadly. As Love writes: "To read Sedgwick always reparatively is to miss the energizing force of paranoia in her work; it also reduces the kinds of relations we might now cultivate with her." Love also observes in the course of this argument that "love means trying to destroy the object as well as trying to repair it." Love, "Truth and Consequences," 240, 239. See also Berlant and Edelman, *Sex, or the Unbearable*, 35–61. The description I give above of Sedgwick's pleasure in "looking out for more" "vectors" echoes a similar account I give elsewhere of (what I argue is) the specifically theatrical structure of pleasure in Henry James: see Jarcho, *Writing*, 23–45.

86. Sedgwick, "A Poem," 139 n. 8.

87. Sedgwick, "A Poem," 124, 126, 134.

88. Lavery, "Egg Theory's Early Style," 395.

89. Lavery, "Egg Theory's Early Style," 395.

90. In fact, Lavery herself observes a version of this sexual posture in a writer whose affinity with Sedgwick we've just remarked: at the end of the "Trans Realism" essay, Lavery observes that as a critic, "one cannot … fail to top James." Lavery, "Trans Realism," 744. Her work, it seems to me, helps reveal a version of the same flushed inevitability in Sedgwick.

91. Sedgwick, "A Poem," 114.

92. Sedgwick, "A Poem," 113.

93. Sedgwick, "A Poem," 140 n. 15.

94. Abdur-Rahman, *Against the Closet*, 14.

95. Jennifer C. Nash, "Black Anality," in *Queer Feminist Science Studies: A Reader*, ed. Cyd Cipolla, Kristina Gupta, David A. Rubin, and Angela Willey (Seattle: University of Washington Press, 2017), 103, 104.

96. Sedgwick, *A Dialogue on Love* (Boston: Beacon Press, 1999), 176.

97. Sedgwick, *Dialogue*, 92.

98. Sedgwick, *Dialogue*, 118–19.

99. Sedgwick, *Dialogue*, 160–61.

100. See the introduction above.

101. José Esteban Muñoz, "Race, Sex, and the Incommensurate: Gary Fisher with Eve Sedgwick," in *Queer Futures: Reconsidering Ethics, Activism, and the Political*, ed. Elahe Haschemi Yekani, Eveline Kilian, and Beatrice Michaelis (London: Routledge, 2013), 103.

102. Muñoz, "Race, Sex," 113.

103. See Sedgwick, *Dialogue*, 179; Robert F. Reid-Pharr, *Black Gay Man* (New York: NYU Press, 2001), 149; Muñoz, "Race, Sex," 103. Ellis Hanson characterizes this project as Sedgwick's "most elaborate reparative project—the one that has attracted the harshest criticism." Ellis Hanson, "The Future's Eve: Reparative Reading After Sedgwick," *The South Atlantic Quarterly* 110, no. 1 (Winter 2011): 109, doi 10.1215/00382876-2010-025.

104. Reid-Pharr, *Black Gay Man*. In addition to Reid-Pharr, Muñoz, and Hanson, see Amber Jamilla Musser, "Consent, Capacity, and the Non-Narrative," in *Queer Feminist Science Studies: A Reader*, ed. Cyd Cipolla, Kristina Gupta, David A. Rubin, and Angela Willey (Seattle: University of Washington Press, 2017), 230–32, and Saketopoulou, *Sexuality*, 113–18.

105. Saketopoulou, *Sexuality*, 116.

106. Muñoz, "Race, Sex," 105–6.

107. Reid-Pharr, *Black Gay Man*, 144–45.

108. Gary Fisher, "Red Cream Soda," in *Gary in Your Pocket* (Durham: Duke University Press, 1996), 38.

109. Fisher, "Red Cream Soda," 38.

110. Fisher, "Red Cream Soda," 39.

111. Fisher, "Red Cream Soda," 40.

112. Fisher, "Red Cream Soda," 37.

113. Fisher, "Red Cream Soda," 37.

114. Reid-Pharr comments on the double significance of throat-fucking in Fisher's work, which (Reid-Pharr suggests) implies both a silencing violation of the subject and an enlivening activation of his organ of verbal expression. Reid-Pharr, *Black Gay Man*, 138.

115. Fisher, "Red Cream Soda," 44.

116. Fisher, "Red Cream Soda," 44.

117. Fisher, "Red Cream Soda," 44.

118. Fisher, "Red Cream Soda," 38.

119. Fisher, "Red Cream Soda," 43.

120. Henry James's *The Beast in the Jungle*, the object of one of Sedgwick's most famous queer readings, would offer another instance of this masochistic structure. See James, "The Beast in the Jungle," in *Henry James: Complete Stories 1898-1910* (New York: Library of America, 1996), 496–541.

121. Irving Goh coins the term "auto-thanato-theory" in reference to "a textual space in and through which it is possible to articulate the truth of longing to die or feeling already dead." Goh, "Auto-thanato-theory: Dark Narcissistic Care for the Self in Sedgwick and Zambreno," in Wiegman, "Autotheory Theory," 206, Project MUSE. Though Goh twice characterizes this discourse as "perverse," he doesn't further specify its perversion; and although narcissism is a central concept for his analysis, he is quick to dismiss the relevance of Freudian thinking for his project, rapidly characterizing Freud's account of narcissism as too normative to be useful in describing the ways some autotheory courts death (199–200).

122. In a parenthesis in the "Fundamental Misrecognitions" section, within a passage in which she is describing the depression of her teenage years, Sedgwick writes: "A

will-to-live, per se, has seldom in me been more than notional, often aggressively absent." "A Poem," 133. Sedgwick later revisits this thought, postdiagnosis, in *A Dialogue on Love*; see especially 16–17 and 69.

123. Sedgwick, "A Poem," 116.

124. Jane Gallop, *The Deaths of the Author: Writing and Reading in Time* (Durham: Duke University Press, 2011), 18.

125. Gallop, *Deaths*, 110.

126. Gallop, *Deaths*, 113–14.

127. Sedgwick, "A Poem," 117.

128. Sedgwick, "A Poem," 138 n. 7.

129. Cavitch observes that "works of autotheory … often dwell on the illusory nature of body intactness and on destabilizations in childbirth and in parent-child relationships"; he argues that this thematic prevalence of the maternal in autotheory is best understood as a sign of the genre's "responsiveness … to widespread displacements (e.g., in psychology, anthropology, and linguistics) of substantivist ontologies by relational alternatives, which makes it harder and harder to speak meaningfully of a monadic ego." Cavitch, "Everybody's Autotheory," 94–95. Here I'm advancing an alternative description both of autotheory and of maternity: not as forms of heightened intersubjective relationality, as nice as that sounds, but as forms of self-destructiveness. I recognize that this difference may be largely—though not, I think, entirely—a matter of mood.

Chapter 5

1. Elizabeth Gilbert, "Elizabeth Gilbert Reveals the Source of True Joy," *O, The Oprah Magazine*, May 2018, https://www.oprah.com/inspiration/elizabeth-gilbert-on -the-source-of-true-joy.

2. Sedgwick, *Dialogue*, 69.

3. Natalie Frank's show *O*, a solo show of drawings, took place at Half Gallery, 43 East Seventy-Eigth Street, New York, NY, in May–June 2018. The drawings have also been published as a book, which pairs each drawing with the passage from the novel that inspired it: Natalie Frank, *Story of O: Drawings by Natalie Frank* (Seattle: Lucia Marquand, 2018).

4. Réage, *Story of O*, 89.

5. Réage, *Story of O*, 185.

6. Réage, *Story of O*, 184–85.

7. Sylvia Day, "Introduction," in Réage, *Story of O*, xxxvii–xxxviii.

8. Réage, *Story of O*, 18, 28, 111–12. For a different reading of the way descriptive details function in the novel, see Musser, *Sensational Flesh*, 58–87.

9. Réage, *Story of O*, 61–63.

10. Réage, *Story of O*, 144, 60.

11. Réage, *Story of O*, 176.

12. Theodor W. Adorno, *Aesthetic Theory*, trans. and ed. Robert Hullot-Kentor (Minneapolis: University of Minnesota Press, 1997), 176–77.

13. Muñoz, *Cruising Utopia*, 21.

14. Réage, *Story of O*, 196.

15. Réage, *Story of O*, 77.

16. Sontag, "Pornographic Imagination," 206, 217.

17. *Buffy the Vampire Slayer*, season 3, episode 1, "Anne," written and directed by Joss Whedon, aired September 29, 1998, on WB; P. J. Harvey, "Happy and Bleeding," on *Dry*, Too Pure Records, 1992; Lana Del Rey, "Off to the Races" and "Gods and Monsters," on *Born To Die—The Paradise Edition*, Interscope and Polydor, 2012, and "Ultraviolence," on *Ultraviolence*, Polydor and Interscope, 2014.

Chapter 5B

1. Hart, *Between*, 205-16; Silverman, *Male Subjectivity*, 389.

2. Rivera, *Model*, 140-47.

3. Chris Kraus, "Emotional Technologies," in *Kink*, 262-63.

4. At the end of this confessional appendix, which Bataille ironically calls a "survey of the high summits of my personal obscenity," he recalls his mother's "manic-depressive insanity (melancholy)." Georges Bataille, *Story of the Eye*, trans. Joachim Neugroschel (San Francisco: City Lights Books, 1987), 87-96.

5. Bersani and Phillips, *Intimacies*, 51, my emphasis.

6. Bersani and Phillips, *Intimacies*, 52.

7. Bersani and Phillips, *Intimacies*, 53-54.

8. Bersani and Phillips, *Intimacies*, 54.

9. It should be noted, though, that the moment of sexual self-shattering for Bersani always also implies a kind of self-discovery; see, for example, Bersani, *Future*, 304.

10. Bersani, *Future*, 297-98. Sontag devotes considerable thought to the book's "heavy use of religious metaphors," arguing that it symptomatizes modern society's lack of vocabularies for expressing "total" or transcendent experience: the novel articulates its "energy … and absolutism" through a religious register because "the religious imagination survives for most people as not just the primary but virtually the only credible instance of an imagination working in a total way." Intent on arguing that "the conventional psychiatric vocabulary" is inadequate for describing the novel's sexual imagination, Sontag also dismisses "masochism" as an inadequate (because conventionally psychiatric) term. Sontag, "Pornographic Imagination," 228-30.

11. Bersani and Phillips, *Intimacies*, 51.

12. Bersani, *Future*, 299.

13. Bersani, *Future*, 292, my emphasis.

14. Bersani, *Future*, 293.

15. Robins, *Ibsen*, 16; see chapter 2 above.

16. Bersani and Phillips, *Intimacies*, 103-4.

17. Ibsen, *Hedda Gabler*, 71.

Bibliography

Abdur-Rahman, Aliyyah I. *Against the Closet: Black Political Longing and the Erotics of Race*. Durham: Duke University Press, 2012.

Abel, Elizabeth, Barbara Christian, and Helene Moglen, eds. *Female Subjects in Black and White: Race, Psychoanalysis, Feminism*. Berkeley: University of California Press, 1997.

Adorno, Theodor W. *Aesthetic Theory*. Translated and edited by Robert Hullot-Kentor. Minneapolis: University of Minnesota Press, 1997.

Als, Hilton. "Adrienne Kennedy's Startling Body of Work." *New Yorker*, February 5, 2018. https://www.newyorker.com/magazine/2018/02/12/adrienne-kennedys -startling-body-of-work.

Aristotle. *Poetics*. Translated by Malcolm Heath. New York: Penguin, 1996.

Artaud, Antonin. *The Theater and Its Double*. Translated by Mary Caroline Richards. New York: Grove, 1958.

Barnett, Claudia. "'An Evasion of Ontology': Being Adrienne Kennedy." *TDR* 49, no. 3 (Autumn 2005): 157–86. https://doi.org/10.1162/1054204054742417.

Barstow, Susan Torrey, "'Hedda Is All of Us': Late-Victorian Women at the Matinee." *Victorian Studies* 43, no. 3 (2001): 387–411. https://doi.org/10.1353/vic.2001.0044.

Barthes, Roland. *A Lover's Discourse: Fragments*. Translated by Richard Howard. New York: Penguin, 1990.

———. "The Reality Effect." In *The Rustle of Language*, translated by Richard Howard, edited by François Wahl, 141–48. Berkeley: University of California Press, 1989.

———. *Sade/Fourier/Loyola*. Translated by Richard Miller. Johns Hopkins University Press, 1997.

Basu, Biman. *The Commerce of Peoples: Sadomasochism and African American Literature*. Lanham: Lexington Books, 2012.

Bataille, Georges. *Story of the Eye*. Translated by Joachim Neugroschel. San Francisco: City Lights Books, 1987.

Benjamin, Jessica. *The Bonds of Love*. New York: Pantheon, 1988.

Berlant, Lauren. *Cruel Optimism*. Durham: Duke University Press, 2011.

———. *Desire/Love*. Brooklyn: Punctum, 2012.

Berlant, Lauren, and Lee Edelman. *Sex, Or The Unbearable*. Duke University Press, 2013.

Bersani, Leo. *The Culture of Redemption*. Cambridge: Harvard University Press, 1990.

———. *The Freudian Body*. New York: Columbia University Press, 1986.

———. *A Future for Astyanax: Character and Desire in Literature*. New York: Columbia University Press, 1984.

———. "Is the Rectum a Grave?" *October* 43 (1987): 197–222. JSTOR.

Bersani, Leo, and Adam Phillips. *Intimacies*. Chicago: University of Chicago Press, 2008.

Blass, Rachel. "Insights into the Struggle of Creativity: A Rereading of Anna Freud's 'Beating Fantasies and Daydreams.'" *The Psychoanalytic Study of the Child* 48 (1993): 67–97. PEP Web.

Blau, Herbert. *Take up the Bodies: Theater at the Vanishing Point*. Urbana: University of Illinois Press, 1982.

Bliss, James. "Hope Against Hope: Queer Negativity, Black Feminist Theorizing, and Reproduction without Futurity." *Mosaic* 48, no. 1 (March 2015): 83–98. JSTOR.

Boumelha, Penny. *Thomas Hardy and Women: Sexual Ideology and Narrative Form*. Brighton: Harvester, 1982.

Brecht, Bertolt. *Brecht on Theatre: The Development of an Aesthetic*. Translated by Jack Davis et al., edited by Marc Silberman, Steve Giles, and Tom Kuhn. New York: Hill and Wang, 2015.

Brenkman, John. "Queer Post-Politics." *Narrative* 10, no. 2 (2002): 174–80. Project MUSE.

Brinkema, Eugenie. "The Violence of a Fascination with* a Visible Form (on Martyrs, Cruelty, Horror, Ethics) [*on and vs. with vs. as]." *Postmodern Culture* 30, no. 2 (January 2020). https://www.pomoculture.org/2021/01/07/the-violence-of-a-fascination-with-a-visible-form-on-martyrs-cruelty-horror-ethics-on-and-vs-with-vs-as/.

Brockett, Oscar G. *History of the Theatre*. Seventh Edition. Boston: Allyn & Bacon, 1995.

Buffy the Vampire Slayer. 1998. Season 3, episode 1, "Anne." Written and directed by Joss Whedon. Aired September 29, 1998, on WB.

Bury, Liz. "50 Shades Makes EL James World's Highest-Earning Author." *Guardian*, August 13, 2013. https://www.theguardian.com/books/2013/aug/13/50-shades-el-james-highest-earning-author.

Butler, Judith. *Antigone's Claim: Kinship between Life and Death*. New York: Columbia University Press, 2002.

Carlson, Marvin. *The Haunted Stage: The Theatre as Memory Machine*. Ann Arbor: University of Michigan Press, 2003.

Caruth, Cathy. *Unclaimed Experience: Trauma, Narrative, and History*. Baltimore: Johns Hopkins University Press, 1996.

Caserio, Robert, Lee Edelman, J. Halberstam, José Esteban Muñoz, and Tim Dean. "The Antisocial Thesis in Queer Theory." *PMLA* 121, no. 3 (May 2006): 819–28. JSTOR.

Cavitch, Max. "Everybody's Autotheory." *Modern Language Quarterly* 83, no. 1 (March 2022): 81–116. https://doi.org/10.1215/00267929-475043.

Chandler, Nahum D. "Of Exorbitance: The Problem of the Negro as a Problem for Thought." *Criticism* 50, no. 3 (Summer 2008): 345–410. JSTOR.

Chavez, Felicia Rose. *The Anti-Racist Writing Workshop*. Chicago: Haymarket Books, 2021.

Chu, Andrea Long. *Females*. New York: Verso Books, 2019.

Coates, Kim. "'Both Sides at Once': Addiction and Autotheory in Paul B. Preciado's *Testo Junkie*." *TSQ*Now*, May 10, 2021. https://www.tsqnow.online/post/both-sides-at-once-addiction-and-autotheory-in-paul-b-preciado-s-testo-junkie.

Collister, Peter. "Henry James, the 'Scenic Idea,' and 'Nona Vincent.'" *Philological Quarterly* 94, no. 3 (Summer 2015): 267–90. ProQuest.

Copjec, Joan. *Imagine There's No Woman: Ethics and Sublimation*. Cambridge: MIT Press, 2002.

Cruz, Ariane. *The Color of Kink*. New York: NYU Press, 2016.

Davis, William A., Jr. "The Rape of Tess: Hardy, English Law, and the Case for Sexual Assault." *Nineteenth-Century Literature* 52, no. 2 (September 1997): 221–31. JSTOR.

Day, Sylvia. "Introduction." In Pauline Réage, *The Story of O*, translated by Sabine d'Estrée. New York: Ballantine, 2013.

Dean, Tim. "Sex and the Aesthetics of Existence." *PMLA* 125, no. 2 (March 2010): 387–92. JSTOR.

De Lauretis, Teresa. *The Practice of Love: Lesbian Sexuality and Perverse Desire*. Bloomington: Indiana University Press, 1994.

Deleuze, Gilles. "Coldness and Cruelty." In *Masochism*, translated by Jean McNeil, 9–138. New York: Zone Books, 1991.

——. *Présentation de Sacher-Masoch: le froid et le cruel*. Paris: Éditions de Minuit, 1967.

Del Rey, Lana. *Born To Die—The Paradise Edition*. Interscope and Polydor, 2012.

——. *Ultraviolence*. Polydor and Interscope, 2014.

de Man, Paul. "Autobiography As De-Facement." In *The Rhetoric of Romanticism*, 67–81. New York: Columbia University Press, 1984.

Derrida, Jacques. *Of Grammatology*. Translated by Gayatri Chakravorty Spivak. Baltimore: Johns Hopkins University Press, 1997.

——. *Writing and Difference*. Translated by Alan Bass. Chicago: University of Chicago Press, 1978.

Diamond, Elin. *Unmaking Mimesis: Essays on Feminism and Theater*. London: Routledge, 1997.

Dickens, Charles. *Charles Dickens: Christmas Books*, edited by Ruth Glancy. Oxford, Oxford University Press, 1988.

Doyle, Jennifer. "Blind Spots and Failed Performance: Abortion, Feminism, and Queer Theory." *Qui Parle* 18, no. 1 (2009): 25–52. JSTOR.

Dustan, Guillaume. *Nicolas Pages*. Éditions Balland, Paris, 1999.

Edel, Leon. "Henry James: The Dramatic Years." In *Henry James: Guy Domville with Comments by Bernard Shaw, H. G. Wells and Arnold Bennet*, edited by Leon Edel, 11–121. Philadelphia: J. B. Lippincott, 1960.

Edelman, Lee. *Bad Education*. Durham: Duke University Press, 2022.

——. *No Future*. Durham: Duke University Press, 2004.

Enelow, Shonni. *Method Acting and Its Discontents: On American Psycho-Drama*. Evanston: Northwestern University Press, 2015.

Fanon, Frantz. *Black Skin, White Masks*. Translated by Charles Lam Markmann. London: Pluto Press, 2008.

Fawaz, Ramzi. "'An Open Mesh of Possibilities': The Necessity of Eve Sedgwick in Dark Times." In *Reading Sedgwick*, edited by Lauren Berlant, 6–33. Durham: Duke University Press, 2019.

Fisher, Gary. "Red Cream Soda." In *Gary in Your Pocket: Stories and Notebooks of Gary Fisher*, edited by Eve Kosofsky Sedgwick, 37–44. Durham: Duke University Press, 1996.

Foucault, Michel. *The History of Sexuality*, vol. 1, *An Introduction*. Translated by Robert Hurley. New York: Vintage Books, 1990.

———. "What Is an Author?" Translated by Josué V. Harari. In *Aesthetics, Method, and Epistemology*, edited by James D. Faubion, 205–22. New York: The New Press, 1998.

Fournier, Lauren. *Autotheory as Feminist Practice in Art, Writing and Criticism*. Cambridge: MIT Press, 2021.

Frank, Natalie. *Story of O: Drawings by Natalie Frank*. Seattle: Lucia Marquand, 2018.

Freeman, Elizabeth. *Time Binds: Queer Temporalities, Queer Histories*. Durham: Duke University Press, 2010.

Freud, Anna. "The Relation of Beating-Phantasies to a Day-Dream." *International Journal of Psychoanalysis* 4 (1923): 89–102. PEP Web.

Freud, Sigmund. *Beyond the Pleasure Principle*. In *The Standard Edition of the Complete Psychological Works of Sigmund Freud*, edited by James Strachey, vol. 18, *Beyond the Pleasure Principle, Group Psychology and Other Works*, 1–64. London: The Hogarth Press, 1955. PEP Web.

———. "A Child Is Being Beaten." In *The Standard Edition of the Complete Psychological Works of Sigmund Freud*, edited by James Strachey, vol. 17, *An Infantile Neurosis and Other Works*, 175–204. London: Hogarth Press, 1955. PEP Web.

———. *Civilization and Its Discontents*. Translated by James Strachey. New York: Norton, 2005.

———. "The Economic Problem of Masochism." In *The Standard Edition of the Complete Psychological Works of Sigmund Freud*, edited by James Strachey, vol. 19, *The Ego and the Id and Other Works*, 155–70. London: Hogarth Press, 1961. PEP Web.

———. *The Ego and the Id*. In *The Standard Edition of the Complete Psychological Works of Sigmund Freud*, edited by James Strachey, vol. 19, *The Ego and the Id and Other Works*, 12–66. London: Hogarth Press, 1961. PEP Web.

———. "Fetishism." In *The Standard Edition of the Complete Psychological Works of Sigmund Freud*, edited by James Strachey, vol. 21, *The Future of an Illusion, Civilization and its Discontents, and Other Works*, 147–58. London: Hogarth, 1961. PEP Web.

———. *The Interpretation of Dreams*. Translated and edited by James Strachey. New York: Bard, 1998.

———. "Ein Kind wird geschlagen." In *Gesammelte Werke: chronologisch geordnet*, vol. 12, 197–226. Frankfurt: S. Fischer, 1968–78. PEP Web.

———. "Das ökonomische Problem des Masochismus." In *Gesammelte Werke: chronologisch geordnet*, vol. 13, 371–83. Frankfurt: S. Fischer, 1972. PEP Web.

———. "Psychopathic Characters on the Stage." In *The Standard Edition of the Complete Psychological Works of Sigmund Freud*, edited by James Strachey, vol. 7, *A Case of Hysteria, Three Essays on Sexuality and Other Works*, 303–10. London: Hogarth Press, 1953. PEP Web.

———. "Psychopathische Personen auf der Bühne." In *Gesammelte Werke: Texte aus den Jahren 1885 bis 1938*, Nachtragsband, 655–61. Frankfurt: S. Fischer, 1987. PEP Web.

Frisina, Kyle. "From Performativity to Performance: Claudia Rankine's *Citizen* and

Autotheory." In "Autotheory Theory," edited by Robyn Wiegman, special issue of *Arizona Quarterly* 76, no. 1 (Spring 2020): 141–66. Project MUSE.

Fu, Kim. "Scissors," in *Kink*, edited by R. O. Kwon and Garth Greenwell, 166–76. New York: Simon & Schuster, 2021.

Fuchs, Elinor. "Presence and the Revenge of Writing: Re-Thinking Theatre after Derrida." *Performing Arts Journal* 9, no. 2/3 (1985): 163–73. JSTOR.

Fuss, Diana. *Identification Papers*. New York: Routledge, 1995.

Gaitskill, Mary. *Bad Behavior*. New York: Simon & Schuster, 2009.

———. "Form Over Feeling: A Review of *Out* by Natsuo Kirino." In *Somebody with a Little Hammer*, 210–14. New York: Vintage, 2017.

———. "A Romantic Weekend." In *Bad Behavior*, 27–48. New York: Simon & Schuster, 2009.

———. *Two Girls, Fat and Thin*. New York: Simon & Schuster, 1991.

———. "Victims and Losers: A Love Story," in *Somebody with a Little Hammer*, 76–84.

Gallop, Jane. *The Deaths of the Author: Writing and Reading in Time*. Durham: Duke University Press, 2011.

Gates, Joanne. *Elizabeth Robins, 1862–1952: Actress, Novelist, Feminist*. Tuscaloosa: University of Alabama Press, 1994.

Gay, Roxane. *Bad Feminist*. New York: Harper, 2014.

Geller, Jay. *On Freud's Jewish Body: Mitigating Circumcisions*. New York: Fordham University Press, 2007.

Genette, Gérard. *Narrative Discourse*. Translated by Jane E. Lewin. Ithaca: Cornell University Press, 1980.

Gilbert, Elizabeth. "Elizabeth Gilbert Reveals the Source of True Joy." *O, The Oprah Magazine*, May 2018. https://www.oprah.com/inspiration/elizabeth-gilbert-on-the-source-of-true-joy.

Gilman, Sander. *Freud, Race, and Gender*. New York: Verso Books, 2007.

Goh, Irving. "Auto-thanato-theory: Dark Narcissistic Care for the Self in Sedgwick and Zambreno." In "Autotheory Theory," edited by Robyn Wiegman, special issue of *Arizona Quarterly* 76, no. 1 (Spring 2020): 197–213. Project MUSE.

Greenwell, Garth. "Gospodar." In *Kink*, edited by R. O. Kwon and Garth Greenwell, 144–65. New York: Simon & Schuster, 2021.

Gunn, Olivia Noble. *Empty Nurseries, Queer Occupants: Reproduction and the Future in Ibsen's Late Plays*. New York: Routledge, 2020.

Hames-García, Michael. "What's After Queer Theory? Queer Ethnic and Indigenous Studies." *Feminist Studies* 39, no. 2 (2013): 384–404. JSTOR.

Hanson, Ellis. "The Future's Eve: Reparative Reading After Sedgwick." *The South Atlantic Quarterly* 110, no. 1 (Winter 2011): 101–19. https://doi.org/10.1215/00382876-2010-025.

Hart, Lynda. *Between the Body and the Flesh*. New York: Columbia University Press, 1998.

Hartman, Saidiya. *Lose Your Mother*. New York: Farrar, Straus and Giroux, 2008.

———. *Scenes of Subjection: Terror, Slavery, and Self-Making in Nineteenth-Century America*. New York: Oxford University Press, 1997.

Harvey, P. J. *Dry*. Too Pure Records, 1992.

Haskell, Molly. Letter to the editor. *New York Times*, March 5, 2021. https://www

.nytimes.com/2021/03/05/books/review/kink-frankenstein-and-other-letters-to
-the-editor.html.

Hedda Gabler. By Henrik Ibsen. Directed by Thomas Ostermeier. BAM Harvey Theater, Brooklyn Academy of Music, Brooklyn, NY, November 21, 2006. DVD. New
York Public Library Performing Arts Research Collections.

Holland, Sharon. *The Erotic Life of Racism.* Durham: Duke University Press, 2012.

hooks, bell. "Critical Reflections: Adrienne Kennedy, the Writer, the Work." In *In-
tersecting Boundaries: The Theatre of Adrienne Kennedy*, edited by Paul K. Bryant-
Jackson and Lois More Overbeck, 179–85. Minneapolis: University of Minnesota
Press, 1992.

Ibsen, Henrik. *A Doll's House.* In *Six Plays by Ibsen*, translated by Eva Le Gallienne,
1–82. New York: Modern Library, 1957.

———. *Hedda Gabler.* Translated by Edmund Gosse and William Archer. New York:
Dover, 1990.

James, E. L. *Fifty Shades Trilogy.* New York: Vintage, 2012.

James, Henry. "The Art of Fiction." In *Partial Portraits*, 375–408. London: Macmillan,
1888. ProQuest.

———. "The Beast in the Jungle." In *Henry James: Complete Stories 1898–1910*, 496–
541. New York: Library of America, 1996.

———. "Nona Vincent." In *Henry James: Complete Stories 1892–1898*, 1–31. New York:
Library of America, 1996.

———. "Nona Vincent" (serialized edition). *The English Illustrated Magazine, 1891–
1892.* London: Macmillan and Co., 1892. 365–76 & 491–502.

———. "On the Occasion of *Hedda Gabler.*" In *Henry James: The Scenic Art*, edited by
Allan Wade, 243–56. New Brunswick: Rutgers, 1948.

JanMohamed, Abdul. "Negating the Negation as a Form of Affirmation in Minority
Discourse: The Construction of Richard Wright as Subject." *Cultural Critique* 7
(Autumn 1987): 245–66. https://doi.org/10.2307/1354157.

———. "Sexuality on/of the Racial Border: Foucault, Wright, and the Articulation of
'Racialized Sexuality,'" in *Discourses of Sexuality: From Aristotle to AIDS* (Ann Arbor: University of Michigan Press, 1992), 94–116.

Jarcho, Julia. *Writing and the Modern Stage: Theater Beyond Drama.* Cambridge: Cambridge University Press, 2017.

Jarvis, Claire. *Exquisite Masochism: Marriage, Sex, and the Novel Form.* Baltimore: Johns
Hopkins University Press, 2016.

Jelinek, Elfriede. *The Piano Teacher.* Translated by Joachim Neugroschel. New York:
Grove, 2009.

Keenan, Jillian. "Finding the Courage to Reveal a Fetish." *New York Times*, November 9, 2012. https://www.nytimes.com/2012/11/11/fashion/modern-love-a
-spanking-fetish-is-not-revealed-easily.html?smid=url-share.

Kennedy, Adrienne. *The Adrienne Kennedy Reader.* Minneapolis: University of Minnesota Press, 2001.

———. *Deadly Triplets: A Theatre Mystery and Journal.* Minneapolis: University of Minnesota Press, 1990.

———. *Etta and Ella on the Upper West Side.* In *He Brought Her Heart Back in a Box and
Other Plays*, 37–72. New York: Theatre Communications Group, 2020.

———. *Funnyhouse of a Negro.* In *The Adrienne Kennedy Reader*, 11–26.

——. *He Brought Her Heart Back in a Box.* In *He Brought Her Heart Back in a Box and Other Plays*, 1–28.

——. *Ohio State Murders.* In *The Adrienne Kennedy Reader*, 151–73.

——. *People Who Led to My Plays.* New York: Theatre Communications Group, 1987.

——. "Unraveling the Landscape." Interview by Branden Jacobs-Jenkins, December 2017. In *He Brought Her Heart Back in a Box and Other Plays*, 29–35.

Kennedy, Adrienne and Adam P. Kennedy. *Mom, How Did You Meet the Beatles?* In *He Brought Her Heart Back in a Box and Other Plays*, 73–115.

Koppen, Randi. "Psychoanalytic Enactments: Adrienne Kennedy's Stagings of Memory." *Hungarian Journal of English and American Studies* 4, no. 1/2 (1998): 121–34. JSTOR.

Kraus, Chris. "Emotional Technologies." in *Kink*, edited by R. O. Kwon and Garth Greenwell (New York: Simon & Schuster, 2021), 242–63.

Kurnick, David. *Empty Houses: Theatrical Failure and the Novel.* Princeton: Princeton University Press, 2012.

Kwon, R. O. "Safeword." In *Kink*, edited by Kwon and Garth Greenwell, 52–65. New York: Simon & Schuster, 2021.

Kwon, R. O., and Garth Greenwell. "Introduction." In *Kink*, edited by Kwon and Greenwell, xi-xii. New York: Simon & Schuster, 2021.

Lacan, Jacques. *The Four Fundamental Concepts of Psychoanalysis.* Translated by Alan Sheridan. Edited by Jacques-Alain Miller. Vol. 11 of *The Seminar of Jacques Lacan.* New York: Norton, 1998.

Lane, Christopher, ed. "The Psychoanalysis of Race," special issue of *Discourse* 19, no. 2 (Winter 1997). JSTOR.

Laplanche, Jean. *Life and Death in Psychoanalysis.* Translated by Jeffrey Mehlman. Baltimore: Johns Hopkins University Press, 1976.

Laplanche, Jean, and J.-B. Pontalis. "Fantasy and the Origins of Sexuality." *The International Journal of Psycho-analysis* 49, no. 1 (1968): 1–18. ProQuest.

Laubender, Carolyn. "Speak for Your Self: Psychoanalysis, Autotheory, and The Plural Self." In "Autotheory Theory," edited by Robyn Wiegman, special issue of *Arizona Quarterly* 76, no. 1 (Spring 2020): 39–64. Project MUSE.

Lavery, Grace. "Egg Theory's Early Style." *TSQ: Transgender Studies Quarterly* 7, no. 3 (August 2020): 383–98. https://doi.org/10.1215/23289252-8553034.

——. "The King's Two Anuses: Trans Feminism and Free Speech." *differences* 30, no. 3 (2019): 118–51. https://doi.org/10.1215/10407391-7974030.

——. "Trans Realism, Psychoanalytic Practice, and the Rhetoric of Technique." *Critical Inquiry* 46, no. 4 (Summer 2020): 719–44. https://doi.org/10.1086/709221.

Lévesque-Jalbert, Émile. "'This is not an autofiction': Autoteoría, French Feminism, and Living in Theory." In "Autotheory Theory," edited by Robyn Wiegman, special issue of *Arizona Quarterly* 76, no. 1 (Spring 2020): 65–84. Project MUSE.

Love, Heather. "Truth and Consequences: On Paranoid Reading and Reparative Reading." In "Honoring Eve," edited by Erin Murphy and J. Keith Vincent, special issue of *Criticism* 52, no. 2 (Spring 2010): 235–41. JSTOR.

Marriott, David S. *Lacan Noir: Lacan and Afro-Pessimism.* Cham, Switzerland: Palgrave Macmillan, 2021.

McPhee, Ruth. *Female Masochism in Film: Sexuality, Ethics and Aesthetics.* Surrey: Ashgate, 2014.

Mendelson, Scott. "Box Office: 'Fifty Shades Freed' Pushes The Trilogy Past $1 Billion Worldwide." *Forbes*, February 10, 2018. https://www.forbes.com/sites /scottmendelson/2018/02/10/box-office-fifty-shades-freed-dakota-johnson -jamie-dornan-universal-el-james/?sh=42b3c6d015c5.

Merkin, Daphne. "Unlikely Obsession." *New Yorker*, "Special Women's Issue," February 26 and March 4, 1996, 98–115.

Miller, Nancy K. *Getting Personal: Feminist Occasions and Other Autobiographical Acts.* New York: Routledge, 1991.

Moi, Toril. "Hedda's Silences: Beauty and Despair in *Hedda Gabler.*" *Modern Drama* 56, no. 4 (Winter 2013): 434–56. Project MUSE.

——. *Henrik Ibsen and the Birth of Modernism.* Oxford: Oxford University Press, 2006.

Mountford, Peter. "Impact Play." In *Kink*, edited by R. O. Kwon and Garth Greenwell, 102–24. New York: Simon & Schuster, 2021.

Muñoz, José Esteban. *Cruising Utopia: The Then and There of Queer Futurity.* New York: NYU Press, 2009.

——. *Disidentifications.* Minneapolis: University of Minnesota Press, 1999.

——. "Race, Sex, and the Incommensurate: Gary Fisher with Eve Sedgwick." In *Queer Futures: Reconsidering Ethics, Activism, and the Political,* edited by Elahe Haschemi Yekani, Eveline Kilian, and Beatrice Michaelis, 103–15. London: Routledge, 2013.

Murray, Timothy, ed. *Mimesis, Masochism, and Mime: The Politics of Theatricality in Contemporary French Thought.* Ann Arbor: University of Michigan Press, 1997.

Musser, Amber Jamilla. "Consent, Capacity, and the Non-Narrative." In *Queer Feminist Science Studies: A Reader,* edited by Cyd Cipolla, Kristina Gupta, David A. Rubin, and Angela Willey, 221–33. Seattle: University of Washington Press, 2017.

——. "The Literary Symptom: Krafft-Ebing and the Invention of Masochism." In *Mediated Deviance and Social Otherness: Interrogating Influential Representations,* edited by Kylo Hart, 286–94. Cambridge: Cambridge Scholars Press, 2007.

——. "Reading, Writing, and the Whip." *Literature and Medicine* 27, no. 2 (Fall 2008): 204–22. http://dx.doi.org/10.1353/lm.0.0034

——. *Sensational Flesh: Race, Power, and Masochism.* New York: NYU Press, 2014.

——. *Sensual Excess: Queer Femininity and Brown Jouissance.* New York: NYU Press, 2018.

Nash, Jennifer C. "Black Anality." In *Queer Feminist Science Studies: A Reader,* edited by Cyd Cipolla, Kristina Gupta, David A. Rubin, and Angela Willey, 102–13. Seattle: University of Washington Press, 2017.

Nelson, Maggie. *The Argonauts.* Minneapolis: Graywolf, 2015.

——. *The Art of Cruelty.* New York: Norton, 2011.

——. "Riding the Blinds." Interview by Micah McCrary. *Los Angeles Review of Books,* April 26, 2015. https://lareviewofbooks.org/article/riding-the-blinds/.

Nordau, Max. *Degeneration.* 2nd ed. Anonymous translation. London: William Heinemann, 1898. Project Gutenberg.

Ohi, Kevin. *Henry James and the Queerness of Style.* Minneapolis: University of Minnesota Press, 2011.

Pellegrini, Ann. *Performance Anxieties: Staging Psychoanalysis, Staging Race.* New York: Routledge, 1997.

Pham, Larissa. "Trust." In *Kink*, edited by R. O. Kwon and Garth Greenwell, 26–51. New York: Simon & Schuster, 2021.

Phelan, Peggy. *Mourning Sex: Performing Public Memories*. London: Routledge, 1997.

———. *Unmarked*. New York: Routledge, 1993.

Pound, Ezra. "Henry James." In *Literary Essays of Ezra Pound*, edited by T. S. Eliot, 295–338. New York: New Directions, 1968.

Preciado, Paul. *Testo Junkie: Sex, Drugs, and Biopolitics in the Pharmopornographic Era*. Translated by Bruce Benderson. New York: Feminist Press at the City University of New York, 2013.

———. *Testo Yonqui*. Barcelona: Espasa, 2013.

Réage, Pauline. *The Story of O*. Translated by Sabine d'Estrée. New York: Ballantine, 2013.

Reid-Pharr, Robert F. *Black Gay Man*. New York: NYU Press, 2001.

Rivera, Takeo. *Model Minority Masochism: Performing the Cultural Politics of Asian American Masculinity*. New York: Oxford University Press, 2022.

Rivkin, Julie. *False Positions: The Representational Logics of Henry James's Fiction*. Stanford: Stanford University Press, 1996.

Robins, Elizabeth. *Ibsen and the Actress*. New York: Haskell House, 1973.

Robinson, Marc. *The Other American Drama*. Cambridge: Cambridge University Press, 1994.

Rodríguez, Juana María. *Sexual Futures, Queer Gestures, and Other Latina Longings*. New York: NYU Press, 2014.

Rubin, Gayle. "Thinking Sex: Notes for a Radical Theory of the Politics of Sexuality." In *Culture, Society, and Sexuality*, edited by Peter Aggleton and Richard Parker, 143–78. London: Routledge, 2006.

Sacher-Masoch, Leopold von. *Venus in Furs*. In *Masochism*, translated by Jean McNeil, 143–271. New York: Zone Books, 1991.

Sade, Marquis de. *Philosophy in the Boudoir*. Translated by Joachim Neugroschel. New York: Penguin, 2006.

Saketopoulou, Avgi. *Sexuality Beyond Consent: Risk, Race, Traumatophilia*. New York: NYU Press, 2023.

Savran, David. *Taking It Like a Man: White Masculinity, Masochism, and Contemporary American Culture*. Princeton: Princeton University Press, 1998.

Schneider, Rebecca. *Performing Remains: Art and War in Times of Theatrical Reenactment*. London: Routledge, 2011.

Scott, Darieck. *Extravagant Abjection: Blackness, Power, and Sexuality in the African American Literary Imagination*. New York: NYU Press, 2010.

Sedgwick, Eve Kosofsky. *A Dialogue on Love*. Boston: Beacon Press, 1999.

———. Afterword to *Gary in Your Pocket*, by Gary Fisher, 282–83. Durham: Duke University Press, 1996.

———. *Epistemology of the Closet*. Berkeley: University of California Press, 1990.

———. "Paranoid Reading and Reparative Reading, or, You're So Paranoid, You Probably Think This Essay Is About You." In *Touching Feeling: Affect, Pedagogy, Performativity*, 123–52. Durham: Duke University Press, 2003.

———. "A Poem Is Being Written." *Representations* 17 (Winter, 1987): 110–43. JSTOR.

———. *Tendencies*. Durham: Duke University Press, 1993

———. *Touching Feeling*. Durham: Duke University Press, 2003.

Sharpe, Christina. *Monstrous Intimacies: Making Post-Slavery Subjects*. Durham: Duke University Press, 2010.

Silverman, Kaja. *Male Subjectivity at the Margins*. New York: Routledge, 1992.

Slavet, Eliza. *Racial Fever: Freud and the Jewish Question*. New York: Fordham University Press, 2009.

Solomon, Alisa. *Re-Dressing the Canon: Essays on Theater and Gender*. London: Routledge, 1997.

Sontag, Susan. "The Pornographic Imagination." In *A Susan Sontag Reader*, 205–33. New York: Farrar, Straus and Giroux, 1982.

Spillers, Hortense. "'All the Things You Could Be by Now, If Sigmund Freud's Wife Was Your Mother': Psychoanalysis and Race." In *Black, White, and in Color: Essays on American Literature and Culture*, 376–427. Chicago: University of Chicago Press, 2003.

———. "Mama's Baby, Papa's Maybe: An American Grammar Book." *Diacritics* 17, no. 2 (Summer 1987): 64–81. JSTOR.

Stanislavski, Constantin. *An Actor Prepares*. Translated by Elizabeth Reynolds Hapgood. New York: Theatre Arts, 1936.

States, Bert O. *Great Reckonings in Little Rooms*. Berkeley: University of California Press, 1985.

Stockton, Kathryn Bond. "Eve's Queer Child." In *Regarding Sedgwick: Essays on Queer Culture and Critical Theory*, edited by Stephen M. Barber and David L. Clark, 181–99. New York: Routledge, 2002.

Szondi, Peter. *Theory of the Modern Drama*. Edited and translated by Michael Hays. Minneapolis: University of Minnesota Press, 1987.

Van Dyke, W. S., dir. *Bitter Sweet*. Warner Bros., 1940. 93 min.

Warner, Michael. "The Mass Public and the Mass Subject." In *Habermas and the Public Sphere*, edited by Craig Calhoun, 377–401. Cambridge: MIT Press, 1992.

Warren, Calvin. "Onticide: Afropessimism, Queer Theory, and Ethics." *Ill Will*, November 18, 2014. https://illwill.com/print/ontocide.

Wiegman, Robyn. "Heteronormativity and the Desire for Gender." *Feminist Theory* 7, no. 1 (2006): 89–103. https://doi.org/10.1177/1464700106061460.

Wilderson, Frank B., III. *Afropessimism*. New York: Norton, 2020.

Wirth, Andrzej. "Vom Dialog zum Diskurs: Versuch einer Synthese der nachbrechsten Theaterkonzepte." *Theater Heute* 1 (1980): 16–19.

Wynter, Sylvia. "Unsettling the Coloniality of Being/Power/Truth/Freedom: Towards the Human, After Man, Its Overrepresentation—An Argument." *CR: The New Centennial Review* 3, no. 3 (Fall 2003): 257–337. https://doi.org/10.1353/ncr.2004.0015.

Young, Stacey. *Changing the Wor(l)d: Discourse, Politics, and the Feminist Movement*. New York: Routledge, 1991.

Žižek, Slavoj. "From Desire to Drive: Why Lacan Is Not Lacaniano." *Atlántica de las artes* 14 (August 1996). zizek.livejournal.com/2266.html.

Index

Abdur-Rahman, Aliyyah, 14–15, 152–53
aberrancy, 71–72
abjection: and Black females, 187n71; and Black masculinity, 12–13, 16–17, 187n71, 202n21; racialized, 15; sexualized, 13
abolitionism, 14, 185n55, 205n93
absolutism, and religion, 215n10
abstraction, 139–53, 209n40; and autotheory, 124, 137, 139, 159; of body, 139; and delimitation, 144; and digital data, 209n33; and domination, 124; and drama, 56; erotics of, 21; and generalization, 133, 137; and intellection, 137, 209n40; and masochism, 51–52, 137–38, 159; and negation, 209n40; and queer theory, 133, 151; and sadism, 137–38; self-, 124, 207n7; and sexual roles, 209n40; and subjectivity, 126; submission to, 124; violation of, 137; and writing, 126, 159; and wrongness, 135
acting, and desire, 118
Actor Prepares, An (Stanislavki), 199n116
Adler, Alfred, 186n64
Adorno, Theodor, 168
Aesthetic Theory (Adorno), 168
Against Sadomasochism (anthology), 22
agency, sexual, 186n69, 200n1
aggression: and autotheory, 137; and masochism, 44–45; Negro's, white

fantasy of (Fanon), 13; and sexuality, 136
Alan's Wife (Robins and Bell), 199–200n132
Alexander, David, 99–100
Alexander, Suzanne, 96–100, 202n22
Alexander Plays (Kennedy), 96–100, 202n22
"'All the Things You Could Be by Now, If Sigmund Freud's Wife Was Your Mother'" (Spillers), 17–20, 88
Als, Hilton, 206n115
alterity, 11, 96, 186n69, 197–98n81
Ambassadors, The (James), 197n76
American Slave Code, The (Goodell), 205n93
amorality, 91. *See also* morality
anachrony, and poststructuralism, 160–61
anality, 127, 141–44, 150–51, 198n98, 210n52
anonymity, 90–91
antagonism, 118–19, 150
anti-Blackness, 89, 118, 155, 182n17. *See also* racism
Antigone, 62, 69, 71, 195n20
anti-Semitism, 17, 182n16
Anzaldúa, Gloria, 126, 207–8n11
Archer, William, 83
Argonauts, The (Nelson), as autotheory, 125–26